S0-AZF-149

What Makes Learning Fun?

What Makes Learning Fun?

Principles for the Design of Intrinsically Motivating Museum Exhibits

DEBORAH L. PERRY

ALTAMIRA
P R E S S

A Division of
ROWMAN & LITTLEFIELD PUBLISHERS, INC.
Lanham • New York • Toronto • Plymouth, UK

Published by AltaMira Press
A division of Rowman & Littlefield Publishers, Inc.
A wholly owned subsidary of The Rowman & Littlefield Publishing Group, Inc.
4501 Forbes Boulevard, Suite 200, Lanham, Maryland 20706
http://www.altamirapress.com

Estover Road, Plymouth PL6 7PY, United Kingdom

Copyright © 2012 by AltaMira Press

All rights reserved. No part of this book may be reproduced in any form or by any electronic or mechanical means, including information storage and retrieval systems, without written permission from the publisher, except by a reviewer who may quote passages in a review.

British Library Cataloguing in Publication Information Available

Library of Congress Cataloging-in-Publication Data

Perry, Deborah L., 1952–
  What makes learning fun? : principles for the design of intrinsically motivating museum exhibits / Deborah Perry.
    p. cm.
  Includes bibliographical references and index.
  ISBN 978-0-7591-0884-4 (cloth : alk. paper) — ISBN 978-0-7591-0885-1 (pbk. : alk. paper) — ISBN 978-0-7591-2128-7 (electronic)
  1. Museum exhibits—Planning. 2. Museums—Educational aspects. I. Title.
  AM151.P475 2012
  069'.5—dc23
                                                                        2011039390

∞™ The paper used in this publication meets the minimum requirements of American National Standard for Information Sciences—Permanence of Paper for Printed Library Materials, ANSI/NISO Z39.48-1992.

Printed in the United States of America

To Allen Milbury,
for starting me on this journey

Contents

List of Strategies

(See Appendix C for the complete *What Makes Learning Fun? Framework.*)

COLLABORATION

GUIDANCE

PERCEPTUAL CURIOSITY

INTELLECTUAL CURIOSITY

List of Figures

Introduction

Imagine the scenario: There's an exhibit, a small unobtrusive unit in the middle of an interactive science gallery at a large children's museum. In your role as volunteer and sometimes teacher of classes, you walk by it often, on your way to the gallery where you usually work. You are always impressed by the number of folks gathered around—and it seems sort of surprising to you, given that it's just a plain white box with some lights shining on it. But people are always busy making hand shadows and seem delightfully surprised when the shadows are brightly colored: red, green, yellow, purple, and pink. They laugh and point and ooh and aah. After a few brief moments, they move on.

One day, you stop briefly at the Parent Information sign that explains, *Colors are subjective sensations that can be produced by light of a certain wavelength and by combinations of different wavelengths. The sensation of yellow can be produced by either light of a wavelength we call yellow or by a combination of more than one [wavelength]* . . . .

"Hmmm," you say to yourself. "I'll stop by later when I have some time, when I'm not in such a rush, and it'll make more sense then." You convince yourself that you are preoccupied and that all you need to do is read the labels and do the hands-on activities, and then you'll get it. You repeat this scenario numerous times, and each time you stall while reading the labels, then convince yourself that all you need to do is spend a little more time with the exhibit.

Eventually that time arrives. You show up for work a half hour early with the intention of reading every label and doing every activity until you understand this exhibit that has this strange pull on you. You dutifully read the label What Is Going On. It shows three colored circles, one being blocked out by a hand, and carefully explains, *Blue and green make cyan, and red and green make yellow.* Wait a minute. From all your days messing around with paint and teaching arts and crafts, you *know* that red and green make brown, not yellow. And you *know* that yellow is a primary color, along with red and blue. But you also seem to remember having heard, someplace, somewhere, long ago, about mixing colors to make yellow.

You read the next label: What to Do and Notice. "Okay," you think, "this should do it. It will walk me through this step by step." You carefully do each of the four steps: 1. *Place your hand over the white tabletop and notice the different colors made by your shadow.* "Okay, I can do this." 2. *The three lights above the table are red, green, and blue. Notice that all three together make the table look white.* "Well, actually the table is white, and the lights make it have a pale pinky hue that changes slightly depending on where I'm standing. But okay, I'll go along with you; it looks white." 3. *If your hand blocks out all three colors then no light hits the table and your shadow is black.* "Okay, I'm having a really hard time making a black shadow, and when I do, how do I know I'm blocking out all three colors? It doesn't look like my hand's blocking out the colors. Hmmm. Okay, I'll take it at its word. But what about the colored shadows? Where do they come from? Maybe the next step will make it clearer." 4. *What colored shadows can you make by blocking different lights? You should see eight colors.* "Huh? I see different colors, but how come I have colored shadows? How am I making them? Aaargh! I still don't understand." At this point, you move back to the Parent Information sign, but it is pretty technical, all about wavelengths and subjective sensations.

Finally, you make it to the computer attached to the table. Maybe this will help. The title screen is called Colored Shadows and asks, *How old are you?* You decide not to be offended and dutifully enter your age: "thirty-two." This gains you access to the next page, a menu of five items to choose from. You select What Is Going On; that is, after all, the big question you've been trying to figure out the answer to. This takes you to a screen explaining that when the red light is blocked out, white minus red equals blue plus green (or cyan). "Huh?" Again, you are confused. You wonder, "How do I know when I'm blocking out the red light? What does it mean that white minus red equals blue plus green?" You do the rest of the computer items, and eventually you start to develop an understanding that, for example, red and green make yellow, but you still don't understand how this exhibit really demonstrates that; besides, this contradicts everything you've learned previously about red and green mixing.

Why can't you figure out this exhibit? You've always thought you were a moderately smart person. You are, after all, working on a graduate degree, and you're in a children's museum, for Pete's sake.

You are starting to feel very inadequate, when it slowly dawns on you that it may not be you after all. Perhaps it is the exhibit design. Granted, it's a very popular exhibit; visitors are constantly flocking around it, and it appears to be used more than any other exhibit in the gallery. Are those other visitors getting something you are missing? By now, of course, you're late for work, and you hurry off.

But the exhibit won't leave you alone. At unexpected moments, your experience keeps coming back to nudge you, to make you pay attention. How can an exhibit that is so popular and "successful" be so frustrating when you're trying to understand it? It gets you wondering what all those other visitors are getting out of it. Do they understand it? What are they learning?

A JOURNEY

This is the story of the *Colored Shadows* exhibit and my journey to understand more about what makes exhibits work for visitors. It is the story of how I went about unpeeling the many layers that make up the exhibit design-and-development process to find out how to design an exhibit not just be popular with museum visitors but rather that will be popular and, simultaneously, educationally effective. In other words, this became my personal and professional journey to discover what makes learning fun.

This journey started at the Children's Museum of Indianapolis when I was a thirty-two-year-old graduate student, part-time volunteer, and teacher. I repeatedly walked by the *Colored Shadows* exhibit until I finally decided to take some time to figure it out. Little did I know then that this would become a many-year journey, one that would reveal much about who I am and how I learn and that would forever shape how I think about the design of visitor experiences. In many ways, the journey continues as I gather new evidence that refines, strengthens, and often causes me to question what I think I know. That is the magic of this kind of journey.

THE EXHIBIT

The exhibit where things began consisted of a large white box, more or less in the shape of a cube, with three floodlights hanging high overhead against a ceiling that was painted black. The lights were red, green, and blue, and they were pointed at the top of the box. Around the beveled edge of the box, or table as it was often called, were two interpretive labels as described above, the messages repeating on opposite sides. There was a stand-alone interpretive label on a movable stanchion reading Parent Information, usually located off to the side of the exhibit but clearly associated with it, and a computer mounted in a cabinet nestled up against the white box (see figure A.1 in appendix A).

Discussions with the gallery curator/educator revealed that the purpose of the exhibit was to teach visitors about mixing colored lights. More specifically, that red, green, and blue lights mix to make white light. A detailed description of the *Colored Shadows* exhibit, its goals and objectives, and some photographs can be found in appendix A (see figures A.1 to A.8)

To the casual visitor walking into the gallery, the *Colored Shadows* exhibit was pretty unimpressive; basically, it looked like a white box. But all one had to do was wave a hand over the top of the box, and brilliantly colored shadows would dance across the flat surface. It was like magic, a surprising and delightful visual experience. This is what made it so popular; it could, in fact, be quite mesmerizing. But I was curious about what people were making of it all. What were they learning? Did they get that this was an exhibit about mixing colored lights?

THE RESEARCH

My research began with observing and talking with visitors to assess and better understand the nature of their enjoyment of the exhibit, as well as their cognitive understandings. Using unobtrusive observations and open-ended depth interviews, I set out to figure out what visitors were getting out of the exhibit. I was surprised to learn that while just about everyone loved it, many of the visitors did not have any idea what the exhibit was about, and even more disconcertingly, they were not particularly interested in trying to figure it out. Was this because visitors are not curious by nature? Or was something in the design of the exhibit contributing? When visitors were asked where they thought the colored shadows on the table were coming from, the range of responses was fascinating: "It's like a mood ring; the colors are responding to heat from my body." "They are being projected from underneath the tabletop." "They are reflecting off my T-shirt." If they didn't understand that the shadows were being created by lights hanging overhead, how could they understand that the exhibit was about mixing colored lights? And how could the exhibit be effective at getting them to think about the wonders of mixing lights to make other colors?

I was fascinated by this exhibit and visitors' responses. Here was a very popular unit that engaged people of all ages and was considered, in many respects, to be quite successful. At the same time, remarkably few visitors understood what the exhibit was about or learned anything new from it, other than, perhaps, that shadows can be colored. Surely it would be possible to increase the "learning" that took place at the exhibit without compromising the delight, awe, and enjoyment. It seemed to me that many principles of instructional design from formal education could be applied, including a more step-by-step approach and improved explanations in the interpretive labels, but one of the delightful things about the exhibit was that it didn't *feel* educational. I wanted the exhibit to work as a stand-alone, casual visitor experience, and I wanted the exhibit to maintain its enchantment. But I also wanted it to be more effective educationally. Was it possible to achieve both?

My challenge, then, was to see what learning theory had to say about educational endeavors that are designed to be fun, then to test these theories by redesigning the exhibit so that its educational effectiveness was increased and the already significant delight and enjoyment were not decreased.

Over the next couple of years, I spent all my free moments tackling this challenge. When I wasn't immersed in the literature, I was at the museum, watching and talking with visitors, implementing relatively minor but research-based revisions one at a time, observing the effects of each of the changes, and making further refinements. The process was sort of like developing a new cookie recipe: mixing, cooking, tasting, revising, and retesting. For each element tested, I asked two questions: (a) Did this change increase learning? and (b) Did it decrease enjoyment and satisfaction? The result of the process was a new exhibit, this one called *The Color Connection*. This exhibit is described in detail in appendix A (see figures A.9 to A.19). While the two exhibits looked similar in many respects—both included the white box and Apple computer—there were many subtle but important differences. For example, the floodlights were replaced with spotlights, the computer modules were totally revised, and new interpretive labels replaced the labels around the side of the white box.

The study concluded with an interrupted time-series, quasi-experimental design comparing the effectiveness (in terms of visitor enjoyment and learning) of *Colored Shadows* with *The Color Connection*. An overview of the primary results is included in appendix B. Briefly, however, the study indicated that enjoyment was equally high at both exhibits and that there was more learning at *The Color Connection*. In addition, the time visitors spent at the revised exhibit tripled, and the quality of social, intellectual, and physical interactions increased. Also, the percentage of respondents who walked away from the exhibit with *no* interest in mixing colored lights was reduced from 15 to 2 percent.

Though interesting, all of this doesn't reflect one extremely important aspect of the research. Throughout the redesign-and-development process, I thought it was essential that the changes implemented not be just trial-and-error design strategies but that they be grounded in a larger theoretical framework. Only with a larger theory guiding my work would it be useful for the field. In other words, it wasn't enough to know that, for example, replacing the floodlights with spotlights worked for this particular experiment. I also needed to be able to tie that particular strategy back to a theoretical framework that would explain why it was successful. Why did the spotlights in *The Color Connection* work better than the floodlights in the original *Colored Shadows*? It's not that spotlights are somehow inherently better than floodlights; rather, the use of spotlights in this situation achieved something that floodlights did not. My job was to ground my work in a theory that would help explain why this was so.

During the time I was becoming interested in the *Colored Shadows* exhibit, I was fortunate to come across research conducted by Mark Lepper and Thomas Malone at Stanford University in the early 1980s. Using current theories of cognition and motivation, they were interested in what makes things fun to learn and had conducted a series of research studies to explore this question. One of their research products was a set of "heuristics for designing intrinsically motivating instructional environments" (Malone and Lepper, 1987, p. 248–249). This was the theoretical framework I was looking for. What if I took their set of research-based heuristics (developed using instructional computer games in classroom settings) and used it to frame the work I was doing in the context of museum exhibits? What aspect(s) of their heuristics would hold up in a museum setting? What would need to be revised, replaced, or refined? My hope was that, if—using the *Colored Shadows* exhibit as a test case—I could use the Malone and Lepper heuristics to guide the redesign of the exhibit, while simultaneously testing and revising the heuristics, I would end up with a research-based framework for designing museum exhibits that maximizes the potential for both learning and enjoyment. That was my charge: to develop a research-based framework for the design of museum exhibits, one with a theoretical foundation in what makes learning fun—that is, one that emphasizes both learning and enjoyment.

This book describes both the theoretical foundation and the detailed framework that grew out of my work on the *Colored Shadows* and *The Color Connection* exhibits.

WHY THIS FRAMEWORK?

You may wonder how this model is any different from the variety of other frameworks and models that currently exist to explain learning in museums and to guide the development of visitor experiences (for example, Hein [1998], Hein and Alexander [1998], Hood [1983], Falk and Dierking [1992, 2000], Wells and Loomis [1998], Silverman [1990], Roberts [1997], Leinhardt and Knutson [2004], Weaver [2007], Carlson [1993], and others). Each of these models takes a unique theoretical perspective and is grounded in a different discipline. For example, Hood's work is grounded in leisure studies, Silverman is from communications, and the Leinhardt and Knutson model comes from sociocultural theory. Only a handful of studies have been grounded in theories of motivation (for example, Salmi 1993; Csikszentmihalyi and Hermanson 1995), and even fewer have come from the field of instructional systems.

The What Makes Learning Fun? framework, however, (a) provides an *instructional-design* perspective; (b) is focused on the *learning* aspects of the visitor experience (it does not deal with, for example, visitor services such as parking or marketing, except to the extent that these influence learning); (c) is grounded in the *motivational aspects* of learning, especially understanding why people learn in certain situations and not others; and (d) uses a *developmental research methodology* to integrate research with practice. Ultimately, the premise is that if we can understand the design elements that contribute to and detract from learning in informal educational environments—in other words, if we can understand what makes learning fun—then we can be more effective at designing museum exhibits that maximize the potential for learning.

Maximizing the Potential for Learning

This section discusses maximizing the potential for learning and not maximizing learning. Museums are many things that are not about learning. This book is not about those things. Because so many rich and meaningful things that are peripheral to learning happen in museums, and so many of these things are out of our control as museum professionals, a museum's goal should not be to guarantee or maximize learning but rather to set up environments that maximize its *potential*. This is not to say that whatever learning happens (or doesn't) is fine or that we don't care what visitors learn. Museums are educational institutions with educational missions. But they are also unique—different from other types of educational institutions with educational missions. As institutions of informal learning, museums specialize in learning that is largely controlled by the extremely diverse audiences that they serve, not to mention influenced by external social and natural pressures such as the economy, politics, and, yes, even the weather. A primary tenet of this book, then, is that museums need to maximize the potential for learning so that visitors who want to learn, can.

HOW TO USE THIS BOOK

This book is divided into two sections. Part I, "Understanding Visitor Experiences," lays down a theoretical foundation and describes the *interpretive activism* perspective that underlies the entire book. In this section, I discuss the social nature of museum visits, as well as what I mean by learning and teaching, and I introduce the concept of interpretive activism. I also describe the Selinda Model of Visitor Learning, briefly unpacking each of its three frameworks.

Whereas the first section of this book is primarily descriptive, Part II, "Designing Visitor Experiences," is highly prescriptive. In it, I describe in detail the motivations, or What Makes Learning Fun?, framework and outline its principles and accompanying strategies. Many examples are included. While most of them were developed primarily for exhibits rather than exhibitions, the reader will note that many of them are applicable on both scales.

I am not a designer, and this book is not intended in any way to compromise or limit the creative design process or dictate how to engage in the process of exhibit design and development. My intention is to provide a summary of some interesting research findings that can inform discussions when museum professionals are faced with tough design decisions and conflicting opinions. I also hope that the book will encourage the reader to become what is described later as an interpretive activist—that is, someone who goes beyond the traditional role of visitor advocate. By advocating for strategic, audience-centered, and research-based exhibit design, interpretive activists maximize the potential for learning while simultaneously enhancing visitors' enjoyment and satisfaction. For the interpretive activist, the book will serve as a reference, a source of research-based principles and strategies to consult when confronted with the challenges of making visitor-centered design decisions. I expect readers will use the strategies as jumping off points for discussion and deliberation, rather than boilerplate solutions. This book is about process and results. In other words, I believe that if the motivations and principles presented here are thoughtfully and deliberately incorporated into the exhibit design process, the outcome will be richer visitor experiences than would have otherwise been possible.

I believe that many of us involved in evaluation can—and do—contribute in important ways to the creation and development of meaningful visitor experiences. In other words, evaluation can (and should) be a tool in the ongoing quest for rich visitor experiences. I—along with many clients and colleagues—have been fortunate to have had the opportunity through evaluation to repeatedly test, refine, retest, and ultimately verify the efficacy of the ideas presented here. I look forward to continuing the journey.

Part I

UNDERSTANDING VISITOR EXPERIENCES

This first part of the book provides an underlying theoretical discussion that sets the stage for a more detailed exploration of specific research-based design principles and strategies in the second part of the book. It summarizes some of what we know about how visitors learn in informal settings but does not attempt to be a comprehensive treatment of visitor learning and experiences.

1

Visitors, Conversation, and Learning

THE SOCIAL NATURE OF MUSEUM VISITS

Leisure studies research has clearly demonstrated that many things contribute to the choice of a particular activity at a particular moment in time (Hood 1983; Hood 1989; Manning 1999; Tinsley and Manfredo 1991; Wells and Loomis 1998). These *experience preferences* run the range from a desire for solitude, privacy, and escape, to that for novelty, creativity, physical activity, or relaxation.

Although people choose to visit a museum for a variety of reasons, for the most part museum visits tend to be driven by a social agenda. In fact, for most folks, visiting a museum is, first and foremost, a social experience. "We wanted to spend time together as a family" or "We wanted to show the museum to our out-of-town friends" or "It's a place I can hang out with my friends" are all common reasons given for visiting museums. Litwak (1993) explains that visitors are "looking to engage in a shared mutual experience with their companions, and they've chosen a museum as the setting for this event" (111).

Museums are also educational institutions, and visitors choose them as good places to spend time together at least partially because they have education at their core. Even though education or learning may not be the primary visitor agenda, it is a highly valued characteristic of museum settings (Hilke 1988). Visitors to museums have a high expectation that they will learn something new; in fact, they are disappointed if they leave thinking they haven't (Falk and Dierking 1992, 142). Learning, then, becomes the vehicle by which visitors achieve their primary agenda of having an enjoyable social experience.

As educational institutions, museum staffs' primary agenda is to educate the public. In exhibit-development meetings, it is very common to hear museum professionals—curators, exhibit developers, and designers[1]—talk about the messages they want to communicate: "We want to teach visitors that . . . " or

"It's really important that visitors learn . . . " are not uncommon refrains. It's not that the museum is not interested in the social aspects of the museum visit; it's just that in many (most?) cases, the social dimension is not the museum's primary agenda. Interpreting objects and artifacts and communicating ideas are. Museum evaluator Randi Korn puts it more emphatically: "After hours of conversations with museum visitors, I started to realize that there is a gulf between the visitor experience from the visitor perspective and the visitor experience from the museum practitioner perspective, and that it is cavernous. . . . [Learning] is our obsession, and it seems to be the single framework we use to develop exhibits" (Kaplan, Bardwell, and Slakter 1993, 15).

Roberts (1997) refers to these different agendas as "the mismatch that arises between a museum's culture and a visitor's culture" (132). Fortunately, these two agendas are not mutually exclusive. McManus (1994, 82–83) suggests that whereas the educational agenda has traditionally tended to dominate the museum field, it's now time to recognize the simultaneous interplay of both. The challenge for museum professionals is to create exhibits that integrate the two agendas in meaningful ways. It's not whether a museum visit is more about the social experience or about learning. It's not about education versus entertainment or learning versus fun; it's about the seamless integration of both. As Roberts (1997) notes, "It's about negotiating [the] mismatch in a way that is respectful of both" (132–33). In other words, it's about how well these differing agendas are attended to and assimilated, for without one, there will not be the other.

LEARNING AS MEANING-MAKING

It's important to be clear about what we mean by "learning." Over the past two decades, there has been an evolution in understanding about what kind of learning happens, and should happen, in museums. Current thinking in museum settings argues for a broad definition of learning that recognizes the visitor as an integral part of the equation (Roberts 1997). While earlier theories of learning focused on an information-processing or -transference model, museum professionals are increasingly embracing active, constructivist, and participatory notions of what takes place within their settings. Not content with merely passing along information to visitors, museum professionals around the world are engaged in discussions about how visitors make meaning of, and develop relationships with, the stuff of museums, and about what the larger implications of this are, as museums tackle their educational functions.

Visitors in museums *make* meaning, rather than 'receive' it. While the 'message' of the museum and/or the object is important to some, it is not always the only source of meaning, and in some cases, it is not very important at all. . . . To operate from a conception of visitors as meaning-*makers* no doubt presents the spectre of a frightening loss of power for museum personnel. On the other hand, to acknowledge, validate, and incorporate other ways of relating to objects and other social functions of museum-going might ultimately democratize the museum experience in such a way that visitors and museum practitioners might all learn more about the variety of ways that things have meaning in our society. (Silverman 1990, 269–70)

Hein (1998, 25) and Hein and Alexander (1998, 33) propose a four-cell matrix to explain learning in museums. Along one axis are theories of knowledge (i.e., whether knowledge is something that resides outside of or within the learner), and along the other axis are theories of learning (i.e., whether one acquires knowledge incrementally by adding bits or by the active restructuring of the mind). Each of the resulting cells—that is, whether one believes that (a) knowledge resides outside the learner and the learning is incremental, (b) knowledge resides inside the learner and learning is incremental, (c) knowledge resides outside the learner and learning is constant restructuring, or (d) knowledge resides within the learner and learning is constant restructuring—implies a specific pedagogy or instructional strategy: didactic, discovery, stimulus response, or constructivism, respectively. Hein and Alexander go on to demonstrate that museums as institutions are becoming increasingly constructivist environments, places where visitors construct their own meanings by actively engaging with exhibits, programs, objects, and phenomena.

Roberts (1997) makes a compelling argument about the evolution of museum learning from traditional models of information transfer and the acquisition of *knowledge* to active and visitor-centered meaning-making, or *narrative*, arguing that the real strength of museums is the setting up of exhibitions and visitor experiences such that visitors create their own story lines, or narratives, and construct their own meanings. Providing a rich and entertaining history of this evolution, Roberts (1997) issues a call to arms to museums "to acknowledge that meaning making lies at the heart of the museum enterprise and that narrative provides the means by which this activity is accomplished" (152). In concert with Silverman (1990), she challenges museums "to take the first step toward truly opening museums to multiple voices and views" (Roberts 1997, 152).

The concepts of meaning-making and narrative are by their very natures broad and all encompassing. Paris and Mercer (2002) summarize learning in museums by suggesting there are three models for how visitors understand the museum objects they encounter. The traditional model of museum learning is *passive reception*, that is, the relatively linear and one-way communication of ideas from the museum to the visitor. This information-processing model underlies much of the way museums have traditionally thought about learning in museums, and it still pervades most museums' pedagogies. Whenever a label is designed to convey information, explain a concept, or argue a point, it is most likely grounded in an information-processing or passive-reception model of learning. This technique has much going for it. It is familiar, comfortable, and efficient. Many creative, catchy, and effective exhibit labels rely on this underlying philosophy of how visitors make sense of the stuff of museums.

More recently, museums have become interested in theories of *active construction* as a useful model of learning. As described by Paris and Mercer (2002), active construction is grounded in the belief that learners are participants in the learning process and that they construct their own knowledges and understandings within the context of the museum setting. This way of thinking is still heavily grounded in the content of the particular exhibit or program, however. It implies that at any particular exhibit, two different visitors may construct slightly different ways of understanding what they are experiencing, but these are just alternative understandings of the topic at hand.

Paris and Mercer (2002) suggest a third model for museum learning, which they call *transactions*. Transactions—also constructions of the learner—are even more highly personalized. The idea of transactions is that the learning process is characterized by a visitor or visitor group engaging in a personally relevant transaction with an object or artifact. These transactions are idiosyncratic and unique to the person or group that is visiting the museum. While the transaction may be generally connected to the object at hand, the meaning-making has more to do with the person or the group than the content of the exhibition. These transactions have much to do with personal identity and can be characterized as confirming what one believes to be true about oneself, disconfirming that belief, or pertaining to the discovery of something new.

The three models described by Paris and Mercer (2002) of how visitors make meaning in museum settings are not meant to imply a hierarchy or chronological progression of sophistication. Rather, they describe three different ways that visitors tend to make meaning: as receivers of information, as constructors of knowledge, and as developers of identity. All three are ongoing throughout a museum visit, and all three are valid and useful to keep in mind as we design and develop exhibits.

To summarize, in this section I argue for a broad definition of learning in museums—for learning as an active process of meaning-making, incorporating many types of learning, including passive reception, narrative creation, active construction, and transaction. Learning in this sense includes knowledge acquisition but is not bound or defined by it.

LEARNING AS CONVERSATION

Museums are increasingly interested in the role of conversation in informal learning. While conversation is often seen as the vehicle by which people learn, an argument can be made that just as learning is both a process and a product, so is conversation. By talking with their companions, museum visitors make sense of their experiences and create deeper understanding, and by engaging with the stuff of museums, they talk more with their companions (Silverman 1990). It's a two-way street. In this sense, learning is conversation, and conversation is learning. "What a group talks about, it thinks about; . . . talking is a tool for socially constructed thought, not just evidence of it; and . . . talk supports the gradual alteration and development of goals during the course of a visit" (Leinhardt and Knutson 2004, 159).

Not all museum conversations, however, carry the same meaning-making function. When conducting research into visitor conversations, Leinhardt and Crowley (1998) limited the focus of their study to *conversational elaboration.* Conversation was defined as "talk that focuses on the meaning and experiential nature of the museum but excludes planning and management decisions," and elaboration was defined as the ways in which conversations about the particular subject of an exhibit or exhibition evolve and become richer and more complex as a result of a museum visit (Leinhardt and Crowley 1998, 5–6). They posit that conversational elaboration is influenced by identity (i.e., who visitors are and what they bring with them), the physical environment (i.e., the objects, interpretation, and spaces and how they are designed), and explanatory engagement (i.e., the conversations that take place) (Leinhardt and Knutson 2004, 18–19).

During research into visitor learning at an outdoor living-history site in the Midwest, researchers found that "a substantial part of family conversation at the museum centered on learning. Parents seemed to be modeling excitement about learning, trying to connect experiences at Conner Prairie with previous learning and giving their children a framework for future learning" (Leinhardt, Crowley, and Knutson 2002, 327).

Emphasizing narrative and conversation is not just a good idea; the research literature has also repeatedly demonstrated their importance as educational strategies. Diamond (1980) found that learning in two science museums took place not from the exhibit unit to the visitor (i.e., the traditional model of passive reception or conveyance of content, as described above) but among the members of the social group within the context of the exhibit. In other words, visitors learned primarily from each other rather than from the exhibit, although they used the exhibit as an important source of information (Diamond 1986, 152–53). In Diamond's research, conversation was an important vehicle for active teaching and learning behaviors among the members of social groups.

Diamond's findings are supported by two studies conducted by McManus (1987, 1988) that examined the difference in visitor engagement, reading of labels, playing, and conversation among different types of visitor groups. She found that different types of visitor groups—for instance, whether the group included children, whether it was composed of an adult couple pair, adult peers, or a single individual—engaged in very different types of social and learning behavior. Whereas singletons tended to spend relatively short periods at an exhibit and read voraciously, groups with children tended to spend long periods, have lengthy conversations, and read very little. When groups with children did read, the adults tended to read "at a glance" to glean quick bits of information that they could rapidly translate and explain to other members of the group. Adult peers, on the other hand, tended not to engage very fully with the exhibits at all, whereas adult couples engaged in little conversation but read the labels quite extensively.

An even more interesting finding of McManus's work was the idea of social cohesiveness as a strong influence on visitor learning behaviors. She found that the more socially cohesive a group was (as measured by physical proximity to one another as well as the extent to which their movements were complementary or independent), the more they engaged in learning-related activities such as reading labels, interacting with exhibits, and having lengthy conversations. McManus (1988) concludes, "Clearly, social group composition affects the strength with which museum visitors work to make their meanings about exhibit communications clear to each other in their conversations" (42–43). According to McManus, conversation is how visitors make meaning, and social cohesiveness is a major influence on how visitors have conversations.

Another study, not from the museum field but from the field of child de-velopment, found that very young children (ages thirty to forty-two months) were able to remember significant events and activities more fully when their mothers engaged in conversations with them about those activities than when mothers did not engage in such conversations (Haden et al. 2001). This rein-forces the findings from Leinhardt and Knutson (2004), who found that what is talked about is remembered, and what is remembered is learned: "What groups talk about in engaged ways and think about, they remember. These memories become connected again through mutually self-referencing discussions to other ideas, activities, and objects. What is remembered is learned" (159).

While Haden et al. focused on young children, Silverman (1990) was inter-ested in the nature of the conversations among adult pairs in museum settings. She found that visitors together created meaning that was idiosyncratic to that particular visitor group. "Visitor pairs filter their competencies and tendencies through the context of their relationship to produce a shared interpretive ap-proach" (Silverman 1990, vii). "Given the social nature of interpretation through talk, it is no longer the individual contributions of the pair members which mat-ter, so much as the joint processes which result" (Silverman 1990, 92).

Other researchers have defined conversation in different ways. Fienberg and Leinhardt (2002, 169–70) describe four specific types of conversation (what they refer to as *explanatory engagement*) in increasing levels of sophistication. The simplest and most direct response to the content of an exhibit—for instance, the identification of an object or the listing of features observed—is called *listing*. When the conversation moves into analyzing some of the underlying features of an object, this type of conversation is referred to as *analysis*, and when multiple ideas from a variety of sources are integrated, this is *synthesis*. The most sophis-ticated type of conversation according to this framework is *explanation*, or the combination of all of the above with the specific intention of helping others in the group understand.

A somewhat similar framework is suggested by Silverman (1990), who con-ducted an extensive study of the conversation of adult pairs at two different art museums. Rather than presenting an organizational scheme of increasing sophistication, as proposed by Fienberg and Leinhardt (2002), Silverman (1990, 90) suggests that virtually all visitors engage in five major *interpretive acts* during their museum visit: establishment, evaluation, absolute object description, relating special knowledge, and relating personal experience. Rather than submitting that

Conversational Acts

Comparing the models described by Silverman (1990) and Fienberg and Leinhardt (2002) adds depth to our understanding of the role of conversation in creating meaning. *Establishment* is similar to *listing* (i.e. the naming and identification of an object). The process of *evaluation* appears to be missing from Fienberg and Leinhardt's framework. It entails offering a judgment or an opinion about an object, such as "It's pretty." Silverman's *absolute object description* closely parallels Fienberg and Leinhardt's *analysis*, referring to the description of an object's key and readily discernable attributes or function. *Relating special knowledge* is similar to *synthesis* in that it draws on knowledge and information not immediately available in the presentation of the object. Finally, *relating personal experience* also doesn't seem to have a place in the Fienberg and Leinhardt model, perhaps because it is assumed under identity in their broader model of conversational elaboration. It includes personal memory or reminiscences. While Silverman's model doesn't have a comparable category to *explanation*, one could argue that all five of these interpretive acts in fact represent the group construction of understanding and meaning.

the individual types of conversation lead up to an ultimate process of teaching and learning behavior, as is implied by Fienberg and Leinhardt (2002), Silverman (1990) posits that meaning-making is what museum visitors do and that *all* conversation is focused on this joint construction of knowledge.

In my research, I have focused on the specific educative value of museum conversations (Perry 1989) and have defined *meaningful social interaction* as those conversations and other educational interchanges that use specific teaching/learning strategies such as directing attention, explaining a concept, listening to an explanation, making an analogy, using metaphor, giving examples, adapting to the developmental needs of different members of the social group, relating to something familiar, employing explaining/teaching behavior, asking and/or answering questions, directing another visitor's behavior, and reading and interpreting labels out loud to or for another visitor. Using a primarily qualitative approach, I observed how the quantity and quality of social interactions were influenced by different exhibit design strategies.[2]

While also interested in the educative nature of visitor conversation, Borun, Chambers, and Cleghorn (1995, 1996) took a slightly different approach by rating visitor groups in terms of the amount of learning evident in the group: low, medium, or high. These ratings were assigned based on the combined richness and complexity of group members' conversations at an exhibit and their responses to interview questions. A low rating was given when answers to interview questions were single-word answers and visitors made few associations to the exhibit content. A medium rating indicated multiple-word answers to interview questions and minimal connections to exhibit content beyond what was in front of them. Like the frameworks proposed by Fienberg and Leinhardt (2002) and Silverman (1990), Borun, Chambers, and Cleghorn placed value on visitors integrating the exhibit concepts with other experiences and knowledge not immediately evident. These types of conversations indicated a high level of learning.

While different researchers have defined meaningful visitor conversations in slightly different ways, when it comes to the process of museum visitors making meaning, it is clear that conversations matter and are worthy of further study.

VISITORS MAKING SENSE OF AN EXHIBIT

As I collected data at the *Colored Shadows* exhibit (see the introduction), I observed a variety of visitor groups and their interactions with the exhibit, some of which provided striking examples of different approaches to learning and meaning making. For example, one carefully dressed father approached the exhibit with his young son, who was probably in the fifth grade. They weren't talking very much as they wandered around the gallery; nor did they seem particularly excited or animated. But as they drew closer to *Colored Shadows*, the father brightened and became visibly interested. As with most intergenerational groups visiting this exhibit, the younger visitor approached first and began waving his hands over the tabletop, making brightly colored shadows. The father excitedly began reading the Parent Information interpretive text that explained—in quite a bit of detail—color and light theory. Although initially intrigued by the colored shadows he was creating, the boy quickly became bored and started to leave the exhibit, whereupon his father called him back and began explaining all that was going on. I could overhear him enthusiastically describing to his son that this was what he did for a living as a physicist: study colors and light waves. He offered a thorough, detailed, and animated explanation about light waves and color theory, pointing to the labels as supporting evidence. The boy stood patiently for a few minutes, shuffling his feet; as soon as there was a break in the conversation, he looked at his father and asked, "Can I go now, Dad?" The father was visibly disappointed as the two of them wandered away.

In a follow-up interview, the father explained that, as a physicist, he specialized in the area of color and light. He then went on to share with me how disappointed he was: he was having difficulty connecting with his son while at the museum, and finally here was an exhibit that had particular meaning for him, but in spite of his best attempts to engage the boy, his son just was not interested.

Fast-forward a few days to when I observed another visitor group composed of a woman with a girl who appeared to be her daughter, about eight years old. They approached the exhibit together, talking among themselves and seeming to have a good time. Again, the younger visitor immediately started waving her hands over the tabletop, making an array of colored shadows, while the adult looked around for some interpretation. The girl quickly asked what was going on and why she had colored shadows. The woman explained that she didn't know but suggested they read the labels together to find out.

The two visitors diligently read all the labels one at a time and tried all the activities, but it was clear that they didn't understand what the exhibit was about. Periodically, the woman would ask the child a question or pose a challenge, and the girl would try to figure it out, but even working together, they were not able to make much sense of things. After a few minutes, they wandered away from the exhibit, again visibly disappointed. In a follow-up interview, the woman told me that she had been teaching elementary school for a number of years and was frustrated because she couldn't figure out what the exhibit was about. She apologized a few times because, as she explained, she wasn't much good at science.

A third group to *Colored Shadows* consisted of an adult man and a group of three boys, probably in middle school or early high school. They approached the exhibit, laughing and talking among themselves. As they came near the exhibit, one of the boys moved his hand over the tabletop and—amid exclamations of "Awesome!" and "Cool!"—the adult pointed up to the ceiling where the three lights were hanging and said, "Look, colored lights!" He asked the boys how many colored lights there were and what colors they were. The boys called out the answers, and the group immediately engaged in a discussion about where the colors were coming from. Ultimately, the conversation got around to how these three colors mixed to make white light and how the different colored shadows came about because their hands were blocking out one or two of the colored lights. The adult showed the boys how to look at the color on the back of their hands to see which colored light they were blocking out. He challenged the boys to "make a yellow shadow," even though there was no yellow light; he encouraged them as they tried different combinations and cheered enthusiastically when one of them was successful. The group stayed with the exhibit for a long time, making interesting hand shadows, arguing and hypothesizing about where the different colors were coming from, and obviously enjoying themselves. In the follow-up interview, the man explained that he was a high school drama teacher who worked with theater lights and that he taught students about stage lighting, a particular passion of his.

These three visitor experiences were markedly different from one another, even though all three took place at the same exhibit in the same museum, and all three involved visitors enthusiastically working to have a meaningful experience. Most folks in the museum field would agree that only the third experience was what we would term "successful." Although the frustrations were different for the first and second visitor groups, neither had satisfying experiences. What made the third experience so much more successful than the first two?

VISITORS AS TEACHERS/LEARNERS

Jerome Bruner (1966) talks about the *natural will to learn* and explains that we are all born with natural curiosity and an inherent ability to learn; we can't escape it, it's ingrained in us, and it's part of what makes us human. I propose that there is also a *natural will to teach*, or at least a desire to help others figure things out. All three groups of visitors described above clearly demonstrated this, although in different ways. The physicist with his son was clearly invested in what others have called identity; this exhibit was about him and what he did for a living. It was an opportunity for him to "teach" his son about something central to who he was, and a way for him to connect with the boy. The elementary school teacher and the drama teacher were also clearly invested in helping others in their group develop an understanding of the exhibit. These are very typical behaviors in museum settings.

When thinking of museum exhibits as opportunities for visitors to engage their natural will to teach, we need to be careful not to think of teaching in a narrow, classroom kind of way. Diamond (1980, 77) claims that "teaching in schools appears to differ substantially from teaching as it occurs spontaneously within family groups." Teaching in informal settings refers to the broad activity of helping others develop a deeper understanding of something, of creating meaning, of making sense. It is intertwined with, and can't be separated from, learning. It's also interesting to note that—at least in a museum setting—teaching is not exclusively, or even primarily, a top-down, from-older-to-younger, from-parent-to-child, from-experienced-to-less-experienced kind of process; rather, it is constantly shifting and reciprocal among all members of the visitor group (Diamond 1980, 70). Rather than talking about the teaching/learning process, Schauble et al. (2002) argue for *supporting learning*. They define learning support as comprising many socially mediated learning processes, including the joint construction of knowledge, asking and answering questions, offering explanations, directing attention, and engaging in rich meaning-making.

In her important research into visitors' teaching behavior in museum settings, Diamond (1980) goes on to explain that different members of visiting social groups tend to engage in different types of teaching activities. She found that adults tended to read exhibit labels and interpret symbolic information for their children, explaining exhibit concepts and phenomena. Children, however, tended to explore and investigate the exhibits, conveying important concrete information about the exhibit back to the adults.

While this natural will to teach in a museum setting is clearly an important component of visitor experiences, it is unfortunately often not accompanied by natural ability. These cases involving the physicist and son and the elementary school teacher and child are clear examples in which a strong desire to help a young charge make sense of what was going on in the exhibit resulted in a frustrating and unsatisfying exchange, in one case because of a lack of understanding about how to engage with the child and in the other because of an inability to quickly glean the content. Unfortunately, these are not isolated cases. Leinhardt, Crowley, and Knutson (2002) write,

> The parents in our study tried earnestly (and repeatedly) on their own to prompt learning exchanges with their children, but more often than not, faced frustrating reticence or outright noncompliance, unless an interpreter had sparked a conversation. (325)

> Parents did not understand what their children did not know, and failed to provide assistance because they were not aware that it was needed. (449)

> Adults in the museum are challenged and sometimes even openly puzzled about how to help children learn in a gallery that affords multiple levels of investigation. Staff and parents clearly appreciated children's spontaneous fascination and sustained engagement with the exhibits, but were not always confident how they could know that children were really learning. . . . For the most part, they were interested in figuring out how to optimize the educational potential of children's

activity by directing it toward finding out, making comparisons, closely observing, or systematically exploring, rather than aimless fiddling or acquiring terms and labels. Many adults—some parents but especially staff—expressed ambivalence or confusion about how . . . adults could offer effective assistance without intruding in clumsy ways on children's self-directed activity. . . . Too often, [the staff] thought, some parents were passively disengaged whereas others tended to be overcontrolling and didactic. (443)

Clearly museum visitors want to engage in meaningful ways that support others' learning, but all too often they are unable to do so, not because they are ignorant or incompetent but because museums haven't provided the appropriate guidance.

Historically, museums have focused on interpretation that conveys information. They've worked hard to figure out how to most effectively arrange objects and write labels, struggling over what level of information is appropriate and how best to structure, organize, and sequence content (Serrell 1996a). But as is clear from the aforementioned examples, while the right objects and the right content at the right level and appropriate organization are essential, they're not enough. The father with the fifth-grade son knew the content very well. But he didn't know how to talk with his son about it. He didn't know what level of explanation was appropriate. He didn't know what questions to ask. Perhaps he didn't even know that asking his son questions was a good thing to do. It was obvious that he was at a loss when it came to knowing how to engage his son in a meaningful way.

The elementary school teacher with her young companion, however, knew about asking questions. She knew about the importance of reading labels and working together to figure out answers. She knew how to give the right level of explanation, and she knew how to engage her youngster in appropriate meaning-making. But she didn't know very much about mixing colored lights or about shadows. She didn't know that red, green, and blue mix to make white. In other words, she knew how to support her child's learning, but she didn't know the content of the exhibit.

The third group, the high school drama teacher with three boys, was fortunate because the group included someone who both knew the content and understood meaningful ways to support the group's learning. As someone who worked with theater lighting, the adult knew about mixing colored lights, and he knew how red, green, and blue combine to make white. But he also knew how to teach. He knew to start with the concrete and to make things relevant and personally meaningful. He knew how and when to ask questions, give explanations, and provide feedback. Of the three groups, this was the only one that successfully integrated both content and pedagogy in an engaging process of socially mediated meaning-making. And ultimately, this was the only one of the three that had a satisfying and successful experience at the exhibit. These three visitor groups clearly demonstrated the importance of not only knowing the content—as the physicist obviously did—but also knowing how to support the group's learning—as the elementary teacher did. The only group able to succeed was the group that included someone who was familiar with both, that is, the drama teacher. But visitors shouldn't have to rely on having someone in their group who already knows both the content and how to support learning. What if exhibits were designed not only to convey the important content but also to guide the meaning-making process?

Another visitor group was composed of a young father and his two-year-old daughter. By this time, the *Colored Shadows* exhibit had been studied extensively, and all the interpretation had been revised to stimulate more meaningful visitor experiences. Although on the surface it looked similar to the original exhibit—the white tabletop was still there, there were still three colored lights, and there was still a computer standing next to the exhibit—in actuality all the interpretation had been overhauled, and it was a very different exhibit, now called *The Color Connection*. Above the computer was a large sign that said "Parent Information" with an arrow pointing down. When visitors approached the computer, they first saw a screen with six menu choices, one of which was "What can I do with my preschooler?" The father initially approached the exhibit by himself, going straight to the computer and immediately selecting the option on preschoolers. The directions were very simple: "Name the colors you see"; "Count the shadows"; "Make hand shadows"; and "Make up stories about the hand shadows" (Perry 1989, 316–17).

After spending a few seconds perusing the computer, the father went and got his child, carrying her over to the exhibit and setting her on the tabletop. Together they did many of the things he had just read about: playing in the lights, naming the colors, dangling hair in the light and shaking their heads. After a little while, the father noticed me watching them. He eagerly scooped up his daughter and approached me. "Is there more exhibits in here like that?" he asked eagerly. When I asked him what he meant, he explained,

As far as where parents can participate like that, you know. . . . Before [my daughter] ever saw [the exhibit], I came over and read what I should be doing with my preschooler. I just did what this said I ought to do. I never have been able to get her involved in the museum [previously] except holding her up and showing her. (Perry 1989, 184)

Here was a dedicated dad in a children's museum who wanted to involve his child in museums at a very young age, and yet, prior to coming to this exhibit, he was at a loss about what to do. He wasn't incompetent; he just needed a jump-start. He needed to know not only the content of the exhibit but also how to engage with his child. I was amazed that he recognized that this exhibit was giving him something crucial. And he wanted more, "more exhibits in here like that."

The adults in the four cases described wanted to facilitate a meaningful, exhibit-based learning experience with their companions. The museum field is full of other similar examples as well.[3] The father's reaction to the redesigned exhibit, however, provided such a stark contrast with those of the groups I observed visiting the original exhibit that it made a powerful impression on me. What would it take to design exhibits systematically to facilitate this kind of positive experience for any kind of exhibit content and any kind of visitor group? Was it possible to make learning fun by design?

NOTES

1. I use the terms *exhibit designer*, *exhibit developer*, and *museum professional* synonymously and very broadly to include all people involved in the decision-making process of developing interpretive exhibits and exhibitions for the public. In this case, "exhibit designer" and "exhibit developer" do not necessarily reference people who hold those job titles but rather all museum professionals who are members of the large team of folks involved in the design and development of a particular exhibit. This includes people who hold the title of designer and developer, as well as curators, educators, evaluators, content developers, research assistants, and so forth.

2. Throughout this book I often refer to teachers/learners and to the teaching/learning process. I use these terms hesitatingly as they connote a structured approach reminiscent of formal educational settings. But I have yet to come across a better description of what goes on as visitors strive to make sense of exhibits. I use these terms very broadly to include the mutually shaping, ever-changing, and fluid meaning-making process that takes place between and among visitors in social groups. Each museum visitor has the capacity to be—and indeed operates as—both teacher and learner, to help others make sense of an exhibit, and to develop deeper understandings through interactions with the exhibit and with other visitors. This important concept is explored in this chapter and also serves as a foundation for ideas presented throughout the book.

3. See, for example, Diamond (1980, 1986); Gottfried (1979); Laetsch, Diamond, Gottfried, and Rosenfeld (1980); Leinhardt, Crowley, and Knutson (2002); Leinhardt and Knutson (2004); McManus (1987, 1988); Perry (1989); Paris (2002); Silverman (1990); Spock (2000); Taylor (1986).

2

Interpretive Activism

Interpretive activism is the process of advocating for and incorporating research-based, visitor-centered exhibit design principles and strategies that facilitate active visitor participation in the interpretive process.

Interpretive activists advocate for and incorporate the kinds of research and strategies addressed in this book, with the intention of facilitating visitor meaning making. This includes visitors having conversations with other members of their social group and being actively involved in teaching/learning processes. I propose that this *is* learning that is fun. The active part of interpretive activism for museum professionals is advocating for and incorporating research-based principles into the design of museum exhibits, with the end goal of engaging the visitor in rich, active, and satisfying meaning-making, conversation, and interpretation.

Our knowledge about museum visitors, their conversations, and how they learn in the museum environment continues to expand as we move the conversation about exhibit design forward into territory that has visitor learning at the center. By understanding and applying this knowledge, we are better able to integrate the largely social agenda that visitors bring with them to our museums with museums' largely educational missions.

When visitors arrive at a museum, research has shown that they want to engage with exhibits, but they don't always have the knowledge and skills to get out of exhibits as much as museum professionals hope they will. We also know that visitors enjoy interacting with their friends and family members who come with them, and in doing so, they use museum labels and interpretation to make sense of exhibits. In other words, we know that learning in museums happens in many different ways, and it is largely mediated through the social context of visitors' experiences. This means that museum visitors who visit in groups often talk their way through exhibits, and their learning is made through their conversations with others.

The premise of this book is that exhibits can be designed to facilitate meaning making on visitors' terms, regardless of the composition of visitor groups or the knowledge or skills they bring with them. To do this requires that we, as museum professionals, expand our repertoire of skills, knowledge, and techniques. If we apply lessons learned from other fields (including instructional design), as well as knowledge gained from research (for example, on intrinsic motivation), and test our design ideas with visitors themselves, the exhibit design-and-development process becomes actively focused on the visitor and what the visitor gets out of the experience. This is what interpretive activism is about. It requires rethinking how all the different exhibit components work together to maximize the potential for each museum visitor to have a personally meaningful experience, where the visitor is actively engaged, learns something, and has fun in the process.

EXHIBITS AS CONVEYORS OF CONTENT

Traditionally, exhibit labels have served primarily to convey information and interpret objects and artifacts. In this role, labels have contributed in significant ways to visitors having meaningful conversations and making sense of the stuff of museums. Ash (2002) claims that good exhibits are the "jumping off points for thematic conversations, by providing strong themes that pervade family conversations in engaging ways" (396). Leinhardt and Knutson (2004) similarly call for exhibit labels that contain "meaningful information for visitors, information that answers their questions . . . information that addresses issues" (160). Leinhardt and Gregg (2002) go so far as to encourage exhibit developers and designers to include labels that embrace controversy. They claim that through controversy, some of the most meaningful conversations take place.

Without labels that convey important, meaningful, and even controversial information, the learning conversations that visitors engage in will not have the richness of understanding that museums desire.

While the importance and necessity of labels as conveyors of information is well established, some researchers have identified problems with this primary role for exhibit labels. This is especially true as museums increasingly adopt constructivist and participatory paradigms for visitor learning. McManus (1990) talks about museums being conversation "hogs"; she explains how members of visitor groups are primarily interested in the social relationships with their companions and how they refuse to allow label writers to monopolize the conversation. In fact, they will choose to not read a label rather than allow it to "hog the language space" (McManus 1990, 5).

Research indicates that one reason many exhibit labels don't work particularly well is that visitors would like more opportunity to participate in the conversation. In an extensive study on the nature of visitor conversation, Hensel (1987, 127) examined issues surrounding the maintenance of conversations in one particular museum. She found that all too often the reading of labels actually interrupted visitor conversations. McManus (1988, 40) goes so far as to suggest that reading labels in a museum setting can be an isolating and antisocial activity.

THE ART OF INTERPRETIVE ACTIVISM

Rather than lecturing visitors and monopolizing the language space, as McManus claims labels too often tend to do, what if museum professionals gave visitors the tools they need to engage in meaningful conversations with their companions? In other words, what if exhibits (including labels, but other components as well) were specifically designed to contribute to visitors' conversations rather than interrupting them? What if those of us involved in the design and development of exhibits served as *interpretive activists*, activating learning conversations and facilitating resultant discussions, providing the necessary support for all visitors to actively engage with the stuff of museums in personal and powerful ways? Visitors are smart and motivated. They don't need oversimplified information. They don't appreciate being lectured to. But we also know that sometimes they need a catalyst, something to get them started in the right direction (or perhaps, more accurately, in *a* right direction, a path that helps them feel safe and smart and that supports them in their desire to be actively involved in the interpretive process). This isn't about dumbing down the text. It's about honoring and respecting visitors, their time, and their agendas. It's about sharing the conversation space with them rather than monopolizing it. Visitors will work amazingly hard to make sense of objects, artifacts, and the phenomena on display. As museum professionals, we need to be working just as hard to design interpretation so that our audiences are able to glean quickly (in seconds or split seconds, not minutes) both content and pedagogy so they can work together to make meaning of what they are experiencing—meaning that is accurate and personally relevant.

This intertwining of content and pedagogy is the foundation for an effective interpretive strategy that moves the field of exhibit design and development from primarily conveying information to facilitating dialogue and meaning-making.

> If visitors are to truly learn from museums, that interpretive activity needs to be coupled with content knowledge. . . . We recommend that museums and museum educators consider how they can enable visitors to develop an interpretive stance toward the museum, a stance that incorporates both content knowledge and a position related to the visitors' own identity. Such enablement will help visitors to enhance both their enjoyment of and their learning from the museum. (Abu-Shumays and Leinhardt 2002, 79)

Museum professionals continue to explore the idea of designing exhibits that support the learning conversations and related teaching/learning activities visitors engage in (Leinhardt, Crowley, and Knutson 2002, 79, 207, 325–28, 395–96, 442, 449). Ash (2002) writes of the "delicate intertwining of content and the method with which it is negotiated" (395). By getting visitors to actively participate not just in the content but also the pedagogy, museum professionals "can help draw the visitor from the periphery of the museum world into a more central conversation with it" (Abu-Shumays and Leinhardt 2002, 79). In discussing living-history museums, Rosenthal and Blankman-Hetrick (2002) argue that we need to spend more time drawing visitors into the "web of the past" and less time "simply covering topics of information" (326).

> Unless careful attention is paid to helping the helpers, the energy and resources devoted to deepening museum learning may be wasted, or at best, underexploited. Museums are contexts where designers give considerable explicit thought to assisting learning via symbol systems and tools, including built environments, texts, activity structures, even color and traffic patterns! However, less thought has been spent on thinking about how to engineer the role of people, including parents, museum staff, and other visiting children. (Schauble et al. 2002, 449)

This important idea of engineering the role of people, helping visitors facilitate learning themselves, is usually overlooked during the design of museum interpretation. The good news is that visiting groups to museums do much of this naturally; they are natural learners, and many researchers have documented this. Hilke (1988) in particular stresses that family visitors naturally engage "in activities which promote both personal and group learning" (124). However, as mentioned, the support they need to engage in rich and meaningful conversations is often lacking.

INTERPRETATION AS CONVERSATION CATALYST

The previous discussion of exhibits as conveyors of information acknowledged the important role of content and described some risks associated with its presentation. How do we take essential exhibit content and treat it so that it facilitates, rather than stymies, conversations?

Research has shown that interpretive labels and other exhibit components can be *conversation catalysts* (Perry 1989). Many visitors—like the physicist father and son—don't know how or where to start a conversation at an exhibit. But in order to design exhibits that help jump-start conversations, the designer or developer must know where visitors are conceptually. What are they thinking about as they approach an exhibit? What do they think the exhibit is about? How do they understand the topic of the exhibit? Where is their attention drawn? And is this where we want them to start?

During the research conducted on the *Colored Shadows* exhibit, for example, I found that while they enjoyed the bright, colorful shadows they produced at the exhibit, most visitors did not learn anything new; in fact, oftentimes they didn't even understand that the exhibit was about mixing colored lights. In analyzing these findings, I found that a good part of the reason for this was that most visitors didn't notice the lights shining on the tabletop. They had no idea that the colors they saw came from colored lights hanging overhead. It became clear

Why Magic Is Not Enough

I am all for creating magic in our exhibits—museums should be about magical experiences—but I also believe that magic is not enough. When the magical experience is as far as visitors can go (as it was for many of the visitors to the original *Colored Shadows* exhibit), especially when they want to go further but don't know how to get there, then we have done them a disservice, and we have not honored their desire to make sense of their world, to learn something new, and to have rich, engaging, active, and meaningful experiences.

that in order for visitors to successfully use this exhibit and learn about mixing colored lights, they first needed to notice the colored lights shining down. Otherwise, the exhibit was simply about magic.

Instead of lecturing his son about color theory, what if the father of the fifth-grade boy had begun his interaction at the exhibit by asking his son a question: Where do the colors on the table come from? Or alternatively, he could have explicitly directed his son to find the three lights shining on the tabletop. In fact, during my research and redesign of the exhibit, visitors' understanding of the exhibit and satisfaction with their experience increased significantly after the addition of a simple label that read, "Look up! Find the colored lights." An appropriate starting point for a visitor conversation was found by analyzing not just the exhibit content but also the learning process. This resulted in higher levels of satisfaction, more meaningful and active learning, and ultimately a more successful exhibit.

What about the directive to look up and find the colored lights helped make this exhibit more successful? Why did this simple label enhance the exhibit experience for so many visitors? I found that this label in particular had a number of things going for it: (a) it contained simple text that could be read at a glance as someone approached the exhibit; (b) it gave visitors actual words to use when talking with each other; and (c) it conveyed pedagogy as well as content. In other words, it served to jump-start a meaningful conversation, a rich and authentic teaching/learning process. With this simple label, as a group approached the exhibit, one visitor (often, but not always, an adult) would usually read the label out loud, and the rest of the group would begin a conversation about where the colored lights were (figure 2.1).

The group would point and debate about what color the different lights were, and they'd argue about which colors combined to make which other colors. The label's simple directive got visitors started on a rich and meaningful learning conversation.

The obvious should be noted here: the resulting conversations were not all exactly the same. Sometimes they were messy, and sometimes they veered off into other areas. Almost always, however, they were rich, personally relevant, satisfying conversations. Most visitors eventually came around to a deeper understanding of how lights mix to produce other colors, and significantly more got to that level of understanding than with the more traditional information-conveying labels. In addition, fewer visitors left the exhibit demonstrating a lack of interest

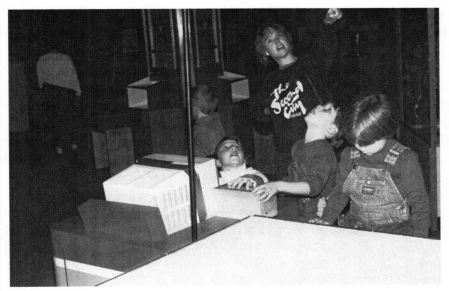

FIGURE 2.1
An adult helps the children find the colored lights.

in the topic of colored lights. An additional benefit of this label was that it quietly modeled an appropriate teaching/learning framework for visitors—that is,
working together, directing attention, and having conversations rather than the
more traditional interpretive strategy of presenting information.

Exhibit interpretation can also be used to facilitate developmentally appropriate interactions among visitors. One of the problems with the exchange
between the physicist and his son was that it wasn't particularly appropriate for
a ten-year-old. This was the same problem implied by the preschooler's parent
who was delighted when the computer's suggestions empowered him to engage
with his daughter in ways he had not been able to before. The simple text quickly
got him started on learning conversations with his daughter at a level that was
perfectly suited to the developmental needs of his child—and, for that matter,
to his developmental needs as a parent. Was the exhibit unsuccessful because
this visitor group did not learn that red, green, and blue lights mix to make
white? Interpretive activists—museum professionals who use research to design
exhibits that actively engage visitors in the interpretive process—would not say
this exhibit failed. Nor would we say that this exhibit should target, for example,
middle school students because that is the age at which children can learn about

color theory. And we would not say that color theory is a difficult concept and beyond the scope of many visitors, so it's okay if folks don't learn much as long as they are having a good time and enjoying the "magic" of colored shadows. Museum professionals, as interpretive activists, would reject these positions in the process of fully embracing museums' educational missions.

I propose that our job as museum professionals is not to ensure every visitor gets the same message, or creates the same meaning, or understands the exhibit in the same way; rather, it is to maximize the learning and enjoyment potential for as many visitors as possible. To do that, we need to recognize that all visitors are different and will create their own narratives. Our job as facilitators of meaningful visitor experiences is to give visitors the support and guidance they need so that they can participate fully in a learning endeavor while having one heck of a time, and to ensure they do not walk away feeling disappointed, frustrated, or incompetent.

Starting Where Visitors Are

The importance of starting where visitors are can't be stressed enough. As museum professionals we often tend to start where we want visitors to end rather than where we want them to begin. We spend long periods wrestling with the exact wording of the "big idea," goals and objectives, and educational messages. And we should. But we need to remember that these are goals, things we are striving for. In other words, goals are where we want visitors to end and not necessarily where they should start. Our job as museum professionals is to help visitors on their learning journeys by joining them where they are and then providing support to get them to where they want to be. When interpretation starts at the end, rather than the beginning, it is no wonder so many visitors get lost.

The way to find out where visitors are, what they are thinking about, and how they understand the topic at hand, is to conduct front-end research. By talking with—and, more importantly, listening to—visitors, we can begin to develop an understanding of visitor *starting points*. A carefully conducted front-end study gives the exhibit-development team valuable information to make informed decisions and ideally illuminates potential interpretive bridges between visitors and the content.

THE DESIGN OF INTERPRETIVE ACTIVISM

Every aspect of a museum visit—including the visitors inside as well as the outside community—contributes to the ultimate meaningfulness of visitor experiences in both positive and negative ways. The weather outside; the makeup of the social group; the design of the exhibit; visitors' backgrounds, experiences, and interests; the state of the economy—all of these aspects of the museum visit serve to either enhance or inhibit how and to what degree visitors have satisfying and meaningful experiences.

Enhancers are all those things that contribute to, or enhance, the probability of a successful and meaningful visitor experience, one in which visitors enjoy themselves, learn something, and leave feeling satisfied. Typical enhancers include well-designed exhibits, an enthusiastic docent, visitors who have studied up on the exhibit before coming to the museum, a community that values museums and museum going, a healthy economy—the list goes on. Anything that enhances the likelihood of meaningful visitor experiences is considered an enhancer.

On the other hand, *inhibitors* are all those things that inhibit the probability of a meaningful visitor experience. Poorly lit artifacts, crowded or broken exhibits, labels filled with technical terms and unfamiliar words, restroom facilities located too far away, not enough spots to rest—anything that interferes with a meaningful visitor experience can be considered an inhibitor.

Some of these enhancers and inhibitors are within our control. Museum professionals engaged in the design and development of museum exhibits select the words to put on an interpretive text panel; we decide how the text is laid out, what colors are used in the exhibition, and how artifacts are organized and illuminated. Other enhancers and inhibitors are not in our control. We have no control, for example, over visitors' prior knowledge, experiences, interests, educational levels, ages, and physical abilities and disabilities. We have no control over the nature of visitors' relationships with others in the social group with whom they visit the museum or what their personal agendas may be. Although these not-under-our-control enhancers and inhibitors have a big influence on the overall experience of any particular group of visitors and are vital, they are not something designers and developers of museum exhibits can do anything about; hence, they are not the focus of this book.

The only thing we, as exhibit designers and developers, have control over is the design of the physical space—in this case, the "learning environment" (Fienberg and Leinhardt 2002, 167), or, in some instances, the "physical context" (Falk and Dierking 1992). While we can't make someone care or learn, we can set up learning environments that maximize the potential for meaningful "conversational elaboration" (Leinhardt, Crowley, and Knutson 2002, 54–56). The job of those involved in the design of an exhibit, then, is to maximize the enhancers and minimize the inhibitors. There is no foolproof way to determine whether something will be an enhancer or inhibitor. In fact, a particular design decision may be an enhancer in one situation and an inhibitor in another. Evaluation (front-end, formative, and remedial) is essential to ensure, or at least maximize the likelihood, that a planned enhancer will in fact serve to enhance the visitor experience.

It should also be kept in mind that a particular design decision will not necessarily be an enhancer or an inhibitor for everyone. An audio tour that provides context and meaningful interpretation for one visitor may inhibit meaningful conversation for another. Being clear about the desired visitor engagements and outcomes and testing with a variety of visitors will help determine the design's ultimate effectiveness at achieving the exhibit's goals and facilitating rich and active visitor experiences.

Can we, as museum professionals, design exhibits that incorporate only enhancers and no inhibitors? As much as we'd like to create perfect exhibits, we know that's impossible. The diversity of museum visitors, the aspects of the museum visit over which we have no control, the fact that sometimes design decisions need to address factors other than those focused on the visitor (e.g., budgets, institutional politics)—these realities mean that the best we can hope for is to create exhibits that maximize the likelihood that visitors will have rich experiences. Interpretive activism provides the background and understanding so that we can make knowledgeable and informed design decisions. By thoughtfully and wisely applying the principles and strategies described in the second half of this book, we can increase the possibility that we will facilitate, through our exhibit designs, meaningful and engaging visitor experiences.

The next chapter introduces a model for looking at the visitor experience using three different frameworks, in terms of (a) what visitors learn, (b) how they engage, and (c) what makes learning fun. From this foundation, we can then discuss principles and strategies for designing intrinsically motivating visitor experiences, experiences that intertwine museums' agendas to communicate content and get visitors excited about new ideas with visitors' agendas to have fun social experiences in the context of cool objects and interesting phenomena.

The PISEC Study

The PISEC study conducted at four institutions in the Philadelphia area[1] is one of a few studies focusing specifically on how design decisions affect the visitor experience. After examining the relationship between learning behaviors and learning outcomes at four informal science institutions, Borun, Massey, et al. (1998) came up with a list of characteristics for *family-friendly* museum exhibits, that is, exhibits that foster social learning in museum settings. They call for exhibits that are (a) multisided, so a family can cluster around the exhibit; (b) multiuser, so that several sets of hands or bodies can use the exhibit simultaneously; (c) accessible, so that it can be comfortably used by children and adults; (d) multi-outcome, so that engagements can be sufficiently complex to foster group discussion; (e) multimodal,[2] so that the exhibit appeals to different learning styles and levels of knowledge; (f) readable, so that text is easily understood; and (g) relevant, so that the exhibit provides cognitive links to visitors' existing knowledge and experience (Borun, Chambers, et al. 1998, 23). These seven characteristics were developed by a team of researchers based on a review of fourteen selected research articles on family learning in museums, then tested in four different informal learning institutions (Borun and Dritsas 1997, 179–80, 193–96).

NOTES

1. PISEC stands for Philadelphia-Camden Informal Science Education Collaborative and included the Franklin Institute Science Museum, the New Jersey State Aquarium, the Academy of Natural Sciences, and the Philadelphia Zoo.

2. Multimodal in this study refers to having a variety of activities that appeal to different learning styles and prior experience. This is a slightly different definition from what is found in the education literature, where modes are defined specifically as audio, visual, and kinesthetic (Fleming and Levie 1978, 46–48).

3

The Selinda Model of Visitor Learning

The What Makes Learning Fun? (WMLF) framework resulted from two years of dissertation research at the Children's Museum of Indianapolis in the late 1980s. To put it in the larger context of visitor learning, I later developed the Selinda Model of Visitor Learning (figure 3.1), which is presented briefly in this chapter before we return to the WMLF framework in the second part of this book. The model consists of three complementary perspectives on visitor learning: (a) an outcomes perspective, (b) an engagements perspective, and (c) a motivations perspective. It can be argued that these are not mutually exclusive or competing perspectives but rather that they work together to describe and mutually shape visitors' educational experiences, and I take that stance in this book. The purpose in presenting the model here is to briefly describe each of the three perspectives, thereby providing a larger context for the focus of this book—that is, motivations, or the psychological preconditions necessary for learning to take place.

In the *outcomes* perspective,[1] the focus is on what visitors take away from their experience. This might be, for example, a new understanding, attitude, interest, or desire to take action, or sometimes it's a new way of thinking about oneself or one's companions. In some instances, a visitor outcome could be a new skill, such as how to develop and test a hypothesis or how to make a puppet or kite.[1]

More recently in the museum field, there has been a push to look at visitor *engagements* and direct experience while in a museum exhibition (Ansbacher 1998, 1999, 2002a, 2005; Simon 2010).[2] Engagements are defined as everything that people do while interacting or engaging with museum exhibits. In the Selinda Model, engagements include four ways visitors interact with an exhibit: physically, emotionally, intellectually, and socially.

The third aspect of the Selinda Model is about *motivations*, the psychological needs and desires that affect visitors' ability to learn while in informal settings.

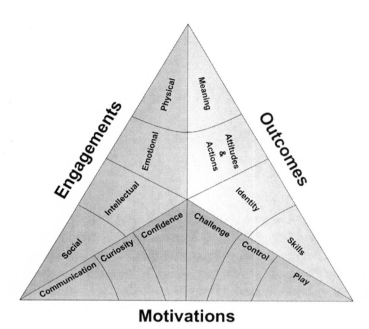

FIGURE 3.1
The Selinda Model of Visitor Learning.

The premise underlying this part of the model is that when visitors are in museums, they expect to have enjoyable and intrinsically motivating experiences, experiences that include learning. As museum professionals, if we understand what intrinsically motivates visitors—in other words, what makes learning fun—then we can ensure that exhibits are designed to include opportunities for these visitor motivations to be met. When these needs and desires are not met, we run the risk of visitors leaving an exhibit feeling less than satisfied. According to the motivations framework of the Selinda Model, museum visitors will be more likely to have satisfying, intrinsically motivating experiences when their engagements with exhibits meet their needs to (a) be part of a communication process, (b) have their curiosity piqued, (c) feel safe and smart,[3] (d) be challenged, (e) be in charge of their learning, and (f) be playful.

Each aspect of the model describes current ways of thinking about and understanding the visitor learning experience, thinking that reflects the museum field's ongoing evolution and shifting. Even though most discussions about visitor learning in museums tend to stress one of the three aspects of the

What Comes First, the Chicken or the Egg?

In considering the order in which to discuss the three aspects of the model, I faced a dilemma. The order of presentation might be perceived to imply a chronology, or a hierarchy, of experiences during a museum visit. Some have argued persuasively that the three aspects of the model should be presented as motivations first (visitors are motivated to attend, engage, and experience), followed by engagements (then visitors engage with the exhibit or artifact), ending with outcomes (and, finally, visitors take something away). However, I have learned that visitor experiences are rarely such neat packages. I know, for example, that it is just as likely that any individual visitor might engage first, become motivated next, and then learn. Or conversely, he or she may learn something by observing another visitor, and that new knowledge might then provide the impetus for engagement—and so on. In the end, I have chosen to present the three aspects of the model in the order in which the professional museum community has embraced them. The outcomes framework (i.e., what visitors take away from their visit and how they are changed as a result of it) is discussed first because that has been the traditional focus when museum professionals discuss learning. The engagements framework (i.e., what visitors do while they are in museums and how they engage within the space with exhibits, artifacts, and each other) is discussed next because this has been a more recent trend among museum professionals. And finally, the motivations framework (i.e., visitors' various psychological needs or preconditions for learning in informal settings) is a more recent trend and the focus of this book.

model, I believe that when describing, defining, assessing, and designing for museum learning, it is essential to consider all three aspects of the model. Together they articulate, as completely as possible, what is going on with visitors. No visitor educational experience can be adequately discussed without understanding and considering all three simultaneously, as all three frameworks are working in concert in all visitor experiences. The remainder of this chapter briefly describes selected components of each of these three ways of thinking about visitor learning in museums.

The Selinda Model: An Educational Model

This model of the museum visitor experience is an *educational* model. It does not provide, for example, a marketing, curatorial, or visitor-services perspective. While sensitive to those aspects of the complete museum experience, the Selinda Model focuses exclusively on designing for meaningfulness and learning, learning in a broad sense that encompasses outcomes, engagements, and motivations and that is fun. The model (and this book) focuses only on those things that affect the direct construction of knowledge and new ways of understanding within the social framework of the museum visit.

OUTCOMES: WHAT DO VISITORS TAKE AWAY?

Museums are wonderfully complex and rich environments where we, as museum professionals, have the good fortune of being able to provide an array of experiences not possible any place else in the world. One of the consequences of such a range of experiences is the concomitant range of visitor outcomes that result: some visitors learn new bits of information, others become interested in stuff they didn't know they were interested in, some may learn new skills, and some may even be empowered to change how they think about something or reconsider the decisions they make in their personal lives. In addition to the more or less traditional types of educational outcomes, such as cognitive, affective, and psychomotor learning, that many museum professionals are familiar with, and in spite of increased attention to the wide range of affective outcomes (Roberts 1991), there is a large assortment of less discussed and less studied outcomes, including, for example, sparking an interest, delayed learning, visceral learning, and wrap-around learning (Perry 2002; Spock 2000; Spock, Perry, and Lewis 1997); adding to the experience bank (Ansbacher 2002b); behavior change (Dotzour et al. 2002); and identity (Falk 2009; Rounds 2006; Silverman 2010).

The following section recasts the more familiar cognitive, affective, and psychomotor learning outcomes into four broad categories of visitor outcomes: meaning, attitudes and actions, identity, and skills. This presentation is a selective sampling rather than a comprehensive description of current thinking.

Outcomes: Meaning

Grounded in theories of constructivist learning, the notion that visitors construct their own meaning is a powerful one that has gained momentum in the museum community (Hein 1998; Silverman 1995; Silverman 2000). How do visitors understand the exhibits they engage with? What meanings do they construct? What messages are they taking away? How do they negotiate understandings and make sense of the exhibition with their visiting companions?

While there are myriad types of meaning-making outcomes, I will discuss two specific ones: islands of expertise and knowledge hierarchies.

Islands of Expertise

Crowley (2000) suggests that learning isn't a linear process from point A to point B but rather a rich and complex process of continuous shaping, which he calls the development of "islands of expertise." Museums can be major contributors to these personalized islands of expertise as children and others negotiate the real worlds they live in and construct their own ways of understanding these worlds. The knowledge outcome of a visit to an exhibit might therefore be less about the acquisition of a particular concept or way of understanding than the furthering of a visitor's own island of expertise about that or a related topic.

> I grew up outside Washington. And I loved going to the Smithsonian. And what I loved was the doll house they had in, I guess, [what] was then called History and Technology and now it's American History. This wonderful Victorian doll house. And I just spent hours staring at that doll house. They had a book about it, and I bought the book. And I looked at the doll house. And then I went home and my father and I built a doll house. And I made it a Victorian doll house, and I read books about doll houses. And I got interested in social history and material culture from looking at this doll house. . . . But because it was a really wonderful object, it was just a wonderful, magical thing that took me in another world, that . . . was really special. It got me interested in museums and material culture, which is what I'm doing now. [PH31–02] (Spock, Perry, Leichter, Gyllenhaal, Forland 1997, ch. 6)

Gyllenhaal (2002a, 2002b) argues for active parental nurturing of children's interests, and shares a delightful story of how his son developed his own island of expertise about dinosaurs:

> As we walked into The Field Museum's temporary exhibit, Ethan was both amazed and a bit frightened by the first thing we saw: a life-sized, moving dinosaur standing

over a nest of babies. It was a few days after his second birthday, so Ethan may have thought they were real. The mother dinosaur looked up, stared past us, and then swung away. The babies popped up, whirred and chattered. Ethan climbed into my arms and wouldn't leave.

We watched, worried, counted the babies, and talked about how Maiasaura, the "good mother lizard," chewed up big, tough leaves, then spat them out so her babies could fit them in their tiny mouths. "They don't drink milk from Mommy, like baby Aaron. She feeds them, but it's different."

We might have stayed in Dinosaur Families for hours, but then Ethan saw the towering, moving model of Albertasaurus (a slightly smaller cousin of Tyrannosaurus rex), and we couldn't leave soon enough. We did stop in the exhibit's gift shop, however, where Ethan selected a plastic Maiasaura and her nest, with two hungry-looking babies molded in place.

After we got home, Ethan pulled a leaf off of a potted plant, tore it into pieces, and fed it to his baby Maiasaurs. This was the first sign that our lives were changing.

A few days later, during our weekly visit to the library, Ethan found two books about dinosaurs and insisted that we bring them home. The following week we borrowed more dinosaur books, and within a month, dinosaur books were the only ones Ethan wanted to borrow and the only ones we really read.

Like the little boy in his favorite storybook, *Patrick's Dinosaurs*, the more dinosaur names Ethan learned, the more kinds of dinosaurs he saw around the neighborhood. On our daily walks, he picked up leaves and sticks and dragged them home. He stacked them in piles—feeding sites for dinosaurs—on our front sidewalk and behind our house. Three-horned Triceratops came to eat his front-yard offerings of plants, plated Stegosaurus munched on plants by the back porch, and tiny Compsognathus hunted for bugs in our garden. He was developing an island of expertise. (Gyllenhaal 2002b)

While Crowley wrote about the development of islands of expertise primarily in terms of how children make sense of their worlds, it can be argued that this process doesn't stop once we become adults. Rather, in informal educational settings in particular, visitors of all ages are often engaged in the active process of constructing rich and complex ways of understanding broad concepts such as volcanoes, evolution, or Monet. Museums function best when they think of themselves as rich settings for contributing to visitors' islands of expertise rather than as teachers of specific information.

Knowledge Hierarchies

Related to the idea of islands of expertise is the notion that—whatever the topic of the exhibit—different visitors are on different learning journeys, learning journeys they may not even recognize themselves. In other words, no matter the topic, everyone comes to understand it over a period of time and in unique ways. You could say that all learning journeys—regardless of the topic—begin with the learner's becoming aware of something, followed by the development of some questions or interest, followed by the acquisition of a conceptual understanding, followed by the development of an appreciation for it. Although presented as linear and sequential, gaining knowledge and developing understandings is not a clean, step-by-step process. Rather, it loops around, in and out, taking detours and side journeys, following myriad whims and fancies, starts and stops, dead ends and tunnels.

Regardless of the specific path it takes, learning is a journey unique to each visitor and visitor group. The dad and preschooler discussed in Chapter 1 were clearly on a different learning journey than the theater teacher with his students. Both, however, had positive—and clearly very different—learning outcomes, outcomes that were specific to each visitor group.

Recognizing that visitors are on unique learning journeys could throw those of us who are responsible for communicating sound educational messages and teaching educational concepts into a tizzy. If all are on their own journeys, how can we design exhibits that start where visitors are and end where museums want them to be? How can we have any hope of designing an exhibit that will succeed with the majority of folks?

One way of meeting this challenge is finding the intersection of the museums' and the visitors' ways of thinking about the content. A number of years ago, the knowledge hierarchy was proposed as a way of assessing visitor knowledge outcomes (Perry 1989, 1993d),[4] and it has been used in numerous research and evaluation studies since then.[5] Rather than assessing whether or not visitors got a particular idea or achieved a particular narrowly defined learning outcome, a knowledge hierarchy articulates a learning journey that captures virtually all visitors' learning or understanding of a particular exhibit topic, no matter where they are on their learning journey. However, the knowledge hierarchy helps articulate not just a visitor's understanding—which can be extremely complex and all over the place—but a visitor's understanding *within the context of the exhibit.*

> The knowledge hierarchy . . . is based on the assumption that inherent in each exhibit is an internal knowledge structure. This knowledge structure is at the intersection of the exhibit developer's, and the visitor's, organization and understanding of the topic. A knowledge hierarchy is simply a description of this range of understandings. It is not the range of knowledge visitors have about a topic, but the range of knowledge within the context of the exhibit. (Perry 1993d)

Most knowledge hierarchies include six or seven levels, and they tend to progress from Level 0 to Level 5 or 6. Although there are wide variations, most knowledge hierarchies also share a similar structure.

- Level 0: I don't know; I don't care.
- Level 1: I don't know, but I'm curious and interested and would like to find out more.
- Level 2: I think I know, but I have a very limited, naïve, incomplete, or inaccurate understanding.
- Level 3: I have a solid but basic understanding of the main concept.
- Levels 4 and beyond represent increasingly sophisticated understandings of the exhibit concept.[6]

Because knowledge hierarchies by definition emerge from visitor-studies data, each hierarchy is unique, even when following the general framework outlined above.[6] For example, let's take the dad and preschooler at *The Color Connection* exhibit. In this situation, we'd all agree that learning that red, green, and blue mix to make white would be an inappropriate knowledge outcome for the toddler. Does this mean that every young child automatically fails at the exhibit? In fact, this visitor group—including the toddler—had a very successful experience. The knowledge hierarchy that emerged for *The Color Connection* is presented below.

- Level 0: The visitor never thought about where the colors on the table come from, and/or they don't care to think about it. For example "It never occurred to me to wonder where the colors come from."
- Level 1: The visitor has thought about where the colors on the table come from, but hasn't arrived at an answer that is satisfactory to them. For example "I don't know where the colors are coming from. That's what I was wondering."
- Level 2: The visitor has thought about the colors, and has come up with an answer, but the answer is wrong, for example "The yellow color is because of light reflecting off my yellow tee shirt."
- Level 3: The visitor has a very basic understanding of the connection between the colors on the table and the lights over the table. For example "The colors come from those lights."
- Level 4: The visitor has an understanding that the red, blue, and green lights mix to make white light.

- Level 5: The visitor has an understanding that the three colors mix to make other colors, for example red and green lights mix to make yellow, red and blue make magenta, and blue and green make cyan.
- Level 6: The visitor has an understanding that the colored shadows are formed by blocking out one of the three lights, and the remaining two lights combine to form a new color. (Perry 1989, 339–40)

This hierarchy describes the learning journey of virtually all museum visitors to this exhibit. The goal of the exhibit, then, becomes not to teach everyone that red, blue, and green combine to make white but rather to recognize the diversity of visitors and to help them along their journey of learning about how lights mix to make other colors. It was clear that the knowledge outcome for the toddler, while her initial knowledge may have been Level 0, was at Level 1 by the time she left. And chances are good that she will remain at Level 1 for a long time. That she didn't achieve Levels 3, 4, 5, or 6 does not mean that she didn't have a successful experience or that the exhibit was in any way deficient.

We have traditionally dealt with this in the museum setting by saying that, well, she wasn't part of the target audience for the exhibit. This may be appropriate for formal educational settings where audiences are composed of learners who tend to share more similar prerequisite knowledge, but informal learning settings demand more. We may find that this same visitor will come back to this exhibit repeatedly in the next three, four, or five years and slowly move from Level 1 to Levels 2 and 3, and eventually on to Levels 4, 5, and 6. During this visit to the exhibit, she clearly learned that colored lights are fun. Some would argue that this is an affective outcome, not a knowledge outcome, but I would argue that in a museum setting, enjoying something is an important part of knowledge acquisition—especially at the beginning of the journey—and not something that can be separated from it.

Now let's look at the teacher with her young companion. In this case, the members of this visitor group obviously wanted to progress beyond their initial Level 1 but were unable to. The *Colored Shadows* exhibit failed them, not because they didn't achieve a basic understanding of colored lights mixing to make other colors but because it interrupted their learning journey. Not only did it not provide the necessary support and guidance for them to develop a greater understanding of colored lights, but in fact it may have had a negative effect by making the visitors feel frustrated and inadequate. Whether or not the teacher felt intimidated by science before the exhibit experience, she clearly was

Do No Harm

Often in museums we are focused on trying to teach visitors what we want them to learn. In our zealous pursuit of increased visitor knowledge and the communication of ideas, we forget that our job is also to do no harm.[7] The case of the teacher and her young companion serves as an example of where "harm" was likely done. How many other situations in museums are like this one? Anytime a visitor leaves an exhibit, exhibition, or museum feeling incompetent, intimidated, or overwhelmed, we have done harm. Anytime a visitor goes backward in their learning journey, we have done harm. Unfortunately, museums don't track these types of experiences, but we all are very familiar with them.

afterwards. Although the study didn't explore this and so can't say definitively, it is feasible that the exhibit actually took this visitor group from a Level 1 ("I'm curious") to a Level 0 ("I don't know and don't care").

Let's go back to the dad and his toddler daughter for a minute. It could be argued that while achieving Level 1 might be appropriate for the preschooler, we also have an obligation to help the dad achieve a Level 3 or 4. In fact, because it wasn't a focus of the study, from the existing data we don't know for certain what his learning outcomes were, except that he left the exhibit at least at a Level 1—that is, enjoying playing in the colored lights. He may actually have achieved a Level 3 or 4, but because he was focused on his daughter, he didn't show evidence of it. More importantly, however, his particular learning journey was more likely about engaging with his daughter, not learning about colored lights. In this case, the job of the exhibit was to not set him back. In other words, due to personal circumstances, not every exhibit will help all visitors progress along the knowledge hierarchy for that exhibit, but if we have done nothing to send them backwards, sometimes that's enough.

On the other hand, if most visitors to an exhibit don't progress, but at least don't go backwards, then we need to ask ourselves if that's good enough or if we have higher aspirations for the exhibit. If an exhibit contributes in meaningful ways to most visitors' learning journeys, however, and few or no visitors slip backwards (i.e., no harm is done), then it could be argued that an exhibit is suc-

Knowledge Hierarchies: Evaluation, Not Development, Tools

Some museum professionals have interpreted the knowledge hierarchy as suggesting the need for writing layered text, or developing labels intended to appeal to visitors who are at a particular level. It cannot be stated too strongly that the knowledge hierarchy was designed to describe visitor learning at an exhibit, not to serve as an approach for developing exhibits. There are many good arguments against targeting interpretation to a particular segment of society, not the least of which is that visitors are not very good at figuring out which part of the interpretation is supposed to be for them, with the irritating consequence that they believe that none of it is. Serrell (1996a, 65–82) presents excellent arguments against the layering of text and encourages planners of exhibits to strive for "inclusive, broad appeal" and to refrain from "segmenting experiences into mutually exclusive audience categories" (77).

cessful, regardless of whether most of the visitors achieve sophisticated—or even basic—understandings of the exhibit content.

Knowledge hierarchies are powerful because they allow us to capture and value at least some of most visitors' knowledge outcomes in a way that satisfies museum professionals' desire for visitors to learn content, while also honoring the diversity of visitors, their personal agendas, and their unique ways of understanding and making-meaning.

This discussion of meaning outcomes (developing islands of expertise and progressing along a knowledge hierarchy) proposes a shift in the way we think about how visitors understand museum exhibits and the messages they walk away with. It shifts the focus from the educational impact of the exhibit on the visitor to how, and how effectively, the exhibit contributes to visitor learning journeys, especially those learning journeys that museums are particularly interested in. It doesn't capture all the ways in which visitors understand or think about the content of an exhibit. Rather it helps the museum professional assess knowledge outcomes in a way that captures much of the richness and complexity of visitor thinking while also recognizing that museums have educational messages they are particularly interested in visitors understanding.

Outcomes: Attitudes and Actions

> The fourth floor of the American Museum of Natural History was the shrine, the principle magic place, the sanctum sanctorum of my youth. I first visited with my father at age five and decided right then to dedicate my life to paleontology. I went back to the dinosaur and fossil mammal halls almost monthly right to the end of high school. I then left New York for undergraduate studies, but returned to do my Ph.D. work at the Museum. I loved the old halls. (Gould 1995, 253)

This story relates an extreme case of a museum visitor taking action as a result of a visit (or multiple visits). There has been increasing interest in the role museums can play in helping visitors to develop caring attitudes to the point that they take some action, whether that action takes the form of, for example, signing up for a drawing class, becoming an active birder, making dietary or other health-related changes, or even pursuing a particular career (Spock 2000). Some zoos and other conservation-minded organizations in particular are actively exploring the relationship between visits to their institutions and the development of visitors' caring attitudes and behaviors toward animals. It is their hope that one of the outcomes of exhibit experiences will be the development of caring attitudes, and ultimately behavior change, among visitors (Dotzour et al. 2002; Gyllenhaal 2001; Irvine, Saunders, and Foster 2000; Saunders, Birjulin, and Myers 1998).

Outcomes: Identity

In the museum literature, *identity* has been variously described as either an input or an outcome. As an input, identity is that part of self that a visitor brings to the museum setting—for example, prior knowledge, experiences, and who the individual is. As an outcome, identity represents what visitors become as a result of their museum visit—for example, how they see their place in the world and in relation to those around them differently. This discussion focuses on the latter: identity as outcome. (See page 51 for a discussion of identity as input.)

Identity as an outcome includes how visitors change in intimate and personal ways that are central to who they are and how they perceive the world. Although there are many different types of identity outcomes, here I briefly mention five particularly salient ones: narrative, restoration, memories, relationships, and personal connections.

Creating Narrative

One outcome of museum visits is the narratives, or story lines, that visitors create from the raw materials of their visit. These narratives go beyond how

Identity as Input

In their contextual model of the museum experience, Falk and Dierking (1992, 25–37) describe the respective influences of the personal, social, and physical contexts, and they describe the *personal context* as all those prior understandings, expectations, and experiences that visitors bring with them. This is similar to Doering and Pekarik's (2000, 261) description of the *entrance narrative*, which is defined as a combination of the information or knowledge visitors have about the world, their framework for understanding that world, and all their personal experiences, emotions, and memories that contribute to those understandings. Similarly, Hilke (1988) posits, "The dominant perspective from which the exhibition is interpreted is more likely to be the visitor's own background experience, own knowledge, and own interests than it is likely to be some common thread or theme of the show" (124–25). Leinhardt and Knutson discuss identity as those things visitors bring with them to a museum visit (for example, motivations, prior knowledge, and roles), although they acknowledge that identity can be shaped by a museum visit. Many museum theorists and researchers have explored the important issue of identity and what visitors bring with them that shapes their museum visit. Falk (2009) devotes an entire book to this issue. In it, he provides one of the more comprehensive explorations into identity and museums and proposes a model for addressing the needs of five different visitor types before, during, and after their visits.

visitors make meaning out of the stuff of museums to include how they see the world and understand their place within it as a result of their museum experience (Roberts 1997). In discussing the importance of conversation and dialogue in a museum setting, Silverman (1990, 191) quotes Fiske (1987, 15): "Discourse not only makes sense of its topic area, it also constructs a sense, or social identity, of us as we speak it." Silverman (1990) explores the issue of conversation and identity in depth in her research and concludes that "the same interpretive frames [i.e., learning conversations] that visitors invoke to make meaning of displayed objects simultaneously make meaning of 'selves'" (246). These narratives that visitors create simultaneously reflect and shape their identities and are an important outcome of museum experiences.

Restoration

Rest and relaxation is another important outcome of a museum visit. By recharging, refreshing, and restoring visitors, the visit shapes visitors' identities (Kaplan, Bardwell, and Slakter 1993). "[A museum visit] may create a sense of peace and calm that permits people to recover their cognitive and emotional effectiveness" (15).

> And at times in my life where . . . I've needed some kind of calming, like right after my divorce, I took a course at the Museum of Natural History, a drawing course, where all you did was sit in front of those exhibits, the exact same exhibits from my childhood, and draw. And it was kind of like a meditation. It was like you'd get deep inside yourself as you sat sort of voiceless, in front of these dioramas . . . that went back so deeply into my life, which I already had several experiences with, as a child and as an adolescent, and just sketch them, so you'd be able to begin to see them in a new way, from the childhood to the adult way of seeing. [PH47–05] (Spock, Perry, Leichter, Gyllenhaal, and Forland 1997, ch. 8)

> I must have been about six years old, seven years old. My father was an architect, so we were all interested in looking at architecture. And I remember, they built a Japanese house in the garden of the Museum of Modern Art, and I remember going to see this house. And what was so wonderful about it was that, as you walked into it, you took your shoes off and they gave you little slippers, so that as you walked on the tatami mats, you weren't wrecking them with your shoes.
>
> But it was a very exciting thing to me to be in this setting, and to be asked to take my shoes off, and given these little shoes, and [to] walk on these surfaces. I can still remember what it felt like and smelled like; and to have these beautiful spaces that were so empty, and so calm and so beautiful in the middle of the museum garden there. So, I always remembered that. [PH49–03] (Spock, Perry, Leichter, Gyllenhaal, and Forland 1997, ch. 3)

Memories

Many museum visits evoke powerful memories and gently shape who visitors are and how they perceive the world. Museum visits are often occasions for reminiscing with one's companions and thereby reinforce social and personal bonds. Falk and Dierking (2000) refer to memories as "that most fundamental of all learning products " (xii) and go on to state, "At the core of all learning are memories, and memories are not permanent entities but rather the creation of new patterns from preexisting patterns" (31). Memories can be powerful outcomes of museum visits as is evidenced by the following two stories of hidden childhood museum memories:

> In my early twenties . . . I was studying anthropology, so I took a walk through the anthropology halls [of the American Museum of Natural History], and I turned this corner and there was this moment, this shock to me, of something that was a very deeply buried image from my childhood that I had never thought about. This image just came back to me with a shock. And it was seeing a diorama of a South American Indian hunter. . . . It was a full size mannequin, and he had a blowgun in his hand and he was aiming it up at this little patch of trees and forest with birds in it, in a very dark hall, with a light on him.
>
> And, as I came upon this in my twenties, it was like some door suddenly opened, and I realized that I had . . . seen this when I was a child. And there was just this recognition of something that was very strange, powerful, a little scary, and also just fascinating. . . . It was something that had obviously made a deep impression, was buried all those years, and I never knew about [it] until I discovered it again. [PH49–02] (Spock, Perry, Leichter, Gyllenhaal, and Forland 1997, ch. 3)

> And I said, "Don't be silly. The Field Museum doesn't have any dinosaurs. I grew up in this museum." He said, "Well, yeah, actually—" and sent me up to Hall 38 which at the time had all the Charles Knight paintings from [19]28 or [19]29. [The paintings] went all the way around. And I got into the hall. And, you know, sure enough, there were a couple of dinosaurs in there. Not a lot of them, but a couple. And then I looked up at these Knight paintings. I started to cry because I realized that the drawings that I have in my head of life in the Mesozoic, that's where I got it from. . . . They're beautiful. I mean, they're kind of misty and—you know, they're a little out of date and they're a little funky. But they really are evocative. And I had them . . . all right here. I just didn't know where I had gotten them from. [PH45–10] (Spock, Perry, Leichter, Ghyllenhaal, and Forland 1997, ch. 3)

Relationships

All of us have had experiences when the museum visit was more about the people we were with than the objects on display. A colleague tells the story of visiting a museum with her daughter:

> We walked into the next [art museum] gallery, and I said [to my four-year-old daughter], "Look around this whole room and just find any painting that you like for any reason at all, and you take me to it." And so she looked around and picked out this seventeenth- and eighteenth-century painting of a boy in very fancy dress.

It didn't look at all like a kid her age. It was a very traditional art painting and she took me over to it and I picked her up and we stood there and looked at it for a while. And I said, "Well, why do you like that painting? What is it about it?" And she said, "Well, he looks sad." And I said, "Well, why do you think he's sad?" And she said, "I think his mom has gone away." And I said, "Were you sad when I was gone last week?" And she said, "Yes." . . . She didn't express her feelings very much, and I don't think she would have said that except [for looking at that painting]. It was like me having a chance to hear her feelings. . . . From that point on it kind of broke the ice for me that I'm here to have an experience with my daughter. Not to be the expert on art, because I'm not. And that's not what she wants. She wants to be with me. . . . I really felt close to her. . . . The picture let me learn about [my daughter] and let me learn about myself and that I'd been ignoring her emotions. (Anonymous, personal communication, July 28, 2006)

This same colleague also shared a story about a museum visit providing an opportunity for her to get to know her dad in a new way:

I knew [my dad] had been in the service, but that's all I knew. He just never talked about it. . . . And then we [went to] an exhibit . . . about what people were doing back at home during the war. . . . And as we went through it . . . my Dad said a few things, but not much. But it was after that that we were back home, and he pulled out a scrapbook that I had never in my life seen or even knew he had. And he started going through this whole scrapbook with us and telling us stories and showing us pictures of people. And it was like a turning point. . . . I remember the door opening and the scrapbooks came out, pictures I had never seen, stories I had never heard. I never had an idea of what he even did. . . . I think it was a real thing that he had been proud of but he thought his family didn't care about. Or he had never talked about. And then it became part of our family. He got a big map of the world, and when he was at the assisted living home, we took that map and he showed me every place that he had fought a battle, and we made a map and put it on there and drew the lines, and people would come into his room then, like the nurses and things, and ask him. So it was like he reconnected to this part of his past, and . . . it's later on that it sparked a conversation that opened a door that wasn't there. . . . Museums have a story to tell, but they're also a context that reminds us and connects with our own histories and gives us a chance to tell our own stories. . . . [They provide a way for] getting to know somebody differently. (Anonymous, personal communication, July 28, 2006)

Two other museum professionals relate stories of how museum visits were influential in their relationships with others:

I grew up in Chicago. And my father . . . was quite the working-class guy. . . . And he was really, you know, "You're gonna get educated, kid, and you're gonna go out there and see the world." And part of his plan about this was that (a) I would not go to Catholic school where they did not have band or art. He was very clear on this point. And (b), he would haul me around to wherever I wanted to go, essentially.

So, we would go to the zoo. And we would go to the lakefront. He loved Buckingham Fountain for reasons unknown to me, but he loved it. And he loved the Museum of Science and Industry. He would tolerate The Field Museum if I really nagged. And he would not step foot in the Art Institute.

So, we went to a lot of these kinds of places. And I had a wonderful time. I associate . . . these trips with him, somehow, and they have a special flavor to them because of that.

And I remember particularly the Museum of Science and Industry, because there were things in there that this guy knew about, you know. They were like his things: they were boy things, man things. He had done sheet metal work, he had done carpentry. There were tools and stuff like that in there. And it was a real connection between him and those things. And he felt very proud to show them to me. (Spock 2000, 33)

My museum learning isn't so much about things as about relationships. . . . I was introduced to museums by an aunt that I had a special relationship with. . . . When I was a little girl and used to go visit my grandmother, my aunt would always take me to the art museum. . . . And this was always a real special trip for us. . . . I came from a big family where you never had family excursions because we didn't all fit in the car, and it was just a very, very special thing. And it had to do with the relationship to this person. The museum was different from anything else in my very ordinary life, and she was different from anything in my ordinary life. And it just represented the whole world . . . that was out there, and all sorts of possibilities. I have absolutely no memory of the art or any of the things that we would do there. It was the act of going that was so special. (Spock 2000, 32–33)

Personal Connections

One of the goals of many museum exhibitions is for visitors to become aware of an issue or a topic and to develop a personal connection with it. The phrase "personal connection," in this case, refers not just to whether something is personally relevant or meaningful—although it includes this—but it describes the various ways in which visitors connect with the topic, in their own words and regardless of how the museum is thinking about it. For example, when planning for the AIDS exhibition at the Museum of Science and Industry in Chicago, the exhibit-development team was interested in presenting a scientific understanding of AIDS. However, the front-end evaluation made it clear that many visitors had formed other personal connections with the topic. These were categorized as follows:

- Emotional: Individuals in this category used many feeling words such as sadness, fear, suffering, and rejection. They often expressed deep empathy for people with AIDS, and described it as "a terrible disease."
- Behavioral: People in this category tended to describe AIDS in terms of the behavior that puts you at risk and what you should do to protect yourself. . . . They talked of how it is difficult to take appropriate precautions "in the heat of the moment."
- Scientific: The scientific perspective emphasizes the biology behind AIDS. People with this connection to AIDS want to know why the disease behaves the way it does.
- Moralistic: . . . These individuals feel strongly that there is right and wrong behavior. . . . [Some] felt that AIDS is primarily a homosexual disease and that homosexuality is bad. They had very little empathy for homosexuals with AIDS and very high empathy for others with AIDS (because they got it through no fault of their own).
- Community/Social/Education/Research: Individuals in this perspective tended to see AIDS from a social responsibility framework. They stressed the need for more education and research (Perry 1993c, 10–11).

While these particular connections emerged as part of a front-end study rather than a summative or outcome study, they still exemplify how personal connections can be a useful way of talking about visitor outcomes. In another study, a summative evaluation of a series of traditional natural history dioramas, three primary personal connections to the exhibition emerged:

- Social: Visiting the dioramas was something to do with friends and family.
- Home: The dioramas depicted scenes specific to the place they lived.

- Learning: The dioramas were opportunities to identify animals and from which to learn new information (Perry, Garibay, and Edington 1995, 3–5).

During research conducted for the *Underground Adventure* exhibition at The Field Museum in Chicago, visitors described seven types of personal connections to dirt and soil. Some respondents described a *sensory* personal connection, talking about smelling the dirt after a rainstorm or walking barefoot and squishing mud between their toes. Others talked about dirt as a *source of leisure activity*—for example, driving fast along dirt roads or hunting, camping, fishing, and gardening. Some visitors talked fondly of *getting dirty* while others didn't like getting dirty. *Playing in the dirt* was a popular personal connection visitors described. Some visitors indicated an *environmental* personal connection and talked about the importance of preserving the planet's resources or not using chemical fertilizers. A few visitors had an *economic* connection with dirt—for example, discussing the economics of organically raised food, and a few respondents talked of a *spiritual* connection with the soil (Perry and Garibay 1996, 32–36; see also Perry, Garibay, and Gyllenhaal 1998, 66). Visitors to the *Hunters of the Sky* exhibition at the Science Museum of Minnesota also indicated a variety of personal connections with raptors and with nature in general (Perry and Niehus 1996).

As can be seen, personal connections aren't necessarily mutually exclusive. However, while visitors may tend to understand and be sympathetic to a variety of perspectives, I have found that each visitor or visitor group tends to develop a single personal connection with the topic. These connections are different from frameworks for thinking about or understanding a topic. Unlike frameworks, connections tend to be very personal and are part of a person's or a group's identity. In other words, a visitor might have three or four different frameworks for thinking about AIDS, depending on the situation they are in. Sometimes they might be coming at it from a behavioral perspective (e.g., how to avoid getting it); at other times, they might be thinking of it from a scientific perspective—for example, as a biological or physiological process. But a visitor's personal connection to a topic is an intimate part of his or her identity.

Outcomes: Skills

In addition to learning something new or developing a richer and more meaningful understanding of something, sometimes the outcome of a museum visit is the development of a new skill or learning of a different way of doing something. This could be as simple as learning how to make a kite or puppet during a museum program or it could be learning how to paint like Monet. At other times, it's about learning a new intellectual skill, like how to engage in the scientific process (including developing skills in observing, hypothesizing, gathering and analyzing data, and experimenting) or how to think like a historian. Skills also include developing a child's learning experience. I mention skills here because they are an important intended outcome of many museum experiences, but I won't discuss them in any detail, as they are covered extensively in other publications.

Thinking about the visitor experience in terms of visitor outcomes is useful as long as they are put in a broad context and one considers a wide range of effects, such as contributing to visitors' islands of expertise, helping visitors as they journey along a knowledge hierarchy, and contributing to the development of personal or group identity. Many other types of outcomes, including sparking an interest and visceral or delayed learning, are not discussed here (Perry 2002). By thinking broadly about the ways museum exhibits contribute to visitors' identities and personal experience banks and how they make a difference in people's lives, we can better understand museums' roles in society and also gain some insights into how we might design effective museum exhibits.

But looking exclusively at outcomes gives us only a partial view of what's important in the visitor experience. Outcomes can help us focus on where we'd like visitors to go and the things we'd like them to learn about or the skills we'd like them to develop, but outcomes provide little concrete direction for how to get there. To get closer to this issue, it's important to look at engagements—that is, what visitors do while at the museum and how they experience their visits.

ENGAGEMENTS: HOW DO VISITORS INTERACT?

> If museums truly want to engage their visitors, then they need to explicitly embrace *process* as a goal—no longer just the means to some other outcome, but something to be pursued in its own right. (Ansbacher 2005, 14)

The previous section discussed in some detail various selected outcomes of museum visits. Traditionally, outcomes have been the focus when contemplating museums' educational functions. "There is considerable pressure for museums to deliver information and to use that as their measure of educational success" (Ansbacher 2005, 13). More recently, however, museum professionals have become increasingly interested in the *process* of meaning-making and

The Selinda Model, the National Science Foundation Framework, and the National Research Council Strands

The National Science Foundation Framework for Evaluating Impacts of Informal Science Education Projects (Friedman 2008) and the National Research Council Strands of Science Learning (National Research Council 2009)—two models of visitor learning currently in use—are important tools for looking at the many outcomes and impacts of science museum visits in particular. The outcomes framework of the Selinda Model encompasses many of the same aspects but is broader in scope in that it doesn't focus primarily on science. At the risk of oversimplification, here is a brief comparison of the three frameworks. Note that in the Selinda Model interest is not separated out but cuts across all types of outcomes (the premise being that in informal settings, curiosity about or interest in something is an integral part of making meaning, developing an attitude, acquiring a new skill, and evolving one's identity.

Selinda Outcomes Framework		National Science Foundation Impacts Framework	National Research Council Strands
Meaning		Awareness, knowledge, and understanding	Strand 2: Understanding science knowledge
Attitudes and actions	Interest	Engagement and interest	Strand 1: Developing an interest
		Attitudes	
		Behavior change	
Skills		Skills	Strands 3, 4, and 5: Scientific reasoning, reflection, and practice
Identity		Other	Strand 6: Identifying

understanding, not just the outcomes (Simon 2010). Some professionals have even gone so far as to say that the process and product of museum visits actually interfere with one another. In fact, Ansbacher (2005) encourages museums "to be more courageous in embracing *process* as a primary goal and willing to let go of traditional 'learning outcomes'" (13).

In this book, I take the position that both process and product, both engagements and outcomes, are essential and intertwined components of museum visits. Rather than sacrificing one for the other, it behooves museum professionals to consider how and to what degree visitor engagements contribute to, and are influenced by, desired visitor outcomes.

How people engage with the stuff of museums is an important aspect of the visitor experience. It can be argued that visitors ultimately make sense of their museum experience through this process of engagement. As they are discussed in this book, engagements are similar to what Leinhardt and Crowley (1998, 10) term *explanatory engagement*. Engagements are about what people do during their visits to a museum, that is, how they interact in time and space; how they engage intellectually and cognitively; how they experience aesthetics, awe, and emotions; and how they engage with each other, their visiting companions.

For many years now, museum professionals have been interested in how to get museum visitors engaged more fully with the objects and ideas presented in their institutions. In discussing science museum exhibits in particular, Screven (1999) paraphrases Miles (1987), stating that "if museums are interested in communicating science, their aims and methods must be replaced from conveying facts to exhibit designs that stimulate and motivate the general public to engage in more active modes of attending that are essential for learning" (Screven 1999, 115). There is no doubt that rich and meaningful visitor engagements result in rich and meaningful visitor experiences. The Selinda Model defines four types of visitor engagements: physical, emotional, intellectual, and social.

Engagements: Physical

Physical engagements refer to all the many ways in which visitors physically interact with an exhibit. Obvious physical engagements include such things as pushing a button, crawling through a simulated cave environment, and manipulating objects in a hands-on science center. But physical engagements also include such things as spending time with an exhibit, reading a label, watching someone else engage, or even standing still and being contemplative. Physical engagements can also include all the ways visitors might engage their senses: touching, looking, listening, smelling, and even tasting. Hensel (1987, 29) differentiates between active and passive physical interactions, although in the Selinda Model, they are not separated.

Physical engagements also include "undesirable" behaviors. In my years of watching visitors in museums, I have seen children grab audio wands and hit each other, I've seen adults kick an exhibit to see if it was made out of sturdy material, and I've seen adult caregivers slap children for pouring sand on the floor.

Whether or not we like to see these types of behaviors, they are also examples of physical engagements, albeit undesirable ones.

While it's most fun to think of ways to design exhibits so visitors will engage in the types of physical interactions that we are most interested in—for instance, stopping, pushing buttons, reading labels, spending time—it is just as important, if not more so, to pay attention to the ways we may inadvertently inhibit the types of physical engagements we are looking for. If visitors don't stop and read a label that we agonized over for weeks on end, it's easy to adopt an attitude that says, "Visitors don't read labels." Instead, if we ask ourselves what about the label's design is inhibiting visitors from reading it, we can see much more clearly what we need to change in order for the label to be effective.

Engagements: Emotional

We all cherish the moments when a visitor is deeply moved or touched by an exhibit. [This] happened about ten years ago when I visited Dublin. I thought, well, I'll go look at the Book of Kells. I'm not interested in medieval manuscripts, I'm not interested in medieval history, I'm not especially interested in medieval Christianity, but [the Book of Kells is] a great object and I should go look at it. . . . I walked up to the case in which it is displayed, and all the hair on the back of my neck stood up and I started to cry. Which was highly unexpected. But I think it was because of the hundreds of years of meaning human beings had invested into the object. And that [was] communicated without any intellectual mediation: I didn't think about it. It was a visceral response to the object itself, which I knew almost nothing about. All I knew was that it was old and it was beautiful, and enormous amounts of time had gone into every tiny little square inch of it [PH59-03]. (Perry 2002, 23)

Emotional engagement is often a difficult thing to design for, much less assess. However, museums are becoming increasingly interested in how visitors engage on an emotional level with their collections. An interesting study conducted at the Brookfield Zoo in Illinois investigated visitors' emotional engagements at various animal exhibits. Emotions examined included "sense of beauty, respect, wonder, peacefulness, special privilege, caring and attraction. . . . Amusement, sense of connection, love, sympathy, and surprise. . . . Concern, fear, disgust, anger and embarrassment" (Myers, Saunders, and Birjulin 2004, 315).

When we watch visitors for any length of time, we will see them be light-hearted and playful, serious and thoughtful; we'll see an exhibit stir long-forgotten memories or remind someone of something sad. Watch visitors, and one is struck by the range of ways they engage emotionally. Sometimes visitors' emotional engagements are deeply personal; other times visitors may feel intimi-dated, frustrated, or even angry.

Although museums readily recognize the importance of using emotion to engage visitors, too often it is seen as the purview of only certain exhibits, such as those in the United States Holocaust Memorial Museum or the *Name Calling School Bus* that used to be at the Children's Museum in Chicago (Finamore and Perry 1995). We need to recognize that all visitor experiences contain some emo-tional components. If we do nothing more than reduce the number of undesired emotional engagements (for example, feelings of intimidation because of overly complex language or frustration because of broken exhibits), we will be heading in the right direction. If we simultaneously enhance powerful emotional engage-ments, we'll be making a huge difference.

Engagements: Intellectual

Whereas physical engagements are often referred to as hands-on, intellec-tual engagements are "minds-on." In other words, intellectual engagements encompass all those cognitive and intellectual processes that are taking place in the visitor's mind. Intellectual engagements include thought processes such as observing, hypothesizing, comparing, analyzing, contemplating, recognizing, wondering, and so forth.[8]

Although most of us want to believe that museum visitors are actively con-templating the stuff of the exhibit, their intellectual engagements may at times have little to do with content. When a parent is preoccupied with planning what the family will have for dinner that evening or a person in a wheelchair is trying to figure out how to get closer to the exhibit, neither individual's intellectual en-gagement is related to the content of the exhibit. In other cases, there may not be much intellectual engagement at all. We've all seen the active child flitting from exhibit to exhibit, pushing whatever button she can find, as an example of high physical engagement but not much intellectual engagement. Csikszentmihalyi (1988, 82) discusses the importance of the learner getting intellectually involved if any learning is to take place. As intellectual engagement is an important com-ponent of the visitor experience, it must be carefully and deliberately designed for; otherwise visitors will fill the vacuum, often with activities that detract from meaningful experiences.

Engagements: Social

Perhaps the most important visitor engagement, and the one that is often the least designed for, is social engagement. Social interactions include all the many ways that visitors engage with one another socially. The most obvious evidence of social engagement is talking with one's companions, but it's important to think beyond just talking. Social engagements include touching, arguing, gesturing, debating, making eye contact, laughing, standing in close proximity to one another, and mirroring body postures. As with the other forms of engagements, social interaction may be more or less educational, or meaningful, and it may or may not have anything to do with the content of the exhibit. When people come to our museum as part of a social group, they will engage socially with one another regardless of how we design our exhibits. This naturally occurring social behavior, however, is an ideal opportunity for museum professionals to capitalize on, in order to maximize the likelihood of meaningful visitor experiences.

During exhibit development and planning phases, rather than focusing primarily on educational messages that need to be communicated, thinking about both desired learning outcomes and intended engagements can result in richer, more effective visitor experiences. Some questions one might ask include the following:

- Intended physical engagements
  - How long do we want visitors to spend with this exhibit unit?
  - What do we want them to do? What will they look at, read, touch, manipulate, smell, or hear?
  - Where will they stand or sit?
  - How will families and other social groups use this exhibit? How close to or far away from each other will group members be?
  - What about visitors with other specific needs, such as those in wheelchairs, those with physical disabilities, those whose primarily language is not English, and those who are very young? How long will they spend with this exhibit, and what will they be doing and seeing?
  - What kinds of physical engagements do we want to discourage or inhibit?
- Intended emotional engagements
  - How do we want visitors to engage emotionally with the exhibit?
  - What emotions will visitors feel while they are engaged with the exhibit? Do we want them to experience excitement, awe, sadness, hope, amazement, disgust? Do we want them to feel empowered, restored, peaceful, energized?
  - What kinds of emotional experiences do we want to ensure visitors do not have?
- Intended intellectual engagements
  - How do we want visitors to engage intellectually? What mental processes do we want them to use (observing, hypothesizing, appreciating, experimenting, comparing, contemplating, etc.)?

- ○ In what ways do we want visitors to think about and make connections between what they already know and what they are experiencing?
- ▪ Intended social engagements
  - ○ How do we want visitors to interact with other members of their social group? What about with other people at the exhibit?
  - ○ What types of teaching/learning and meaning-making interactions do we want them to participate in? Directing attention? Explaining something? Asking or answering questions? Giving encouragement?
  - ○ What do we want visitors to talk about, and how will they talk about it?
  - ○ What types of social interactions do we not want visitors to be engaged in?

MOTIVATIONS: WHAT MAKES LEARNING FUN?

In addition to discussions about visitor outcomes and engagement, museums have become increasingly interested in exploring issues surrounding the motivations of visitors. Visitor motivation has been studied for many years, although somewhat sporadically and definitely not comprehensively (see, for example, Carlson 1993; Csikszentmihalyi and Hermanson 1995; Nedzel 1952; Perry 1992; Salmi 1993; Screven 1974, 1992). Only more recently have issues surrounding motivation become a foundation for exhibit design and development (Fenichel and Schweingruber 2010). While summarizing the important work on motivation in museums is beyond the scope of this book, it is nonetheless useful to outline some of the issues examined recently.

Much of the discussion about museum motivation stems from the age-old debate on intrinsic versus extrinsic motivation. With intrinsic motivation, the reward is in the doing. Visitors will learn because they find it enjoyable and satisfying. They will engage with the exhibit because it's fun. They will spend time at the exhibit because they're having a good experience. If they are not enjoying themselves or find that learning is not pleasurable or satisfying, they will go find an activity that is. With extrinsic motivation, on the other hand, the reward is externally imposed. Field-trip visitors often learn or attend because their teacher will give them a good grade, or they will earn a certificate.

Some studies have varied the nature of the stimulus and the reward for visitors to learn something in a museum gallery or at a museum exhibit. Most of their results indicate that this reward/punishment model does not tend to work very well for museums. For example, a series of pilot tests showed no significant difference in learning when visitors were able to earn differing amounts of cash for learning new material at a museum exhibit (Screven 1974). In a different study,

Callison (1983) found that even though participants were offered a certificate for using a prototype exhibit, very few respondents indicated that their engagement with the exhibit was due to external factors (such as earning a certificate); instead, they indicated that their motivation was simply to learn something new. A wealth of research has also shown the various effects of extrinsic motivation on intrinsic motivation (see, for example, Greene and Lepper 1974 and Iyengar and Lepper 1999).

Why motivation? Talking about visitor outcomes and even engagements seems to make sense to many museum professionals, but why do we need to focus on visitor motivations? Intrinsically motivating museum environments are satisfying places where visitors' needs and expectations are met. This is not to say that they are always comfortable environments (consider, for example, the Holocaust Museum or the Museum of Tolerance). But they are places where visitors engage in meaningful ways and leave with a sense of satisfaction that their time has been well spent and that they have learned something new or experienced something worthwhile. Intrinsically motivating settings are not constrained environments but ones where learning happens naturally, within the context of the visitor's agenda, whether that is to come to the museum on a weekend outing with a partner, friend, or children; as an individual with a special interest in the topic; or as a host showing off the sights of the city to out-of-town guests.

How many of us have heard (or said) the following: "We'll put this information on the label so that it will be there for visitors who want it." Or maybe, "We'll add this detailed explanation for those people who are interested." And then, when the exhibition opens, we find that no one bothers to look at the information.

Our jobs as creators of rich visitor experiences is not to make stuff available in case someone *might* want it but rather to help visitors care enough so that they *will* want it. Too often we find that our making stuff available in case someone might want it is exactly what leads to visitors deciding they don't want to find out any more about the topic. All too often it is exactly these labels that subtly communicate to visitors that this topic is complicated, difficult, or for someone else. Our job as museum professionals is to give visitors a reason to care, not to lament that "visitors don't read labels." That is just untrue. Visitors do read labels if they have a reason to. It is, however, true that visitors don't read labels that aren't interesting or don't attract their attention. In other words, if visitors aren't reading our labels, or paying attention to our exhibits, or spending time doing what we want them to do, we might need to give them a better reason. Our job is to create intrinsically motivating environments, spaces where visitors want to learn and figure things out, places where they want to engage physically, intellectually, emotionally, and socially. If we don't understand what kinds of things motivate visitors, what makes things fun to learn, it's difficult to design effective museum exhibits.

A number of years ago, two researchers at Stanford University conducted a series of experiments to determine what makes things fun to learn (Lepper and Malone 1987; Malone 1980; Malone 1981; Malone and Lepper 1987). They took popular educational computer games (games that children chose to play during their free time at school) and analyzed them to identify their common motivational characteristics. Malone and Lepper developed a set of "heuristics for designing intrinsically motivating instructional environments" (Malone and Lepper 1987, 248–249). Following up on their research, I tested these heuristics in a museum setting to come up with a new framework specifically for the design of museum exhibits (Perry 1989, 1992). (See appendix B for a description of this research study.)

The premise of this model is that six motivations (communication, curiosity, confidence, challenge, control, and play) work together, resulting in intrinsically motivating visitor experiences. In other words, when folks go to a museum, they want and expect to be part of a successful dialogue between themselves and the museum (communication), to be surprised and intrigued (curiosity), to feel safe and smart (confidence), to be challenged and exposed to new ideas (challenge), to feel in charge of their experiences and to have free choice over what they do and where they go (control), and to be playful and have fun (play). The results of the research indicated that when these needs were met, visitors engaged with the exhibit in meaningful ways for extended periods and walked away with new understandings and with new interests and deeper appreciations for things they did not even know they were interested in.

The third framework of the pyramid that comprises the Selinda Model describes these six motivations. I outline them only briefly below because they are fully unpacked and defined in Part II, "Designing Visitor Experiences."

Motivations: Communication

Communication is an essential intrinsic motivation for informal learning environments. A primary reason for visiting museums is often a desire to be part of a communication process—communication between an exhibit and the visitor, communication among the members of the group with whom one is visiting, communication as part of a guided tour. Visitors who leave a museum feeling they have not been part of a communication process often express disappointment: they might say, "Well, I didn't learn anything new," or "I'd like to come back some other time when I don't have my children with me," or "I tried to figure out what the exhibit was about but couldn't."

Motivations: Curiosity

The curiosity motivation basically states that in order for people to engage with an exhibit or exhibition, in order for them to enjoy themselves and learn something new, they must be curious about it. This could be an innate curiosity—for example, some personal interest that a visitor brings to the museum—or, as is more often the case, a curiosity that is aroused by the museum visit itself. Visitors to museums desire and expect that their curiosity will be piqued.

Motivations: Confidence

In addition to being curious about something, visitors must also feel confident about their ability to succeed and have a good time. When visitors feel safe and smart, they will engage with an exhibit and have a good time while doing so. There are many opportunities for confidence to be undermined in museum settings, such as exhibit text written at too high a level, unfamiliar terrain, not enough places to rest, and poor lighting. All of these erode visitors' feelings of confidence.

Motivations: Challenge

While visitors need to feel safe and smart in order to engage successfully with a museum exhibit and to have a meaningful visitor experience, they also need to feel challenged. It is imperative that visitors feel they will be able to succeed and that they know how to engage with an exhibit; it is equally imperative that they perceive some challenge or a goal. When things are too easy—too simple, boring, or babyish—visitors won't engage. There needs to be just the right amount of balance between visitors feeling confident about their ability to engage meaningfully with the exhibit and their feeling challenged in an area that isn't totally comfortable for them.

Motivations: Control

Unlike many educational settings where learners have relatively little control, informal settings are predicated on visitors' ability to take charge of their own experiences. Although it is not the only characteristic—and definitely not the most important one—a defining distinction of museums is the notion of free choice. When visitors feel powerful and in charge, when they perceive that they have meaningful and appropriate choices to make, they will engage for longer periods and in more meaningful ways.

Motivations: Play

The final motivation is often neglected—or, alternatively, given only cursory attention—in much of the non-children's museum exhibit-development process. Play in this case is something that is important not just for children but for every visitor. When visitors feel playful—even if only in their minds—they will have more successful and satisfying experiences. In learning new things, regardless of the age of the learner, one of the initial stages of engagement is play and exploration. And play doesn't stop when a person moves from being a novice, to being experienced, to being an expert. Play is as essential for scientists, art historians, and expert gardeners as it is for someone brand new to an experience.

These six motivations are not mutually exclusive. They are, however, essential. That's not to say that every visitor experience has to have equal amounts of each at all times. Just as each visitor experience is unique, so too is the specific combination of each of these motivations during any particular visit. It's when visitors perceive that the balance is out of whack, when one or more of these intrinsic motivations has been violated, that the visitor experience becomes uncomfortable and the visit itself unsatisfying.

By consciously designing for communication, curiosity, confidence, challenge, control, and play, museum professionals will significantly increase the likelihood that visitors will have enjoyable, educational, and ultimately deeply satisfying and meaningful experiences in museum spaces.

NOTES

1. I am using a broad definition of outcomes compared with the more specific descriptions put forth by the Institute of Museum and Library Services in its important publication on outcomes-based evaluation (Sheppard, Weil, and Rudd 2000) and similar to follow-up publications by Wells and Butler (2002, 2004). In the Selinda Model, outcomes include all the ways visitors are changed—in a relatively permanent way—as a result of their visits to an exhibit or exhibition. Outcomes, as discussed in this book, focus on the individual and group and do not include the many related outcomes for communities and the museum field.

Many professionals also refer to this as the *impact* on the visitor. I steer away from the use of that term, as it unintentionally implies a somewhat unidirectional and linear approach to learning that I believe doesn't adequately capture the deeply personal and mutually shaping contributions of exhibits to visitors' lives.

2. While Ted Ansbacher and, more recently, Nina Simon have been leading proponents in this area, many others have joined in the discussions. See, for example, Ansbacher et al. (2000) and Dierking et al. (2002).

3. Thanks to Paul Martin, then exhibit developer at the Minnesota History Center, who used this phrase to guide the exhibit development of *Minnesota A–Z,* a wonderful example of a museum exhibition designed with the visitor in mind.

4. Note that the term *knowledge hierarchies* as I am using it refers to something different than Gagné's *learning hierarchies* from the field of education (Gagné 1965; Gagné and Briggs 1979).

5. See appendix D for samples of knowledge hierarchies from actual visitor studies.

6. Note that although it is described in visitor terms, the knowledge hierarchy is for the exhibit, not the visitor. In other words, it describes a learning journey *in the context of the exhibit.* It is not a description of a visitor. Each exhibit unit should have one, and only one, knowledge hierarchy, ideally based on a well-defined main message or big idea.

7. "As to diseases, make a habit of two things—to help, or at least, to do no harm" (Hippocrates, Epidemics, Bk. I, Sect. XI). See also Cedric M. Smith, "Origin and Uses of *Primum Non Nocere*— Above All, Do No Harm!," *Journal of Clinical Pharmacology,* December 3, 2004, http://jcp.sagepub .com/cgi/content/abstract/45/4/371.

8. Carol Fialkowski at the Chicago Academy of Sciences developed a list titled "12 Skills for Thinking" that was used to guide much of the museum's exhibit development and programming. This list includes observing, communicating, identifying, comparing/contrasting, classifying, hypothesizing/predicting, experimenting, analyzing, synthesizing, conceptualizing, evaluating, and applying/transferring (Perry and Edington 1995, 30). Although far from exhaustive, this list is a good starting point for thinking about some of the types of intellectual engagement that are desirable for science exhibits in particular. Housen (1992) describes intellectual skills for viewing art that vary by stage of development: observing, making personal associations, creating narratives, reflecting, judging, interpreting, and so forth.

Part II

DESIGNING VISITOR EXPERIENCES

The second half of the book devotes a chapter to each of the six motivations in the Selinda Model of Visitor Learning. Each chapter defines and describes the motivation and presents supporting research-based principles and strategies for designing intrinsically motivating museum exhibits. The principles and strategies presented here are, like our profession, dynamic and evolving as we learn from each other and from our visitors. This is just the beginning of the conversation. Ongoing design discussions will advance the conversation and contribute to the evolution of these ideas and to the development of additional concrete examples and techniques. Visit www.selindaresearch.com/wmlf for further examples, photographs, and discussion.

4

Communication

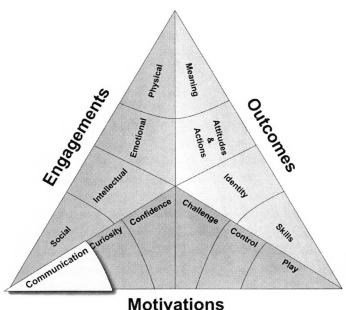

Motivations

Communication is one of the six basic motivations visitors bring with them to museum settings. When discussing communication in museums, we often think specifically of social interaction (Perry 1992; Litwak 1993). But as McManus points out in the quotation below, social interaction is not an end in itself but a means to an end, that is, communication.

The social aspect of visits to the Museum is not a mere enjoyable overlay adding pleasure to the museum experience for visiting groups. It is, rather, at the core of that experience and a fundamental source of satisfaction in museum visiting which is brought to the museum. As such, designers should capitalize upon it as much as they are able. The social aspect needs to be taken into account seriously in their work since it permeates the communicative situation in the museum. Both group composition and quality of social interaction with groups affect independently the manner in which visitors take information from exhibits. Additionally, social group structure affects the strength with which people work to make meanings clear to each other. (McManus 1988, 43)

All museum visitors, whether visiting alone or in a social group, share the motivation for and expectation of communication. Bruner (1966) refers to this need as "reciprocity." Whether engaged in an enthusiastic conversation with one's visiting companions, thoughtful discussion about an exhibit artifact, or the careful and thorough reading of an exhibit label, visitors to museums have a need for communication. As museum professionals, we have all seen wonderful examples of visitors passionately working to make sense of the objects and phenomena with which they are engaged. The four visitor groups to the Children's Museum of Indianapolis described in chapter 1 are clear evidence of people actively pursuing their need for meaningful communication.

But how do we know when meaningful communication has taken place? Is it when visitors learn the intended messages of the exhibit? Is it when they are satisfied with their experience? What if visitors learn the educational messages but don't feel satisfied? Is this meaningful communication? What if they feel satisfied with their experience but have not achieved any of the goals of the exhibit? For the purposes of this book, meaningful communication is when both the visitors feel satisfied with the communication process they have been part of and the museum is satisfied that the visitors have learned (broadly defined) something of merit. Without expressed satisfaction on the part of both the museum and visitor, meaningful communication has not taken place. In other words, the fact that visitors have learned the exhibit messages does not mean that their need for communication has been fulfilled. At the same time, just because visitors feel satisfied with their experience at the museum, this doesn't mean that the museum has successfully engaged them in meaningful communication. Satisfaction, both on the visitors' parts and in the museum staff's eyes, is essential for communication to be achieved.

Furthermore, meaningful communication is not strictly limited to the exhibit's intended messages. Sometimes communication takes place that is satisfying to both the visitor and the museum, but it is on the edge of the exhibit goals.

Leinhardt, Knutson, and Crowley (2003, 29) present a clear example of this when they describe two women sitting on a bench looking at a museum display about recycling that included a large wall of stacked Coke cans. One woman began reminiscing about a childhood memory of one of her father's friends who had a wall of stacked beer cans in his basement. While both museums and visitors value such personal memories in exhibitions, and while these types of communications might be deemed meaningful in many instances, if this was always the sole or even primary type of communication taking place, the exhibit team might rightly decide to redesign the exhibit so that more visitors had meaningful conversations that incorporated aspects of the main exhibit message, unless of course the main message was about personal reminiscing.

The remainder of this chapter presents two educational principles—collaboration and guidance—and with them, interpretive strategies for achieving meaningful communication in museum settings. Similar to *explanatory engagement* (Leinhardt and Crowley 1998), collaboration and guidance focus on the processes used to achieve meaningful communication. Because most visitors come to museums as part of small social groups, and because meaningful communication is such an individual and personally driven experience for single visitors, this chapter focuses on group meaning making. These communication principles and strategies, however, while designed with groups in mind, also work well in most instances with individual visitors.

PRINCIPLE 1: COLLABORATION
Meaningful communication is enhanced when visitors collaborate on a group task or meaning-making venture.

Put more simply, this principle states that when visitors work together, they learn more. Increasingly, collaborative learning in museum settings is not only being discussed but also valued. Due to the social nature of most museum visits, museums are natural environments for collaborative learning to take place. In fact, Diamond (1980, 1986) found that the learning that happened among the respondents in a science museum study was a function of the collaborative social interactions that took place between adults and children in the presence of an exhibit, as opposed to a direct communication between the exhibit and the visitor. Furthermore, Vygotsky (1978, 1986), in discussing how children learn, suggests that every individual has a zone of proximal development (ZPD). He posits that every child is capable of a certain level of understanding about any particular concept when left to her or his own devices, but when paired with someone more knowledgeable about that concept, the child will be able to achieve much higher levels of understanding. This difference—between what one is capable of on their own and what one is able to achieve when working alongside someone more knowledgeable—is the learner's ZPD. Having exhibit spaces that are carefully designed to include opportunities for collaboration is an important way to enhance and maximize rich meaning-making at museum exhibits.

In her study on family learning, Hilke (1988) explains that a naturally occurring dynamic in museum settings is that less and more experienced members (e.g., adults and children) tend to pair up: "Specifically, children were much more likely to choose parents as interactive partners than they were to choose their siblings. Similarly, parents were much more likely to choose their children as interactive partners. . . . Such a cross-generational bias in choosing interactive partners enhances the learning potential of the family experience by putting individuals with the least common experiences and knowledge in direct contact" (123–24). This merging of diverse experience banks resulted in "augmenting the information that would have been available to family members had they been visiting the exhibition alone" (Hilke 1988, 123). Using Vygotsky's language, these are naturally occurring groups that contain multiple ZPDs.

These findings support the extensive work conducted by Brown and others on *communities of learners*, an attempt to provide richer and more meaningful classroom experiences for school students. Brown and Campione (1994) describe four characteristics they strive for when setting up communities of learners: ritual, familiar participant structures; a community of discourse; multiple zones of proximal development; and the seeding, migration, and appropriation of ideas (234–237). All of these are naturally occurring phenomena in museum settings (Ash 2002, 358–64).

In a research study that was part of the Museum Learning Collaborative,[1] Fienberg and Leinhardt (2002) shared an example of a conversation in a museum in which each visitor contributed something different to the group understanding of the exhibit; they concluded that a collaborative experience such as this "can build on the joint experiences of visitors to create a much richer experience than any individual could have alone" (209).

Given that museums are natural settings within which meaningful, socially constructed learning can and does take place, and because the visiting public has a strong motivation for communication, it makes sense to ensure there are plenty of opportunities for visitors to collaborate on the joint construction of knowledge. When visitors work together, learning increases. The following section discusses some strategies for maximizing the likelihood that visitors will work together.

Strategy 1.1: Design spaces that encourage members of
visiting social groups to stay together and in close proximity.

McManus (1987, 1988) did extensive research on the learning behavior of social groups in museum settings. She identified four types of behaviors directly associated with museum learning: reading exhibit labels, engaging in conversation about the exhibit topic, spending time at the exhibit, and using exhibit interactives. She was also interested in group cohesiveness—that is, a measure of the social intimacy among group members—and divided her respondents into three levels of group cohesiveness:

- Poor: Group members were more than one meter apart and likely to be acting independently.
- Good: Group members were close to one another, and movements were made in tandem with or complementary to those of other group members.
- Very good: Group members were moving shoulder to shoulder and/or touching unconsciously.

Investigating the relationship between group cohesiveness and each of the learning-related behaviors, McManus found no relationship between group cohesiveness and the use of exhibit interactives, but she did find highly significant relationships between group cohesiveness and the other three learning behaviors: label reading, length of conversation, and time at exhibit. About the reading of exhibit labels she explained that "groups showing very good cohesive behaviour were more likely to show comprehensive reading behaviour" (McManus 1988, 39). At the same time, those groups that demonstrated poor group cohesiveness were much more likely not to read labels. Similarly, McManus found that as group cohesive increased, so did the length of conversation about the exhibits, and she pointed out that "many poorly cohesive groups did not talk at all and those that did tended to have short conversations" (McManus 1988, 40). Finally, the relationship between time at exhibit was also positively significant—that is, highly cohesive groups tended to spend longer periods at the exhibit, and poorly cohesive groups spent significantly less time (McManus 1988, 40).

While some of a group's cohesiveness is determined by the social intimacy members bring with them, McManus encourages exhibit designers and developers "to plan exhibits so that the united focusing of a group on the exhibit reinforces social intimacy within the visiting group" (McManus 1988, 40). In other words, if we design exhibits to encourage groups to stay in close proximity, social intimacy will be maximized, and learning-related behaviors will increase.

Like McManus (1987, 1988), Hensel (1987) also investigated group behavior in museums with a focus on interactions with, and conversations at, exhibits. Drawing on work by Argyle and Kendon (1967), Hensel (1987, 95–98) discusses F-formations, those communicative stances that are formed when people face each other: "Kendon identified a body of spatial arrangements between interactants in which two or more participants [maintain] jurisdiction and control over transactional space between them" (Hensel 1987, 96). She goes on to define an F-formation:

> An F-formation [occurs] 'whenever two or more people sustain a spatial and orientational relationship in which the space between them is one in which they have equal, direct and exclusive access' (Kendon 1977, 179). . . . Cooperation for maintaining the F-formation is accomplished by changes in stance, location and/or orientation which is compensated for by other members of the group. (Hensel 1987, 96–97)

Hensel (1991) found that "conversations [in museums] do not just happen. They are rule-bound, structured, and follow predictable patterns" (14). However, she also found that the design of an exhibit had a major impact on the occurrence of F-formations and the resulting conversations. For example, she found that all too often, the reading of interpretive text served to interrupt or interfere with—rather than support or enhance—meaningful conversations among visitors (Hensel 1987, 127). When visitors went looking for graphics or labels to assist their conversations, they often had to leave the F-formation to search for text, resulting in the premature termination or interruption of the communication process. Hensel found that many of the visits to an exhibit ended at least partially because visitors' conversations ran out of material. Because of this tendency, Hensel (1987) encourages exhibit designers to "place information within visual range of places visitors will congregate to observe exhibits" (220). But she goes further than this and explains that all aspects of the exhibit need to be within easy reach of the intact visiting group. When this is not the case, visitor conversations tend to be organizational in nature rather than educational. She posits that when visitors are talking about logistical and organizational issues, they aren't talking about educational and exhibit-related themes; exhibit designers should work hard to design spaces that reduce this switch from educational conversations to organizational ones. "Since exhibit related talk is desirable, care should be taken in the design of exhibits that this takes precedence over organizational talk" (Hensel 1987, 217).

Although Borun and Dritsas (1997) do not discuss the idea of F-formations per se (see chapter 2's sidebar, "The PISEC Study"), they call for exhibits to be multisided so that family members can cluster around them. Such multisided exhibits serve to enhance F-formations by providing visitors with easy opportunities for face-to-face interactions.

Obviously, it's not feasible, or even desirable, for all museum exhibits to be multisided. In many situations, keeping group members in close proximity with others in their social group is best achieved by other means. In addition to making sure labels and interpretation are readily at hand, as suggested by Hensel (1987, 1991), seating can be designed to encourage groups to stay close together. In some museums, for example, short wooden stools with carrying slots cut into the seat are plentiful and often found clustered around computer interactives. Curved rather than straight benches can help maintain F-formations and contribute to groups staying together. The creative use of flooring, color, and sound can also unobtrusively encourage people to stay in close proximity.

A summative evaluation I conducted at the Science Museum of Minnesota compared visitor interactions at three experiment benches with interactions at two traditional stand-alone exhibit interactives (Perry 1994b). Housed in the physical sciences gallery, *Experiment Benches* was a series of open-ended exhibits that provided visitors with many objects and components related to a particular physical construct (e.g., electricity, sound, optics), as well as the opportunity to explore the phenomenon. For example, in the case of the *Electricity Bench*, visitors could connect wires to batteries, light bulbs, and fans; in the case of the *Optics Bench*, visitors could manipulate lenses and a light source. Each bench was composed of a large tabletop, objects and components that could be manipulated and arranged in various configurations, and a long bench that could easily accommodate two or three visitors, all surrounded by a short, white picket fence. While deliberately designed to foster meaningful social interactions, the space enclosed within each experiment bench area, it was noted, was somewhat cramped.

The results of this study indicated that there was indeed a difference in the social interactions that occurred at the experiment benches compared with the stand-alone exhibit units. More specifically, a greater and more meaningful range of social interactions took place at the benches compared with the stand-alone exhibit units. In other words, when visitors talked at the benches, they discussed a wider range of topics and talked about them in more meaningful ways than did visitors to the stand-alone exhibits. However, it was also interesting to note that a larger percentage of visitors to the benches did not talk at all with their visiting companions. While the reasons for the greater percentage of silent visitors at the benches was not explored in this study, one could speculate that it was easier to maintain an F-formation communicative stance as described by Hensel (1987) when clustered around an exhibit unit than when seated next to one another on a straight bench. What if the sitting benches had been curved to enable visitors to face each other more directly? Or what if the spaces had been opened up a bit to allow more people to cluster around the bench?

When spaces are designed to keep members of visiting groups in close proximity with one another and to encourage the development of F-formations, social interaction and collaboration are enhanced, and the potential for meaningful communication is maximized.

Strategy 1.2: Ensure there is something for everyone.

Many museum professionals interpret this strategy of including something for everyone to mean they should design different exhibits for different audiences. Hein (1998) also suggests separate venues for different groups or perhaps different exhibits within a single gallery for different members of the audience. However, Hein (1998, 175) acknowledges that, although a potentially rich and rewarding approach, this strategy would take too much time and money to implement consistently. Another, perhaps more serious limitation is that while designing different exhibits or even exhibitions for specific audiences can be useful in some situations, it tends to split the visiting group rather than keep it together, making communication difficult. A more useful technique (although also difficult to implement) is to design exhibits to engage visitors in ways that work simultaneously for all ages. Hein (1998) offers a few concrete suggestions for how one might design such an exhibit, including "minimizing reliance on words, or choosing standard display characteristics" (175).

While it may seem an impossible task to ensure there is something for everyone, this opportunity exists in more exhibits than we may think. Hensel (1987) suggests including what she calls "child engagers" as part of museum exhibits in such a way that "all family members can share in the discovery process utilizing a variety of skills, senses and interests" (223). She calls for "hands-on, exhibit-related devices, artifacts, models, illustrations and try-ons" that are included as an integral part of the exhibit so that "the group can attend to both the exhibit and the device" (Hensel 1987, 223). This approach ensures there is something for everyone, it keeps the group intact, and it maximizes the potential for meaningful communication. Hensel also advocates for exhibits designed so that all group members can simultaneously and easily see into them. When it's not possible to have "open" exhibit bottoms so young children can have easy visual access, she suggests adding "steps, shelving, ramps, and perches" or sight-line directors such as tubes, telescopes, and directional arrows (Hensel 1987, 217–18). As another advantage, including something for younger visitors allows them to explore and manipulate while freeing up the adults to read and observe (Hensel 1991, 14).

If we deliberately search out creative ways to engage all members of the group regardless of their age, background, or experience, we may find that there are many opportunities to keep the visitor group together, interested, and engaged in the content of the exhibit—more than we thought possible. It may not be easy, but it is necessary if we are to maximize the possibility of visitor collaboration and communication.

Strategy 1.3: Pose a problem that encourages
input from a number of visitors working together.

To stimulate most collaborative ventures, two things are required: a common goal, or problem to be solved, and an opportunity for more than one visitor to participate.

In their discussion of cooperation, Malone and Lepper (1987, 243) distinguish between endogenous and exogenous cooperation[2] and advocate for the

more educationally effective endogenous cooperation. Endogenous, or de-
pendent, cooperation is collaboration that is integral to a task at hand and to
which everyone contributes equally.[3] For example, most museum professionals
are familiar with the classic *Whisper Dish* exhibit at many museums around
the country: large parabolic dishes located across the room from each other
are positioned in such a way that when someone whispers into one, a person
at the other will be able to hear them. This exhibit requires the participation of
two visitors in order to work. Contributions from both individuals are equally
important, or the exhibit doesn't succeed.

Another classic exhibit that requires input from numerous visitors is the *Build
an Arch* exhibit found at many children's or science museums. This exhibit includes wooden or foam blocks that are stacked on top of each other, ultimately
to form an arch, usually requiring two sets of hands to complete. Both of these
exhibits share the feature of having a common goal, or something to work
toward—that is, hearing a whisper from across the room in the first case and
completing a self-standing arch in the second.

The Color Connection exhibit (described in the Introduction and in Appendix
A) encouraged collaboration via a computer program that gave parents directions like "Have your child stand on the steps. Ask them: Where do all these
colors come from?" (Perry 1989, 316). This part of the exhibit set up a special
type of cooperative venture, one whose common goal was for the visitor group
to engage in a teaching/learning process. I discuss this example in more detail
under principle 2, "Guidance."

While exhibits that require visitors to work together can effectively enhance
cooperation and collaboration, many exhibits can be designed to encourage
cooperation without requiring it. In fact, many museum exhibits are natural
candidates for cooperative visitor experiences, and sometimes the content naturally lends itself to visitors working together. For example, in the *Hunters of the
Sky* exhibition at the Science Museum of Minnesota, a computer interactive
posed two brief video scenarios, one from the perspective of a lumberjack and
one from the perspective of someone trying to save the habitat of the spotted
owl. After viewing the two perspectives, visitors were asked to vote on whether
a particular area should be logged. The questions posed were designed to get
visitors to think carefully and critically and to understand the complexity of the
issue more fully, rather than to respond immediately and emotionally without
considering the consequences of their decision.

Visitor groups to this interactive were repeatedly observed piling onto the stools at the exhibit, sometimes with two or even three visitors to a stool. As in McManus's work, we found that when visitors were piled on top of each other (i.e., physically touching), the level and intimacy of discussion, debate, and thoughtful argument was impressive.

While it could be argued that this was an example of exogenous cooperation (i.e., each person voted independently), the real strength of the interactive lay in the discussion and debate that ensued as visitors tried to figure out how to vote. The voting itself turned out to be relatively minor. While cooperation was not a requirement of this exhibit, much evidence suggested that it enhanced the visitor experience.

At the Indianapolis Museum of Art a number of years ago, a retrospective exhibition on the sculpture of Jackie Ferrara was on display. Visitors were encouraged to view the exhibition and then go outside—where precut, 2" × 2" pieces of lumber in different lengths were housed—to put together their own Ferrara-inspired sculptures. Although no explicit directive stated that visitors should work together, in many instances they clearly saw this as an opportunity to work collaboratively (figure 4.1), often building elaborate structures that would have been much more difficult to achieve if they had worked separately (D. Fischer, personal communication, January 28, 2006).

Another example of an exhibit that stimulated visitor collaboration without requiring it was the *What's Hot, What's Not* exhibit at the Exploratorium in San Francisco (Humphrey and Gutwill 2005). Visitors sat in front of an infrared camera that was mounted atop a large monitor and observed which parts of their bodies were hot and cool. As part of the experience, tools such as a hair dryer were provided to warm and cool hands, faces, and elbows. Visitors naturally worked together to compare the temperatures of different people's noses and fingers, and also to figure out the answer to the question "The whiter it is, the hotter it is, right?" (Humphrey and Gutwill 2005, 38). The common goal was to compare what's hot and what's not, and the exhibit was carefully designed to encourage participation by many visitors at the same time; it even incorporated activities for visitors left standing when the bench was already filled with other visitors.

It could be argued that many (most?) exhibits in museums are already cooperative or collaborative ventures simply because they are in public spaces, visitors tend to come in groups, and most groups tend to approach an exhibit with the common goal of figuring out what it is about. All too often, however, because most exhibits

FIGURE 4.1.
Dan Gleason and Jordan Fischer work together on a sculpture at the Indianapolis
Museum of Art. Photo courtesy of Daryl Fischer.

haven't been designed with the specific goal of encouraging cooperation and collaboration, visitors revert to individual and noncooperative use of the exhibit. Or
they try to be collaborative but have a difficult time coming up with a common
problem or goal or figuring out how to engage with the exhibit together, a difficulty similar to that faced by the physicist and his son described in the section
Visitors Making Sense of an Exhibit in chapter 1. When exhibits are designed deliberately to elicit cooperation and collaboration with clearly discernible common
goals, visitor communication and meaning-making are enhanced.

The hand-shadow label at *The Color Connection* exhibit is a good example of a
label that elicited cooperative behavior with a minimum of intrusion on the visitor experience (see figure A.14). By observing pictures of hand shadows, visitors
immediately understood the common goal to "make a hand shadow." Another
example is the I Spy labels at the Detroit Institute of Arts, where visitors are
encouraged to locate different objects in a gallery. This activity naturally evolves
into a collaborative experience.

An interesting example of how some simple design strategies can significantly influence visitor behavior was used at the Chicago Children's Museum during a Designing for Conversation workshop (Perry and Morrissey 1999). The museum's *Dinosaur Expedition* exhibition includes a recreation of a 1997 dinosaur expedition that resulted in the unearthing of a Suchomimus dinosaur. The exhibition includes an excavation pit with a dinosaur skeleton embedded in the floor and covered with chipped tires, simulating an active dinosaur dig. Plenty of excavation tools are available for visitors to use to uncover the skeleton. The workshop began by observing visitors to this gallery, which provides a prime opportunity for visitors to work together. We found that young visitors tended to climb into the excavation area and start digging while their adult caregivers pulled up a chair and watched from the sidelines. There was little collaboration taking place, even though the pit was plenty big enough to accommodate all the visitors and provided clear opportunities for adults and children to work collaboratively at uncovering their piece of the dinosaur skeleton.

During a discussion among the workshop participants about why this had turned into an individual rather than a collaborative experience, it was suggested that there were two inhibitors to collaboration: adult visitors didn't know (a) if they were supposed to be in the space with their children or (b) what they were supposed to be doing if they were in the pit. For many adults, it was easier—and safer—to remain on the sidelines and observe the activity. The

Maximizing the Potential

During the workshop, participants also suggested a possible third inhibitor: the adults were just tired and looking for a place to sit down and relax while their children were occupied with something else. Occasionally this is indeed the case; everyone needs a break sometimes. The role of the label was not to force visitors to do things they didn't want to do. Rather it was to maximize the exhibit's potential. In other words, for those adults who wanted to do something more but didn't know how, the new label provided the information they needed to have the type of experience they wanted. The fact that with the addition of the label many adults climbed into the pit indicates that without the label the exhibit hadn't reached its potential for meaningful communication.

workshop participants decided to see if they could enhance more collaborative experiences with the addition of a simple directive. They posted a large sign on the back wall of the excavation pit that said, *Work with your child to uncover the Suchomimus skeleton.* The difference was striking. All of a sudden, the pit was filled with small groups of two and three people working together, talking quietly, and sharing their discoveries. There was also more conversation about the fact that this was a Suchomimus dinosaur skeleton in particular, not just a generic fossil.

PRINCIPLE 2: GUIDANCE

Visitors will experience more meaningful communication when they engage in active teaching/learning processes, guidance, and direction.

While collaboration and cooperation are essential for meaningful visitor experiences in museum settings, just working together on something isn't enough. Vygotsky (1978, 1986) makes clear that it isn't just the act of collaboration or working together that helps learners achieve what they are capable of; rather, it is collaboration coupled with guidance and direction—for example, asking and answering questions, directing attention to important attributes, explaining salient ideas, and relating the content to something personally meaningful. Vygotsky explains that this structuring and nurturing of the teaching/learning process is essential for children to move beyond the limits they experience when working alone.

It must be noted that Vygotsky focused exclusively on children's learning and development. He was interested in the development and schooling of children, not the education of museum visitors. However, by looking at the essence of what he was talking about, we can apply his core ideas to (a) learning in museum settings, and (b) learning among visitors of all ages, not just children. The implication of Vygotsky's ideas is that people learn in informal, socially oriented public spaces such as museums; furthermore, they have the potential to learn more when with others, provided at least one member of their social group has more experience or a deeper understanding of the content. In fact, in most small social groups that visit an exhibit, the chances are excellent that there are different levels of understanding among the members of that particular group.

Taking this idea a step further, you could argue that in the best situations, the exhibit unit itself becomes an active member of the social group. What if rather than just presenting information to visitors like a textbook (even a beautiful, interactive, and creative textbook), the exhibit served as a more knowledgeable and experienced member of the social group? What if instead of "lecturing" visitors, the exhibit was designed to provide the guidance and direction that is essential for visitors to develop their conceptual understandings and move further along in their learning journeys? What if the exhibit asked and answered questions, directed attention, explained the most salient ideas, and made personal connections. Remember the physicist and his young son who visited the *Colored Shadows* exhibit back in chapter 1? Their experience at the exhibit was missing guidance and direction. What if the exhibit served at least some of that function?

When I write about guidance and direction and teaching/learning behavior, I am referring to a very specific technique that is not used often in the museum context. Because I have found very few successful museum exhibit examples, most of my examples in the following section come from the *Colored Shadows* and *The Color Connection* exhibits on which I did my research at the Children's Museum of Indianapolis. There, I was able to test these principles and strategies thoroughly, discarding ones that at first appeared to have potential but later proved not to work with visitors.

Strategy 2.1: Guide the visitor group
through a successful teaching/learning process.

> Family conversations [in a museum] are inherently educational. They are characterized by participants organizing and playing the part of learners and teachers as they ask and answer questions for each other. The information is provided via readings or tellings and may come from labels, observations, or out of one's head. (Hensel 1987, 215)

Hensel points to a fluid dynamic discussed in numerous literatures, although museum professionals are rightly hesitant to use the words "teacher" and "learner" because of the strict formal educational and instructional baggage they carry. In the absence of better words, I use them here to describe the rich, complex, and ever-changing meaning-making process that takes place among all visitor groups, regardless of whether they are composed of close familial relationships, friendships, or even casual acquaintances. As described in chapter 1, the human species is predisposed, particularly in museums or other informal educational settings, to engage in teaching. Unlike in many formal educational classrooms, in museum settings the teacher/learner dynamic is constantly shifting. As is characteristic of many learning conversations, at one moment a particular individual may be playing the role of a learner, then switch into the teacher role and back again (Feher and Diamond 1990[4]; Perry 1989). As became clear from the four visitor groups described in chapter 1, however, while most visitors have a wealth of experiences in the learner role, they are not always as adept when it comes to playing the teacher role. Although the physicist wanted very much to engage his son in a meaningful way at the *Colored Shadows* exhibit, he, like many visitors, fell back on what he knew to be a teacher's role, that is, explaining or lecturing rather than initiating a more engaging and collaborative communication.

Wood, Bruner, and Ross (1976) introduce the concept of scaffolding as an effective instructional technique, one that has been discussed extensively in the education literature.[5] They suggest the scaffolding process includes six steps that would be performed by a "teacher," or an individual more expert in the content. These teaching steps are recruitment, or getting the learner's attention and interest; reduction in the degrees of freedom, or chunking the lesson into manageable pieces to enable feedback and success; direction maintenance, or keeping the learner on task; marking critical features, or giving feedback as the learner is progressing; frustration control, or helping the learner overcome frustration; and demonstration, or modeling appropriate solutions. While the researchers used scaffolding techniques specifically in the study of children performing a particular problem-solving task, much of what they found is directly applicable to the type of guidance and teaching/learning processes museums would like to foster among their visiting groups—that is, to providing gentle guidance and feedback, drawing group members along a learning journey, chunking the exhibit content into appropriate sized bites and building on what visitors already know, and challenging group members to learn something new, while maintaining interest and enthusiasm and reducing frustration.

As is typical with most exhibit-development projects, during the development of *The Color Connection* exhibit, the educational messages were designed after a careful analysis of the content goals and objectives and visitors' connections to the content. At the same time, a similar process was also used to design the pedagogy of the exhibit. In other words, the exhibit was envisioned as playing the role of teacher, mentor, or expert guide. The educational or pedagogical process was divided into useful learning chunks, each standing alone but also contributing to the exhibit's big idea about lights mixing to make other colors. Ultimately, there were at least six learning chunks, six ways someone could "enter" the exhibit: the hand-shadows activity described previously, finding the colored lights and trying to make different colored shadows as described on a label, the computer interactive activities, "reading" a didactic but simple graphic explanation of the exhibit, or just waving one's hands over the tabletop and making brilliant colors.

Each of these learning chunks had guidance at its core. For example, the brief computer unit called Where Does This Happen in My Home? consisted of eight screens (see figure A.19) designed both to present content and simultaneously to provide guidance by using a variety of pedagogical strategies, such as asking and answering questions, directing attention, providing feedback, relating the exhibit to something familiar, and stimulating conversation.

The research showed that in a typical interaction at this computer module, one visitor would read the screen text, especially the questions, out loud to other members of the group, who discussed, debated, and tried to figure out the answers. During the prototyping we attached a magnifying glass to the computer monitor at the exhibit, but this idea was abandoned because the high resolution of the screen made it difficult to see the colored dots. As it turned out, this resulted in another pedagogical strategy, that of extending visitors' learning beyond the walls of the museum by encouraging them to look at their TV sets when they got home (see strategies 5.2 and 6.5).

Museum professionals may protest that such a directed teaching/learning sequence is too structured, too linear, thus inappropriate for a museum setting. I am not suggesting that this technique be used on all exhibits or at all times. Rather, the technique was demonstrated to enhance an exhibit and add value in a way that has not been tried very often within the museum community. The findings from the research indicated that visitors to the Children's Museum actually appreciated having this type of guidance and direction when they were trying to figure out the exhibit, especially when they were trying to engage other members of their social group. As one visitor stated, "It's nice to be a teacher even if you're just reading the screen" (Perry 1989, 184). Another visitor also expressed appreciation for the computer program: "It explained to you what you can do with the kids to help them understand what was going on" (Perry 1989, 184). In fact, if we as museum professionals saw visitors engaged in this type of learning exchange at an exhibit, we'd be delighted. The trick is to keep it short and simple. The activity described above comprised only eight screens, a focused and straightforward concept, and simple vocabulary. The challenge for exhibit developers and designers is to (a) identify the situations in which this type of guidance can be useful, (b) explore creatively how to implement it in a meaningful way appropriate to informal learning settings, and (c) test it vigilantly with visitors before the exhibit is finalized. Each of the many different learning chunks mentioned above was carefully and repeatedly vetted with different visitors over long periods until it worked just right.

Thinking back to the high school theater teacher with his three students, we can see that this group was successful because its members were able to engage in meaningful collaboration that was possible because one member of the group (the teacher) could provide the appropriate level of guidance and direction. As was noted, however, he was an unusual case as he brought this skill and knowledge with him. Most visitors do not. The research clearly demonstrated that when the exhibit was revised to guide visitors deliberately through a teaching/learning process, they spent longer periods with it and learned more, without a reduction in their feelings of enjoyment and satisfaction (Perry 1989).

Guiding a group through a successful teaching/learning process need not be as directed and structured as the example given. Sometimes visitors just need a jump-start. For example, simply posting the hand-shadow graphics at *The Color Connection* exhibit (figure A.15) helped visitors embark naturally on a meaningful teaching/learning process. They needed no additional guidance and ended up going beyond the few examples provided. Another example was the label reading, *Look up! Find the colored lights* (see figure A.13). As described earlier, we found that it, too, was effective at starting a teaching/learning process that visitors were able to take further on their own. The message here is that each exhibit is an opportunity for visitors to engage in teaching/learning processes. We need to provide the minimum amount of interpretation that will jump-start and then guide visitors in these processes. At the same time, it is not intended that these are the only conversations, or even the most important conversations, visitors have about the content of the exhibit. As Ash (2002) describes, "there is a delicate intertwining of content and the method with which it is negotiated" (395). Based on her research examining the ways visitors negotiated meaning in an evolution exhibition at the California Academy of Sciences, she posits that "good exhibits, then, are the jumping off points for thematic conversations, by providing strong themes that pervade family conversations in engaging ways" (Ash 2002, 396). In other words, the role of the exhibit is to start a conversation and a meaning-making process, a teaching/learning exchange that will be rich, meaningful, satisfying, and ultimately unique to that particular visiting group.

Strategy 2.2: Model appropriate teaching/learning strategies.

Bandura is a leading developer of social learning theory and a proponent of observational learning (Bandura 1977; Chance 1979, 192–99). In his theory, he outlines the importance (and efficacy) of people learning from each other.

According to social learning theory, four conditions must be met for people to learn from each other: (a) the learners must pay attention and notice some particular behavior; (b) they must practice or rehearse this behavior, although this rehearsal can be imaginative or verbal as well as physical; (c) they must have the ability to actually perform the behavior; and (d) they must have the motivation to actually do the behavior.

When we design museum exhibits to model and engage visitors in appropriate teaching/learning behaviors, three desirable outcomes are achieved. First, visitors are shown how to engage with other members of their social group. Like the father of the preschooler who explained that he never knew quite what to do with his daughter other than holding her up and telling her to look at things, many adults at museum exhibits crave direction about how to interact meaningfully with their younger charges (Perry 1989, 181–84). Museum visitors will welcome exhibits that appropriately model these behaviors (Koran et al. 1988).

Second, by engaging in appropriate teaching/learning behaviors, visitors can be immediately successful at participating in a rich meaning-making venture with their social group. And when visitors feel successful and confident about adopting the teaching/learning strategies they see modeled in exhibits, they are more likely to carry those teaching/learning and meaning-making behaviors into other exhibits and settings.

Finally, a third outcome of modeling teaching/learning behaviors is that when visitors engage in these behaviors, they themselves model them to other visitors. Other visitors who want to engage in meaningful ways with their group will see these visitors doing so, and they will pick up these behaviors and also use them.

The Where Does This Happen in My Home? example given above was a relatively didactic teaching/learning process. Another, more collaborative model of teaching/learning was used in the computer module called What's Happening? (see figure A.18).

Notice that this series of computer screens effectively models an appropriate teaching/learning sequence focused on the main message of this exhibit, that is, that lights mix to make other colors. It chunks learning into easily manageable units; it directs attention to the important features of the exhibit; it asks and answers questions; it offers explanations; it guides the learner through a series of steps. Furthermore, it is particularly effective for a museum setting because it maximizes the potential for success (it was extensively tested and revised until it worked with every visitor group); it's short and simple—composed of only eleven screens—and doesn't take very long to do; it's collaborative; and visitors

Labels as Conversation Catalysts and Pedagogical Tools

At the Michigan State University Museum in East Lansing, a large elephant's head skeleton greets visitors at the top of the stairs. Mounted atop a short box, the head boasts long, glorious tusks that curve out toward visitors, beckoning them to look closer. Visitors love the elephant's head, and they love the fact that they can get so close to it, close enough to touch the tusks and feel how silky smooth they are. But for years, visitors were confused by this exhibit. Not knowing if it was okay to touch the tusks, two behaviors often resulted: either a child would touch a tusk, and the accompanying adult would immediately admonish him or her for doing so, or, after looking around furtively to see if anyone was watching, the adult would say nothing but would keep an eye out in case a museum staff member approached. During an exhibit-update meeting (involving the curator as well as representatives from the education and exhibits departments), it was decided that visitors needed some guidance about how to engage with the tusks. The label was revised and tested, ultimately resulting in the following: *Touch the tusks! Tusks are teeth.* This brief label quickly modeled to visitors how to engage in an appropriate teaching/learning experience by (a) letting them know it was okay to touch the tusks, and (b) jump-starting a conversation about teeth. The result was more meaningful physical, social, intellectual, and emotional engagements (K. Morrissey, personal communication, April 11, 2011).

had fun with it. By modeling all the appropriate teaching/learning strategies, the exhibit served to facilitate rich group meaning-making at the exhibit, while also enabling adults to engage meaningfully and informally with children.

While I have seen some exhibits that try to give teaching/learning guidance to adults by having labels that provide vague directives such as *Talk to your child about . . . .* I have found that most visitors queried don't find these particularly helpful, and in some cases they even resent being told what to talk about. On the other hand, the directive *Ask your child, Where do you think the colored shadows come from?* was successful at jump-starting meaningful engagements with the exhibit and eliciting appropriate learning outcomes, and visitors also appeared to appreciate it.

There are two important caveats when using this technique. First, this approach could get very tiresome if every time visitors approached an exhibit in a museum, they encountered a guided sequence. Whenever possible, the minimum amount of explicit modeling should be used in order to achieve the desired visitor engagements. In many cases, the modeling can be very subtle, and other instructional strategies can be interspersed as well (as is exemplified by the entire *Color Connection* exhibit). In some instances modeling can be progressively disclosed (see strategy 4.2b)—for example, with computer screens and flip labels.

Second, it must be stressed that all exhibit strategies benefit from thorough testing with visitors before they are adopted. *The Color Connection* exhibit was repeatedly designed, tested, and revised over many months. Far more "excellent" ideas were discarded than made it into the final design because, in spite of thorough thinking and good intentions, they just did not work. No matter how good an idea is, if it doesn't work with visitors, it doesn't work.

Strategy 2.3: Use visitor-spoken language.

Most strategies dealing with label text are described in detail as part of the confidence motivation described in chapter 6. Using visitor-spoken language is included in this chapter because it is so much a part of providing appropriate teaching/learning guidance.

Research has demonstrated that visitors read labels seeking information to help them understand museum objects and exhibits. In fact, it is common to find text echo in visitor conversations (McManus 1989; Rowe 2003). Studies suggest that typical visitor behavior includes children rushing up to an exhibit to touch or manipulate something while the adults accompanying them quickly scan the area for interpretive text so they can explain what the exhibit is about (Perry 1989).

Museum exhibit labels are often spoken aloud. In many instances, you'll also hear visitors interpret the words into more familiar and easier-to-understand spoken language (Rowe 2003). This instant translation is beautiful when it happens well and painful when it happens poorly. Too many times, visitors struggle over the pronunciation of a particular word or become distressed trying to come up with a useful way of explaining what the exhibit is about to another visitor. What if simple interpretation were written using visitors' natural language, language that visitors could skim, understand, and use immediately to engage in meaningful discourse about a topic about which they knew little? We know that visitors—especially adults with children but also children-only groups and adult-only groups—scan exhibit text looking for quick information so they can understand what's going on and simultaneously interpret/explain it to others in their group. If exhibit text includes words that visitors can read at a glance and use to explain to others in their group without having to go through the step of translating it into spoken language, the meaning-making and teaching/ learning capacity of that group is immediately enhanced. Some folks criticize this approach, accusing it of dumbing down the information. In fact, it does the opposite. It gives visitors credit for being as smart as they are. They don't need lengthy explanations on walls in order to understand museum exhibits and exhibitions. They do need quick, easily understood language so that they can couple it with what they already know and engage in meaningful conversations with their visiting companions.

Conclusion

Visitors are smarter than we think they are and they know less than we think they do. One of our goals as museum professionals should be to design interpretation that gives visitors what they need to start a naturally occurring meaning-making process with their companions. When we do this, museums will have honored these visitors; respected their backgrounds, experiences, and intelligences; trusted their learning capabilities; and stimulated an intrinsically motivating and highly personal opportunity to engage in appropriate meaning-making with members of their social group. Somewhat counterintuitively, there is strong evidence that visitors will learn more when they encounter interpretation that is designed to (a) be spoken, not read (think plays, not novels); (b) be read at a glance, not as one would read a book; (c) jump-start a conversation that goes off in its own direction, rather than lecturing visitors or handing them information on a platter; and (d) provide learning guidance as well as content.

At *The Color Connection* exhibit, one reason for the effectiveness of the label directing visitors to look up (figure A.13) was that it jump-started a learning conversation by giving them words they could immediately use to engage with the exhibit. The original label that it replaced (figures A.2 and A.3) tended to shut down conversation.

The label directing visitors to look up incorporated additional important design characteristics not found in the original label. It could be read at a glance as someone was approaching the exhibit. It gave parents (and other visitors of all ages) words to use when talking with other members of their group. And it contained pedagogy as well as content.

The other effective thing about this label was that it immediately modeled a more appropriate teaching/learning framework for museums (i.e., working together, directing attention, and having conversations), as compared with the more traditional interpretative strategy of explaining (i.e., conveying messages). In other words, the label honored and respected visitors' intelligence and eagerness to learn and figure things out, while recognizing the limitations of their preexisting knowledge.

Visitors are very capable of engaging in meaningful conversations and working hard to make sense of the objects, artifacts, and phenomena on display when museum professionals give them the space to talk. As mentioned in chapter 2, McManus talks about museums being conversation hogs. She posits that when museums are talking at visitors, visitors aren't talking among themselves. Most visitors need a jump-start, something that shows them where and how to begin a conversation about the exhibit. They need to be able to glean quickly (i.e., in seconds or split seconds, not minutes) both content and pedagogy so they can work together with their companions at making sense of what they are experiencing in a meaningful and personally relevant way. Having interpretation that can be spoken out loud, without requiring translation, is essential for stimulating and facilitating meaningful communication.

One last note: Some folks might wonder how we knew that the *Look up! Find the colored lights* label was the right place to start. The answer is that we talked with many visitors and found that this was the point at which they began misunderstanding the exhibit. In other words, by talking with visitors about the exhibit, we quickly came to realize that many of them didn't understand that the colors on the table were coming from the colored lights hanging overhead. They thought the colors were being projected from inside the table, or that the heat from their hands was creating the colors, as happens with a mood ring, or that the colors were reflecting off their clothes. Once we helped them overcome this basic inhibitor to understanding the exhibit, they could be far more successful. This was not dumbing down the content; rather, it was recognizing and accepting where visitors were coming from, then using this as a jumping-off point to begin a successful communication process. And when visitors are part of a successful communication process, they are more likely to have a successful and satisfying visitor experience.

NOTES

1. The Museum Learning Collaborative, based at the Learning Research and Development Center at the University of Pittsburgh and funded by Institute of Museum and Library Services, National Science Foundation, National Endowment for the Humanities, and National Endowment for the Arts, was an extensive research collaborative that explored museum learning.

2. The terms *collaboration* and *cooperation* are used interchangeably in this section.

3. In exogenous cooperation, each person accomplishes something independently and contributes it to the larger goal. One example of this would be a game in which each person's high score is added to a larger pot to see how high an overall score can be achieved.

4. In her work on human social learning, "Diamond found that the transfer of information within family groups is strikingly bi-directional occurring as often from children to parents as vice-versa. This finding contrasts with the commonly held notion that teaching is the passage of information from a wiser to a more naïve person" (Feher and Diamond 1990, 27).

5. Although Vygotsky didn't use the term per se, scaffolding is often associated with his above-mentioned concept of the zone of proximal development.

Curiosity

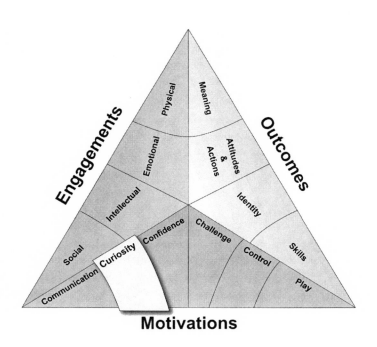

Curiosity is a strong driving force, a prerequisite, one might say, to engaging with exhibits in meaningful ways. Bruner (1966) claims that we all arrive on this planet with an innate sense of curiosity, a natural desire to explore our environment and to learn about the world. All too often, however, this natural curiosity is pushed aside, and work is required to stimulate and engage it. Curiosity in museums is both a prerequisite for and, as described in chapter 3, an outcome of visitors' meaningful experiences. This chapter's discussion focuses on curiosity and a sense of intrigue as necessary conditions, or prerequisites, for engaging with a museum exhibit. It addresses the questions of how to attract—and how to hold—visitors' attention in ways that help ensure meaningful engagement (Shettel et al. 1968; Bitgood 2000).[1] Two types of curiosity are discussed: perceptual (or sensory) curiosity and intellectual (or cognitive) curiosity.

PRINCIPLE 3: PERCEPTUAL CURIOSITY
Visitors will be attracted to an exhibit when their perceptual curiosity is aroused.

Before a message can be attended to or any learning takes place, visitors must first perceive the thing they need to pay attention to. Perception is the (often incredibly complex) process by which we become aware of items within our environment. In museum settings, this usually entails a combination of senses, including sight, touch, sound, and sometimes even smell and taste.

Perceptual curiosity is a powerful force influencing where visitors' attention is drawn. It is often what draws a person in to investigate an exhibit further. There has been extensive research about what stimulates perceptual curiosity in humans: moving objects, blinking lights, enticing smells, interesting sounds, bright colors (Fleming and Levie 1978). Drawing from the formal education research and literature, Malone and Lepper (1987) describe sensory curiosity in the following way.

> Sensory curiosity involves the attention-attracting value of variations and changes in the light, sound, or other sensory stimuli of an environment. The sort of factors that influence this form of curiosity have been discussed in detail as "collative variables" by Berlyne (1960). Colorfully illustrated textbooks and educational manipulatives (e.g., Cuisenaire Rods, Diene's blocks, or Montessori materials) are examples of instructional materials designed to stimulate sensory curiosity (Malone and Lepper, 1987, 235).

In many ways, humans' responses to these perceptual and sensory stimuli are physiological and not really under the individual's control.[2]

Strategy 3.1: Stimulate perceptual curiosity
by using audio, visual, and other sensory effects.

During the research conducted on *Colored Shadows* and *The Color Connection*, one of the design characteristics visitors mentioned most frequently was the tabletop lit up with bright colors. As one visitor said, "It's neat. It's bright and pretty and it catches your eye" (Perry 1989, 187).

Visual appeal and attractiveness are techniques frequently used by exhibit designers and developers, but perceptual curiosity is not limited to what we can see. Many museums also use audio effects to attract attention. *The Coal Mine* at the Museum of Science and Industry in Chicago, for example, uses a loud screech to announce itself periodically. Nearby, a Boeing 727 exhibit is accompanied by a rousing musical call to attention as it simulates a jet coming in for a landing.

Touch can also be used to stimulate perceptual curiosity, for instance, by allowing visitors to feel a walrus hide or the fine serrations along the edges of the immense teeth of a Tyrannosaurus rex. Clear evidence of the power of touch to arouse sensory curiosity is found whenever a bronze sculpture is placed within visitor reach, whether it is Brighty the burro, displayed at the North Rim Lodge at the Grand Canyon, or Bob Newhart at the entrance to Navy Pier in Chicago.

With notable exceptions, museums have been less willing to use smell and taste to stimulate perceptual curiosity, but these can also be powerful motivators and attention grabbers as well. Many living-history sites use the smells of freshly baked bread and the fire from a blacksmith's shop to attract attention and draw visitors in for a closer look.

One interesting aspect of perceptual curiosity is the element of surprise. At the original *Colored Shadows* exhibit, if no one was making colored shadows, visitors often walked by the plain white tabletop, barely noticing it. If, however, they happened to wave a hand over it as they were passing by, they would be instantly surprised and delighted to see brilliantly colored shadows. This surprise element grabbed visitors' attention and got them to engage. There were limitations, however. First, this experience required that the visitor already be at the table. Second, the visitor had to pass a hand over the tabletop; otherwise it was just a plain white table. When these two things happened, visitors loved it. But more often, the exhibit sat unused because of its rather bland appearance and limited attractiveness (see figure A.1).[3]

In an attempt to stimulate perceptual curiosity (among other things), the floodlights in the original exhibit were replaced with spotlights that created three overlapping colored circles of light with a large white area where they intersected (see figure A.11). With this revision, the three circles of bright color were easily seen from a distance, and the exhibit gained visual appeal and attracting power. As one visitor explained, "[The exhibit] kind of pulls you in" (Perry 1989, 187).

Interestingly, despite concerns to the contrary, there was no significant loss of the original version's element of surprise. This was most likely due to the fact that visitors didn't expect to see something other than a single black shadow, so were still surprised when they saw multiple shadows in many colors.

[It was fun] because you can see three shadows. (188)

[I liked] the shadow. You know it has two and three. (188)

This revision of the exhibit maximized the use of visual effects both to attract visitors and to surprise and intrigue them once they started interacting. In the original version of the exhibit with the floodlights, although visual effects were used effectively to surprise and intrigue, the attracting power of the exhibit was severely limited. While it was tempting to be satisfied with the fact that some visitors were delighted by the serendipitous discovery of colored shadows, careful analysis of data from the original exhibit enabled a redesign that used visual effects to significantly increase the attractiveness of the exhibit from a distance without significantly reducing surprise and intrigue (Perry 1989, 258).

Strategy 3.2: Use a variety of these effects, but use them wisely.

While using a variety of audio, visual, and other sensory effects can go a long way toward stimulating perceptual curiosity, it's important not to overuse them. If every artifact in every exhibit demands attention, visitors can easily become overwhelmed and confused about where to direct their attention (Bitgood 2009a, 2009b, 2009c). Not only can such an environment be physically uncomfortable, but overuse of audio, visual, and sensory effects can also be educationally counterproductive. Research has demonstrated that each of our senses has a load limit, or a maximum perceptual capacity, and each of us "can attend to only a limited amount at a time" (Fleming and Levie 1978, 8). In the museum setting it is particularly easy to bombard visitors with so many stimuli that they have little capacity left to attend to the educational messages. On the opposite end of the spectrum, of course, are those staid environments where everything seems to blend together and nothing jumps out to invite one to engage or to hold the visitor's attention.

The lessons for the designers are double edged; s/he must not exceed the perceptual capacities of the audience, but neither can s/he allow those capacities to be so underemployed that a more stimulating message will be selected. (Fleming and Levie 1978, 9)

Sometimes the sensory effects used to pique visitors' perceptual curiosity backfire by getting visitors to pay attention to the technology, or glitz, rather than the educational message. The result is that they engage rather intensely with the superficial aspects of the experience while, for the most part, ignoring the content of the exhibit.[4] Some high-tech theater experiences are particularly prone to this phenomenon. For example, it's not unusual for visitors to recall in vivid detail being scared by a sudden, loud clap of thunder, or having their seats vibrate, or getting splashed by water, but then have little recollection of what the presentation was about. In other situations, the mere presence of a computer as part of an exhibit causes visitors to focus on the technology rather than the content. Some of the most effective uses of computers occur when their presence is greatly downplayed and the computer itself is perhaps even hidden from view. The message here is to avoid using computer technologies to attract attention, as doing so will almost always prove counterproductive—unless of course, it's an exhibit about computers.

An example in which technology itself was literally larger than life—but in this case effectively stimulated perceptual curiosity—was in the *Underground Adventure* exhibition at The Field Museum. Using realistic-looking but oversized robotic critters in a recreated underground environment, the exhibit brought these animals to life, and all of the movement drew visitors in for a closer look.

The summative evaluation conducted on this exhibition showed no indications that visitors were overly focused on how the technology worked; rather, they appeared to use the robots as an opportunity to engage in conversations about bugs and life underground with other members of their visiting group (Schaefer, Perry, and Gyllenhaal 2002). Perhaps this was because the technology didn't overwhelm the space. Instead, a limited number of robots were nestled in among other interactive devices, wall text, and oversized dripping roots and fungal hyphae.

In summary, the judicious use of visual, audio, and sensory effects can create an intriguing environment. It can surprise and delight visitors without startling them. It can pique curiosity without overwhelming. And it can draw visitors into a meaningful learning experience. The line is fine between the deliberate planning for and the careful and controlled use of audio, visual, and sensory effects and exhausting or overwhelming the visitor, but it is an important balance to strive for.

PRINCIPLE 4: INTELLECTUAL CURIOSITY

Visitors will become interested in and engage with an exhibit when their intellectual curiosity is piqued.

Stimulating perceptual attention is an essential precursor to any visitor learning, but it's not enough. Whereas perceptual curiosity tends to attract visitors to an exhibit, often it is intellectual curiosity that engages them and encourages them to stay longer. Intriguing aesthetics, moving objects, and interesting sounds will all draw people in to an exhibit, but visitors will quickly get bored if their intellectual curiosity is not also engaged. Without intellectual curiosity, we end up with empty engagement. Jerome Bruner (1966) talks about the lure of perceptual curiosity and describes it as "the passive attraction of shininess and the vivid" (117). Arguing that in order to sustain intrinsic motivation during an educational endeavor, a smooth "transition from the passive, receptive, episodic form of curiosity to the sustained and active form" is essential, he suggests that such a shift takes place "with ideas and questions . . . that provide such a disciplining of the channeling of curiosity" and advocates for shifting passive curiosity "into more powerful intellectual pursuits" (Bruner 1966, 117). Three strategies are effective for facilitating this shift from passive perceptual curiosity to active intellectual surprise and intrigue.

Strategy 4.1: Present information that contradicts what visitors already know.

One particularly useful strategy for stimulating intellectual curiosity is presenting information that contradicts what visitors already know. For example, in an exhibition at the Glenbow Museum in Calgary, two small works of art were displayed side by side; one was a drawing of an intricate pencil-sketched female nude, and the other, a simple painting of some flowers. A label above the artwork asked visitors, "What was the gender of the artists who painted these works?" When you lifted the flip label next to the art, you found that the nude was done by a female artist and the flowers by a male artist. The exhibit then asked, "Do you think they were self-taught or professionally trained?" The questions elicited many interesting conversations about our preconceptions of art and what it means to be an artist.

Another example of using contradictions is the *Water Standing on Air* exhibit at the Exploratorium in San Francisco. In this exhibit, visitors flip a tube half full of water in such a way that, due to the competing forces of the surface tension of the water and the pressure of the air, the water rests on top of the air.

Although a useful technique, presenting contradictions does not always translate into more sophisticated (or accurate) understandings. Borun, Massey, and Lutter (1993) conducted a series of studies about visitors' naïve understandings of scientific phenomena. They took a common naïve notion—that air is necessary for gravity to work—and designed an exhibit to clearly demonstrate that when air is removed from a tube (via a vacuum hose), a ping-pong ball will still fall to the bottom. In other words, gravity works, even in the absence of air. When presented with this direct challenge to their understanding of the relationship between gravity and air, most visitors were able to move beyond their initial, limited understanding. However, it was interesting to note that, after using the exhibit, a full 13 percent of respondents still expected the ping-pong ball to float, even though they had just been confronted with a direct, contradictory experience.[5]

Despite the fact that some visitors will tenaciously hold on to their preconceptions, even in the face of contradictory evidence, providing that evidence is still an effective way of stimulating intellectual curiosity. In the end, it is more important to stimulate curiosity about the relationship between air and gravity (in this example) than to move all visitors from thinking air is necessary for gravity to work to understanding that the two are independent phenomena. While it is certainly desirable for an exhibit to correct misconceptions and evolve naïve understandings, the mere act of stimulating intellectual curiosity is an important contribution to meaningful and long-lasting visitor experiences with the stuff of museums.[6]

The Color Connection exhibit also presented information that contradicted what visitors already knew (see figure A.14). In this case the label on the side of the exhibit presented information not to address any existing misconception, naïve notion, or stereotype but rather to expand on existing and accurate knowledge. It referred to the fact that mixing colored lights (something most of us are relatively unfamiliar with) is different from mixing colored paint (something many people have some firsthand experience with). In other words, when mixing, for example, red and green paint one will get brown, but when mixing red and green light, the result is yellow. The computer program accompanying the exhibit explained why this is so. One visitor explained what they learned about this:

> If I mix green and red [paint] I get brown. So light is different from pigment and that is very funny because pigments absorb light so it's almost the reverse . . . You mix them all together here, you get white and when I mix all my pigments together I get black because it absorbs all the light. That's pretty neat. (Perry 1989, 188)

■

Formative Testing: An Essential

Because of the inherent challenges of exhibit strategies that present information that contradicts what visitors already know, formative testing is particularly important. In an interesting aside in the work cited above, Borun, Massey, and Lutter (1993) found that a prototype label reading, "Gravity does not depend on air," tended to reinforce the idea that it does. In other words, respondents who used the exhibit with that label were then asked if gravity needs air to work and incorrectly answered yes. Borun, Massey, and Lutter (1993) write, "The impact of the word 'not' seemed lost on readers, and the label succeeded in reinforcing the association of gravity and air!" (210). Alternatively, a label reading, "Gravity makes objects fall," was more effective at helping to reduce the misconception. Borun, Massey, and Lutter (1993) concluded that "(1) We cannot simply tell people a naïve idea is not so, (2) negative statements are easily misread or misinterpreted, and (3) formative evaluation of labels is necessary" (210).

■

The Color Connection included another example of presenting contradictory information. The accompanying computer program explained, *The screen looks white, but there are no white dots!* (Perry 1989, 313) (see figure A.19). It included an invitation to look closely at a television monitor with a magnifying glass, whereupon the visitor would observe that although the screen looked white, there were in fact only red, green, and blue dots. Mixing red, green, and blue light makes white light.

> I did not know that if you looked at your TV screen with a magnifying glass you would see the little dots on it. I was . . . wondering where did I put my magnifying glass. (Perry 1989, 188)

Other contradictions that stimulated intellectual curiosity in that exhibit included (a) getting multiple shadows, and (b) getting shadows in different colors.

> [This exhibit] is neat. When you put your hand over [the table], you get one, two, three hands.

I just always thought shadows were just either black or white. I didn't know you could do them in color. (Perry 1989, 188)

The strategy of presenting contradictory information can appear deceptively simple and straightforward, but it can also be difficult to use effectively. When designing contradictions and surprises in order to stimulate intellectual curiosity, we run the risk of (a) reinforcing naïve understandings, and (b) confusing and frustrating visitors. It is important, therefore, to use the technique strategically for a specific purpose and to test multiple versions of the contradiction thoroughly with visitors before putting them on the museum floor. In summary then, using contradictory information is a powerful tool for stimulating and engaging intellectual curiosity, but it can achieve the opposite outcome if it is not carefully designed and tested.

Strategy 4.2: Present incomplete information.

This strategy evolves from a discussion put forth by Malone and Lepper (1987) in which they argue that "people have a cognitive drive to bring 'good form' to their cognitive structures and that instructional environments can stimulate curiosity by making people believe that their existing knowledge structures are not well-formed" (236). This is directly congruent with Bruner (1966), where he posits that because of peoples' innate curiosity and will to learn, they will continue to engage in intellectual pursuits until "the matter at hand becomes clear, finished, or certain" (114). The natural conclusion is that if people perceive that something is "complete," they will be less likely to engage. In museums, this would have the effect of dampening intellectual curiosity .

Curiosity can be stimulated, therefore, by designing environments that make people think their knowledge structures lack one or more of these characteristics [completeness, consistency, parsimony]. (Malone and Lepper 1987, 236)

In developing a set of guidelines for designing effective exhibits, Jones (1987) also recommends that designers and developers of exhibitions "arouse curiosity and imagination by not giving all the related facts or details . . . [and] by indicating there is more to be learned about the subject" (4). I further discuss this second point, about letting visitors know that there is more, as part of the confidence principle, strategy 6.5: "Never dead-end the visitor."

Strategy 4.2a: Leave some things unsaid.

While it's important to avoid frustrating visitors (see strategies 5.1 and 6.2), choosing selectively what information to include in an exhibit can be an effective way to increase intellectual curiosity. At *The Color Connection* exhibit, for example, a decision was made early on in the revision process not to include any information about rainbows, even though it became clear from talking with visitors that many people thought about them as they engaged with the exhibit. This decision was made partly because it was thought that explaining the scientific phenomenon of rainbows (i.e., the refraction and separation of light into its component colors) would detract from the main message about colored lights mixing together and partly because the exhibit was effective at stimulating visitors to be intellectually curious about this on their own. In fact, although many respondents indicated that the exhibit made them think about rainbows, none expressed any frustration with the lack of information about them. To the contrary, one young respondent explained that the exhibit made her think of rainbows and that she intended to look them up in her encyclopedia when she got home. When asked directly if not having all her questions answered at this exhibit bothered her, she replied, "I think it's fun that you can't answer them because then you have more things to think about" (Perry 1989, 188).

Strategy 4.2b: Use progressive disclosure.

Progressive disclosure is an instructional technique frequently used in many formal educational endeavors. It enables the presenter of information to selectively reveal important concepts and control the pacing of the information so that curiosity is maintained. In a museum setting, progressive disclosure can also be used to maintain attention by hinting that there is more to come. This is described in more detail under strategy 9.2.

The Color Connection exhibit used the progressive-disclosure technique effectively (see figure A.14) (Perry 1989, 277). A label on the side of the table started off with a question: *Did you know?* It was followed by graphics demonstrating that red and green make yellow, red and blue make pink, and so forth. Off to the side, it asked, *Is this different from what you have learned in school?* followed by a direction: *To find out why, do Primary Colors [computer module].*

The research indicated that this label piqued many visitors' curiosity to explore this issue, partly because it pointed out a contradiction (as described in strategy 4.1) but also because it indicated that there was more information elsewhere. Placing all the information on the label would likely have served to dampen curiosity rather than stimulate it.

Presenting incomplete information can seem counterintuitive to developing good museum exhibits, and, in fact, doing so can easily have the opposite effect. Presenting incomplete information must be carefully balanced with confidence principles 6: Success, and 7: Expediency (described in chapter 6). This strategy is an opportunity to carefully design interpretation so that (a) visitors' intellectual curiosity is piqued in such a way that they then explore the exhibit further to uncover hidden information (see also challenge principle 9: Uncertainty), or (b) they leave the exhibit satisfied but hungry for more.

Strategy 4.2c: Use questions to stimulate
intellectual curiosity, but use them carefully.

Questions can be a powerful technique for stimulating curiosity . . . sometimes. Serrell (1996a, 105–10, 168–70) presents an excellent discussion about the use of questions to stimulate and engage visitors :

> While asking questions may be a good idea, it is important to recognize that there are good and bad questions. Some work better than others. The best questions are those that visitors themselves ask. (105)

At the original *Colored Shadows* exhibit, one label asked, *What color do you think your shadow will be when you block one or more colored lights with your hand?* This was definitely not a question that visitors were asking themselves. Instead, during the testing of this label, we found that visitors would read it and try to answer the question, but they didn't have enough background information to come up with a viable answer; instead, they left the exhibit feeling frustrated and incompetent. In analyzing the data, we found that most visitors did not notice there were three colored lights shining on the tabletop. In fact, they did not understand that when they waved their hands over the tabletop, they were blocking out a colored light (or lights). And to complicate matters, many did not fully understand that shadows are created by the absence of light. The label had too much incomplete information and left visitors feeling frustrated.

In the initial stage of revising the exhibit, we replaced the original label with one asking, "How many different colored shadows can you find? Where do they come from? How many colored lights are there? What colors are they?" We quickly found that these questions were no better and also left the visitors feeling frustrated. We kept working until we finally came up with the text *Look up! Find the colored lights.* This was followed by text and a graphic: *Put your hand in the blue light. Can you make shadows in these colors? Why? To find out, do [the computer program] Colored Shadows.* This label was more effective. The right information was incomplete at the right level to stimulate rather than shut down intellectual curiosity.[7]

PRINCIPLE 5: INTEREST
Visitors will be attracted to and engage with an exhibit that deals with a topic that is already of interest to them.

I include this principle here to remind ourselves that what is interesting to museum professionals is often less interesting to museum visitors. As we design visitor experiences, it is essential to ensure the exhibits and programs are interesting to our audiences; otherwise, visitors will choose to go somewhere else and engage with something more appealing to them (Rounds 2000). Three general strategies can help ensure an exhibit is interesting to visitors.

Strategy 5.1: Cover topics that are already of interest and relevant to visitors.

Designing exhibits that deal with topics that visitors are already interested in (e.g., dinosaurs, mummies, live animals) is a surefire way to draw large crowds. Museums have capitalized on this phenomenon by mounting exhibition blockbusters on such topics as Jacqueline Kennedy's dresses, King Tut, the Titanic, Monet, and sharks. Shettel (1973) refers to these as "intrinsically interesting" exhibits (33), although, unlike the present discussion, he distinguishes between these intrinsically interesting exhibits and those that have "an instructional or educational role." Topics that are already of interest to visitors can also be used to draw visitors into areas of learning and understanding about things that they didn't know they were interested in. In other words, the topic of sharks can be a useful vehicle for visitors to learn about issues of biodiversity; Monet can become a vehicle to learn about color theory. Collins and Loftus (1975) discuss this as the spreading-activation theory; they found that people became interested in new information related to topics they were already interested in.

Obviously, covering only topics that are already of interest to visitors is not possible or desirable. One of museums' primary functions—and strengths—is getting people interested in things they didn't know they would be interested in. While mounting exhibitions about the inner workings of the human body, Degas' ballerinas, the lions of Tsavo, and Abraham Lincoln's deathbed are important undertakings, museums can also effectively portray content that is less enticing. With every popular exhibit topic, no matter how inherently interesting it might be to a majority of visitors, there will also be some visitors who are not interested at all. While choosing an interesting topic may result in a popular exhibit, it remains a challenge to ensure the exhibit becomes interesting to the visitors for whom it is not immediately so.

Another caveat is that visitors are often less interested in a particular topic than we as museum professionals think they are. Front-end research won't tell us what topics to cover, but it will tell us what visitors are interested in. More importantly, however, it will illuminate how the general public thinks about the topic so that strategies can be employed to help maximize the possibility that the content will become interesting, even to those for whom the topic was not initially appealing (Korn 1998). I discuss this in more detail in strategy 6.2a.

Strategy 5.2: Relate new information to past knowledge
and things that are already familiar to the visitor.

Another way of making sure an exhibit will be interesting to museum visitors is to relate new and unfamiliar things in the exhibit to things that visitors already know about. A strong body of research supports the use of this strategy (Fleming and Levie 1978), and museums have been active advocates of this approach for many years. For example, one way that was used to make the *Colored Shadows* and *The Color Connection* exhibits more interesting was to make a connection between what visitors were seeing and their home television sets (Perry 1989, 312).

Another example is an exhibit on the periodic table of elements at the Museum of Science and Industry in Chicago. Although the exhibit is now somewhat outdated, it strives to help visitors make the link between different elements and things from everyday life. For example, the 29 Cu Copper display includes a penny, copper pipes, and some copper wire. The Ag Silver display includes earrings and 35 mm film.

It's important to assess accurately whether and what information is familiar to visitors. Front-end and formative research studies are important tools for identifying and testing what visitors will already know about (Beck and Cable 2002; Dierking and Pollock 1998).

Strategy 5.2a: Use metaphors and analogies,
but choose them carefully, and use them wisely.

Metaphors and analogies can be powerful strategies for enhancing visitor
experiences by making unfamiliar things more familiar. While there are many
different definitions of metaphors and analogies, one provided by a museum colleague is straightforward and clear: "a physical experience that draws a comparison or parallel between two largely unrelated things" (G. Dillenburg, personal
communication, January 19, 2007). A metaphor or analogy, as presented here, is
not simply an example, illustration, or model.

Martin and Briggs (1986, 379) stress the importance of using analogies to
arouse and maintain interest, as well as to make abstract concepts more concrete.
Ash (2003) also stresses the importance of using analogies and advocates for the
use of *personal analogy*, that is, using human beings as an analogy for how other
animals might grow and behave, especially when talking with children.

Unfortunately, the use of metaphor and analogy has often proven trouble-
some in museum environments as it can easily distract visitors and ultimately be
counterproductive to learning goals, especially when visitors pay more attention
to the metaphor than the exhibit content.

> Analogies used in museum exhibit labels require people to retrieve memories of
> the analogy's subject—its structure and meaning—and then compare it to the
> subject at hand and analyze the appropriateness of comparing the two and decid-
> ing if a new insight was indeed reached in the process. This is additional mental
> work in a setting where people are spending very little time (seconds) reading.
> Furthermore, analogies can and do provoke vivid mental pictures, and those visu-
> alizations can compete with the highly visible nature of museum exhibitions (e.g.,
> looking at real objects, artifacts, art, phenomena), and thus can be distracting to
> the concrete context at hand when the analogy is distinctly different, as they often
> are. (B. Serrell, personal communication, January 15, 2007)

In thinking about using analogies as an interpretive strategy, it's useful to
explore them a little. Analogies are composed of the target, or the new object,
artifact, phenomenon, or concept, and the source, the thing it is being compared
to. "An atom is like the solar system" compares a new and unfamiliar target,
an atom, with a familiar source, the solar system. Research in cognitive science
suggests that the effectiveness of any particular analogy depends on the degree

of similarity between the target and the source; that is, the more superficial and structural characteristics these components share, the more effective analogies tend to be (Dunbar and Blanchette 2001). For example, an atom and the solar system share both superficial and structural characteristics; hence, this analogy is frequently used in instructional materials.

A number of years ago in an exhibition about beavers, a large display compared different parts of a beaver with carpenter's tools. One analogy compared a beaver's front teeth with a chisel. The only two characteristics that beavers' teeth and a chisel share are (a) a general physical resemblance, and (b) a common use for cutting wood. But it is difficult to imagine a carpenter using a chisel to cut down a tree. More distracting, however, was the disparity between how the two are used to cut wood: beavers use a gnawing, clamping motion, while a carpenter pounds on a chisel with a hammer. The chisel analogy conjured up a beaver acting more like a woodpecker and did little to communicate how beavers use their teeth to fell a tree. In other words, the target and source in this analogy shared some superficial characteristics but few structural ones, making the "distance" between the target and source too great. Another limitation of this particular analogy has to do with the extent to which a chisel is familiar to the public. Any analogy that will effectively aid interpretation must in fact have a source that is more familiar to visitors than the target, which, in this case, was questionable.

An example of an effective analogy was provided by a tiger exhibit at a zoo. The tiger was on display behind a thick, floor-to-ceiling glass wall, and it was sleeping peacefully right up front, its huge paws splayed against the glass. A young mother with her two- or three-year-old daughter was crouched down, her hand pressed against the glass and aligned with the tiger's paw, as she talked to her child. She encouraged her daughter to notice how the tiger's paws were just like their cat Fluffy's. The two were then able to engage in a conversation about the number of toes, retractable claws, soft pads, and other ways the tiger and their house cat were similar and different. This analogy was effective because the target and source shared so many critical characteristics, both superficial as well as structural, and Fluffy was so familiar to the little girl.

The message here is that analogies and metaphors can be an effective interpretive strategy to help make unfamiliar things familiar to museum visitors, but they must be carefully chosen to ensure the greatest superficial as well as structural similarities between the source and the target. When chosen wisely, analogy and metaphor can enhance learning; otherwise, it's best to avoid them.

Strategy 5.2b: Display the artifact or object in context.

An effective and powerful way of relating objects to things familiar to the visitor is to place the object or artifact in context. Visitors are more likely to understand the relevance and meaning of a particular object when they see it as part of a larger diorama, in a life-size photograph, or as part of a video showing the object being used. The Field Museum uses this strategy very effectively in the large entrance gallery to its Africa exhibition. The exhibit is rich with large photo cutouts of residents engaged in daily activities involving tea sets, washbasins, and other real objects that are on display, as well as with video segments of exhibited musical instruments being played. And at the newly renovated Detroit Institute of Arts there is an engaging video presentation of shadow figures using a variety of ancient urns and jugs, with the actual vessels on display right in front of visitors.

Incorporating context doesn't have to involve a slick or expensive treatment. At the Capitol Reef National Park Visitor Center in Utah, a tool made from a sheep's horn is displayed in front of a simple and yet elegant close-up drawing of a hand using the tool to cut hide.

Strategy 5.3: Balance the familiar with the novel.

As effective as it is to relate concepts, objects, and artifacts to things visitors are already familiar with, at the other end of the continuum is using novelty and that which is unfamiliar to stimulate intellectual curiosity. Providing novelty in this sense entails deliberately presenting things that are new and different, that are not familiar to visitors. This can be an important and powerful strategy as well, and in fact, it is one of the major strengths of many museum exhibits—that is, visitors see something they've never seen before or learn something they didn't know they didn't know about. Using things familiar to the visitor can help create intellectual interest by providing important hooks for developing understanding, but using novelty or things that are unfamiliar can be a useful strategy for keeping things interesting. On the other hand, too much change and novelty can easily overwhelm and frustrate the visitor, so striking an appropriate balance is key.

Fleming and Levie (1978) talk at length about the importance of novelty in designing educational events both for attracting attention and maintaining interest among learners. They caution, however, against using change for change's sake and emphasize that "change or novelty should *direct attention to the most relevant ideas* in a message rather than the marginal or superficial" (Fleming and Levie 1978, 26; italics in the original).

Strategy 5.4: Ensure that the exhibit is
personally meaningful and relevant to visitors.

While museum professionals sometimes readily see why a particular object, artifact, or idea is important or at least interesting, the general public often does not share this perception. A subtext running through conversations with visitors dissatisfied or unimpressed with a museum exhibit is often "So what?" or "Why should I care?" The importance of making an instructional unit relevant to learners has been discussed at length by Keller (1983, 1987a, 1987b). Relevance according to Keller (1983) is the perception that "*important personal needs* are being met by the learning situation" (406, italics in the original). He suggests that we can increase the likelihood that people will be interested in something if they perceive that it is relevant to them in some meaningful way, and he suggests a number of strategies to achieving this, including tying the experience to the learner's experiences. When asked why he selected the Where does this happen in my home? unit on the computer at *The Color Connection* exhibit, one respondent explained, "Frankly that's the most immediate and intriguing thing" (Perry 1989, 186).

Keller (1987b) also cautions the designer "never [to] try to motivate an audience that is already motivated; just get on with [it] and do not de-motivate them" (4).

Strategy 5.5: Ensure that the exhibit includes things of interest to everyone.

"Chill, Brian. This is the only exhibit Mommy wanted to see ."—Mother to young son (Serrell, Ratcliffe, and Prager 2001, 1)

Unfortunately, this scenario—in which one person wants to visit an exhibit that holds little interest for other members of the visiting group—is an all-too-frequent occurrence in museum settings. Young ones are admonished to "behave" (or, in this case, "chill"), and disinterested parties reluctantly plod along. Whether we like it or not, people often (usually?) visit museums in diverse, intergenerational social groups. Just because an exhibit has a defined target group of, for example, adult women, or six to twelve year olds, or people interested in ships, we need to acknowledge that a much wider range of visitors will actually come through the doors, and, even more importantly, most visitors will come as part of a small but diverse social group. Furthermore, unless they are visiting alone, most visitors will be in the company of others who have more or less interest in and experience with the particular exhibition topic. For this reason, every exhibit must have something for everyone.

Going back to *The Color Connection* exhibit at the Children's Museum of Indianapolis, it became obvious that one reason it worked so well was that there were many opportunities for visitors of all ages and backgrounds to learn something new and experience the exhibit in their own ways. Visitors could make hand shadows, crawl through the colored lights, name the colors, experiment by systematically turning different colored lights on and off, compare how this was different from mixing colored paints, or learn new ways of interacting with a child. No matter what their background or particular interest, visitors encountered multiple ways to engage with the exhibit, all of which focused on the main idea of the exhibit, that is, that colored lights mix to make other colors in surprising and delightful ways.

One of the more difficult challenges facing museum professionals is designing exhibits that pique and maintain the curiosity of all (or at least many) members of a visiting social group. Most exhibits tend to be perceived as targeted toward one particular type of visitor: "This exhibit is for people who are interested in ships"; "That's a children's exhibit"; "I'll visit that exhibit some other time, when I don't have my children with me."

As noted earlier, most visitors come to museums as members of small, intergenerational social groups with a wide range of interests and abilities. There is some evidence that these visitor groups tend to leave an exhibit when one of the visitors becomes bored and wants to move on (Hensel 1987; Tisdal and Perry 2004). Regardless of whether they are young or old, departing visitors usually leave when they perceive that there is no longer anything of interest to them. Exhibits are more likely to maintain interest when they include a range of activities and topics for a range of ages and interests—for infants, toddlers, young children, teens, adults, and senior citizens (Perry 1989, 196).

An often neglected audience in museums includes babies and toddlers. When conducting the research on *Colored Shadows*, I was continually surprised by the number of visitors who expressed frustration because there was nothing for their young children. As one respondent put it, "All of the exhibits are wonderful, but they leave a lot to be desired for preschoolers" (Perry 1989, 192).

Some museums address this issue by designing a space specifically for the little ones. As mentioned in chapter 4 on communication, this can be a useful strategy in some instances. However, invariably this particular audience is in the company of older siblings, teenage caregivers, and/or parents and other adults. When an exhibit is designed to be of interest to babies, there is usually nothing for other members of the social group, and vice versa: when an exhibit has nothing for the little ones, it is often difficult for any of the other visitors in that social group to do anything more than give the exhibit their cursory attention. If we want to pique visitors' curiosity and get them to engage with an exhibit for a meaningful amount of time, it is imperative that there be something for everyone, including the little babies.

While there is a lot we don't know about how babies and toddlers learn, we do know that they are egocentric, they like to use their senses, and they like to use their whole bodies. Rather than segregating the baby visitors into play areas, what if museum exhibits included something at toddler/stroller eye and/or hand level? Some diorama exhibits do this now with Plexiglas barriers that go all the way to the floor so people of all heights can see the animals and plants (Hensel 1987). This technique could be supplemented with different textures embedded in the exhibit case walls, or puppets on string, or even interesting visual patterns. The possibilities are endless.

And what if museum exhibits provided opportunities for little ones to experience the exhibit with their whole bodies? At *The Color Connection* exhibit we added a short computer unit called What can I do with my preschooler? It encouraged visitors to put their little ones on the tabletop and let them crawl around in the colored lights. It suggested dangling hair in the light and noticing the shadows that were made, naming the colors they saw, or playing in the lights with crumpled tinfoil. In this way, adults, children, and babies were all able to engage with the exhibit together. As one parent commented,

> I liked the way it involved all age groups. There were lots of things to do that were interesting and different. She had fun with some of the things that she could do and I had fun with other things that I could do. (Perry 1989, 192)

NOTES

1. See also Bitgood (2011, 230–313) for an extensive discussion about research into attracting and holding visitor attention. In this discussion, he presents an "attention-value model" and argues that visitors choose to pay attention to things in their environment that provide high value.

2. See Fleming and Levie (1978, 1993) for more detailed discussions about people's physiological responses to perceptual stimuli from an educational perspective. Other discussions include Malone and Lepper (1987, 235–36), Keller and Suzuki (1988, 408), Abbey (1968), Bitgood (2011) and Koran and Koran (1983).

3. The original exhibit had high attracting power when other visitors were already using it. In those situations, folks from across the room could see the colored shadows on the tabletop and were readily drawn to it (Perry 1989, 256–58).

4. Mac Fleming, emeritus professor of instructional systems technology at Indiana University, called this "the slickness factor."

5. This finding is supported by an exploration of middle school students' understandings of the causes of the seasons. A documentary about the study (A Private Universe) is available online at www.learner.org/resources/series28.html# (free registration required). The same site includes a description of a one-hour program about children's learning about photosynthesis, *Lessons from Thin Air*, available at www.learner.org/resources/series26.html#.

6. When presenting information that contradicts what visitors already know, it is essential to conduct front-end research. Museum professionals often find themselves in situations where they are confident they know how visitors think about the content of an exhibit, only to find that what they thought they knew was itself a misconception or naïve notion.

7. For a more detailed discussion of the use of questions as an interpretive strategy, see Serrell (1996a) and also strategy 9.1: Ask questions.

6

Confidence

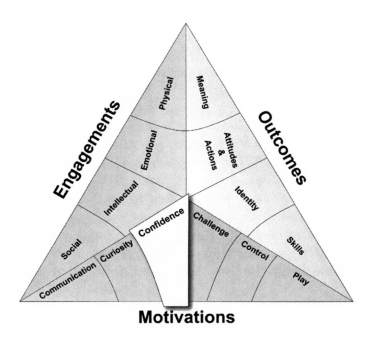

Motivations

Visits to museums can sometimes be intimidating and frustrating for visitors. For those of us who work in museums, it can be easy to forget how daunting the trip up the steps and through the front doors of many museums feels, especially to a novice visitor. Where am I supposed to go? What am I supposed to do? Where am I not supposed to go, and what am I not supposed to do? (Rand 2001).

We may neglect these concerns in our in the rush to meet deadlines, mount exhibitions, and develop programs, but these feelings are often the reason many potential museum visitors choose not to enter our institutions in the first place or, once they do walk through the doors, fail to enjoy their visit. For museum visitors to have powerful and meaningful experiences, they must feel comfortable and competent. Other museum professionals have described this as visitors feeling safe and smart[1] or physically and psychologically comfortable (Serrell 2006a, 41; Weaver 2007, 85–93). Hein and Alexander (1998, 11–12) talk at length about the importance of creating comfortable environments that are conducive to learning. And a large body of research demonstrates that being comfortable and competent is an essential precursor to learning in informal settings. So how do we help visitors feel safe and smart?

PRINCIPLE 6: SUCCESS
Visitors will feel confident and competent when they experience success.

Keller (1983, 418) encourages educators to "increase expectancy for success by increasing experience with success." Martin and Briggs (1986, 133) also discuss research that demonstrates that success begets subsequent success, and in an evaluation study of an exhibition about calculus, Gyllenhaal (2006) found that visitors "tended to stay engaged when they experienced success" (352).

It quickly becomes obvious that if we want visitors to feel successful—hence capable of learning—we must make sure that they are in fact successful. During the research conducted on the *Colored Shadows* exhibit, however, it was interesting to note how easy it was to unintentionally convince visitors that, in fact, the opposite was true—that is, that they were not capable of succeeding (Perry 1989).[2]

> I was looking up there seeing where [the lights] were coming from and trying to see where I could place my hand, and I just couldn't seem to do it. (186)

> It said you could block out all and get black, and I couldn't do it. That was what I was trying to do was block them all out and [get] black and I couldn't do it. (186)

> Well, it did say if you put both hands over it, it would turn black. It didn't turn black. So I said well, never mind. I didn't press it. I thought something was wrong with me. Okay, [it] didn't turn black, let's just keep [on] walking. (186)

Most visitors who were not successful at an activity at the exhibit put the blame on themselves rather than attributing it to some shortcoming of the exhibit. They made comments like "I wasn't doing it right," or "My son is too young," or "I'm not very smart when it comes to scientific things" (Perry 1989, 197). Four strategies are outlined here to help visitors experience success at an exhibit.

Strategy 6.1: Use clear, straightforward, and easy-to-read text.

Even though many museum exhibits focus on complex and often abstract ideas, it is imperative that text on interpretive labels be simple, straightforward, and easy to understand. When it's not, visitors feel overwhelmed, intimidated, and incompetent. There is strong support for this in the research literature (Borun et al. 1997; Borun and Dritsas 1997; Felker et al. 1981; Hood 1989; Keller and Burkman 1993; Taylor 1986).

Following are five specific techniques to help ensure exhibit labels are easy to read and understand: simple vocabulary, short sentences, chunked information, reduced concept density, and definitions and pronunciation guides.[3]

Strategy 6.1a: Use simple and nonexclusionary vocabulary.

It is useful to think of an interpretive label as something to be spoken out loud, not read silently. Labels are most effective when they include vocabulary and the actual words people use when talking with each other.

An example of this is an interpretive label for a Mohawk airplane that states, *Its primary role was as a photo observation and electronic reconnaissance*

"Easy to Read" versus "Easy to Say"

On page 93, I presented strategy 2.3, "Use visitor-spoken language." On the surface, the two strategies may appear similar. To distinguish between them, it is helpful to think about the motivation associated with each and how it relates to visitors and their experience. "Easy to read" is associated with confidence. By using familiar and straightforward words, we help visitors feel safe and smart. "Easy to say," or visitor-spoken language, is associated with communication and is a strategy designed to facilitate meaningful social interactions. Like all the motivations presented in this book, these two strategies have in common a focus on the visitor's positive experience, but they are distinct from each other because of their intended effects.

airplane. Even though it is a single sentence, the label is not easy for most of the general public to understand quickly, and it's even harder to read out loud. An alternative label could be as simple as *It was a spy plane.* If necessary, this simple, easy-to-understand, easy-to-say-out-loud statement could be followed by *Its primary role was photo observation and electronic reconnaissance.* Unless you are familiar with spy-plane technology, however, the two phrases photo observation and electronic reconnaissance are likely to be unfamiliar and difficult to understand. As mentioned previously, when things are difficult to understand, visitors tend to blame themselves; they often end up feeling that the content is beyond them and that they are incompetent. This is a direct violation of principle 6, which states that visitors will have a more meaningful experience when they experience success.

A simple guideline for making text more readable to ensure visitors will experience success is to replace longer words that have more syllables with shorter words of fewer syllables. While the process of arbitrarily replacing, for example, three-syllable words with two-syllable words and two-syllable words with one-syllable words can result in uninteresting text, when this technique is used judiciously and retains the primary message, it can greatly increase the understanding of many visitors.

Another real-life example comes from Michigan State University Museum (K. Morrissey, personal communication, April 11, 2011). The text shown in figure 6.1 was on a label in front of a complete elephant skeleton.

The text was rewritten with the intention of retaining most of the original content but making it more familiar and understandable for visitors by using simpler language. In the rewrite of the original label shown in figure 6.2, the main ideas were retained, but visitors' ability to quickly read and understand its meaning was greatly enhanced.

In a research study conducted at the Steinhart Aquarium at the California Academy of Sciences, Taylor (1986) found that when visitors read labels, they would often translate them into simpler language for others in their visiting group (137–138). Some examples of these translations included replacing "crevices" with "cracks" and "more potent than a cobra" with "more powerful than a cobra."[4]

Interestingly, this study also found that when encountering a difficult word or one that was hard to pronounce, many visitors just left it out. "Most frequently, when an out-loud reader comes to a word that she can't pronounce, she then stops reading the label (and acts like there really wasn't anything else interesting in the label anyway)" (138–139). Taylor goes on to encourage developers of labels to use simpler words that can be understood "by a wider range of visitors,"

> An elephant's skeleton must support an enormous weight (1 ton). This requirement, more than any other, seems to affect the design of the limbs. The elephant's limb is like a building column with each bone directly above another bone. The toes radiate out to provide additional support and distribute weight. In life, a large pad of connective tissues cushions the bottom of the foot and acts as a shock absorber. Limbs constructed like building columns can only be moved in certain ways. We could hardly imagine an elephant sprinting or jumping.

FIGURE 6.1
Original interpretive text accompanying a complete elephant skeleton.

even when some of the original words "might not seem difficult (e.g., swifter, stun, capturing)" (139). If our goal is for visitors to read labels, writing text that visitors can easily and quickly read and avoiding text that results in visitors prematurely terminating their reading will help us achieve our objective.

Strategy 6.1b: Use white space to chunk information.

Another often promoted technique for helping visitors feel safe and smart is to chunk information and include plenty of white space. A long paragraph of text becomes immediately more understandable—and more likely to be read—when it is chunked. (See Serrell [1996a] for a more detailed discussion on chunking.) Taking the aforementioned example from Michigan State University Museum, we can make the label even more understandable by using white space to separate the information (figure 6.3).

> Look at the toes. Does it look like this elephant is standing on its toes? In life, there's a thick pad of tissue behind the toes. When the elephant walks, this cushions the foot and works like a shock absorber.

FIGURE 6.2
First revision of interpretive text. Notice the use of more familiar and less academic—although still accurate—language.

Look at the toes.

Does it look like this elephant is standing on its toes? In life, there's a thick pad of tissue behind the toes.

When the elephant walks, this cushions the foot and works like a shock absorber.

FIGURE 6.3
Possible additional revision of interpretive text. Notice how adding white space increases the readability of the label.

As in much of design work, what's not there is as important as what is there. In this case, even though both examples use the exact same text, the second label is easier to read because it uses white space to chunk the information. Note also the ease with which this label can be read out loud compared with the original label.

Strategy 6.1c: Use short sentences.

Another strategy that was effective in the above label example was the use of shorter sentences. In the original label (see figure 6.1) sentence length ranged from nine to twenty words. In the revised labels (see figures 6.2 and 6.3), the shortest sentence contained four words and the longest fourteen. Research has repeatedly demonstrated that shorter sentences are easier to read than longer ones:

> Readers can take in only so much new information at one time. At the end of a sentence, readers pause to chunk together what they have just read. If you write short sentences, your readers will be able to do this easily. (Felker et al. 1981, 41)

One easy test to see if a sentence can be shortened is to remove some words and see if the sentence means the same thing. Another effective technique is to take a single compound sentence and divide it into two.

Strategy 6.1d: Minimize concept density.

While shortened sentence length, chunking of text, and simple vocabulary all help to make visitors feel safe and smart and increase confidence and motivation, research has shown that the density and complexity of information contained within a piece of text also has a significant impact on the ease with which a reader can make sense of it (Felker et al. 1981, 43). A useful test for concept density is to count the number of likely-to-be-unfamiliar concepts within a particular sentence or text. For example, take the first sentence in the original elephant label (see figure 6.1): *An elephant's skeleton must support an enormous weight (1 ton).* This short sentence contains four distinct, somewhat unfamiliar concepts: (a) elephant's skeleton, (b) support, (c) enormous weight, and (d) one ton. While none of these are terribly difficult concepts for many visitors, introducing them all in the first sentence taxes visitors' cognitive capacities.

A likely internal (and to some extent unconscious) thought process might go as follows: "Oh, okay. This must be an elephant's skeleton. How does a skeleton support something? Oh yeah, when muscles are attached, the skeleton supports the muscles. Enormous weight? That must mean that there's a lot of muscle. A ton is heavy. That's like the weight of a small car?" And all this mental effort is just to get through the first sentence.

On the other hand, consider the first sentence in the revised label (see figure 6.3): *Look at the toes.* This sentence has just two concepts—look and toes—both of which are immediately familiar to visitors. Whereas the cognitive task with the original label was to figure out all the information contained in the sentence, with this simpler, less-concept-dense revised label the cognitive task becomes figuring out which parts of the skeleton are toes. The first unfamiliar concept in the revised label is *thick pad of tissue*, and this comes quite late, after visitors have had numerous opportunities to be successful.

When designing successful visitor experiences, it's important to remember that as concept density increases, readability (and hence visitors' motivation) decreases.

Strategy 6.1e: Define unfamiliar terms and include pronunciation guides.

Because museum labels are so often read out loud by visitors, one way of ensuring success is to include definitions and pronunciation guides. Be sure to test these with a range of visitors, though, to make sure they help rather than hinder the reading process At the Old Faithful Visitor Education Center in Yellowstone National Park two versions of a prototype label were tested, one with the pronunciation (figure 6.4), and one without. When the pronunciation was present, even young visitors could read the label smoothly, but without it, most visitors, including many adults, stumbled. The results clearly indicated the importance of including a pronunciation guide (Gyllenhaal and Perry, 2005, 21–24).

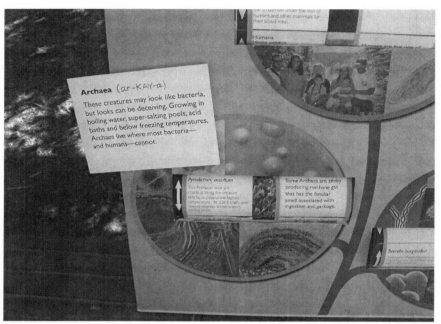

FIGURE 6.4.
The pronunciation guide on this prototype label helped visitors.

As mentioned, these five techniques—simple vocabulary, short sentences, chunked information, reduced concept density, and the inclusion of definitions and pronunciation guides—will not guarantee effective museum labels, but they will go a long way toward helping visitors feel safe, smart, and confident, a precursor to visitor learning, motivation, and ultimately satisfying experiences. Another useful tool for achieving clear and easy-to-understand text is a readability index.

Strategy 6.1f: Use readability indexes, but recognize their limitations.

Readability indexes serve a useful function in writing museum interpretation by identifying when a particular sample of text will be difficult for the general reading public. In general, the lower the readability level, the more visitors will be able to quickly grasp the intended meaning and, ultimately, the more visitors will be motivated to engage. However, readability indexes need to be used with caution. One limitation of these indexes is that most were designed to determine the difficulty of text that is read while one is sitting down and relaxing or studying. It is highly likely that most readily available readability indexes actually overestimate the ease with which most of the visiting public is able to access the information on a particular museum exhibit label.

In informal educational settings such as museums, material that could be comfortably and easily read by an individual sitting in an armchair in a quiet living room becomes impossibly difficult to read while standing and being tugged on by a demanding three-year-old. Because different readability indexes are developed for different purposes, when choosing which one to apply, it's essential to examine the context within which the reading will take place. For example, of three well-known and often used readability indexes, the Fry Index was designed to assess instructional reading. By definition, instructional reading is usually done by a student or employee; the purpose of the reading is to learn or do something specific, and the reader usually has help readily available (for example, a teacher, boss, or more experienced colleague). The Fry Index is most useful for printed documents like textbooks and training manuals.

Another popular readability index, the FORCAST Index, assesses technical reading. Technical reading is done (a) by a person with technical knowledge, and (b) for the purpose of understanding technical material. The FORCAST Index has been found to be most useful for professional journals, military documents, and technical manuals.

An index more closely aligned with informal educational settings is the Fog Index, which is used for what is termed "independent reading." The Fog Index was created by Robert Gunning (1968) to indicate the amount of "fog" in written material. The audience for this type of reading is the general public; the purpose of the reading is recreational, and it's usually undertaken with little or no help. This intended audience more closely parallels the audiences of museums. Examples of writing assessed by this index include popular magazines and instruction manuals. Even with the Fog Index, however, the expectation is that readers will be sitting down with few distractions. Because of this, the resulting readability level needs to be interpreted conservatively.

Gunning's formula for calculating the Fog Index is based on two factors: (a) the number of sentences in an approximately one-hundred-word block of text (more—i.e., shorter—sentences are better), and (b) the number of hard words (fewer are better). Hard words are defined simply as words of three or more syllables. Gunning (1968) contends that if you replace words with many syllables with words with few syllables, and if you keep sentences as short as possible, the resulting text will be easier to read.[5]

Any readability index must be used in conjunction with other criteria. It is only one source of data, and it is of limited applicability when used alone. To be of use, it must be considered alongside variables such as the graphic design of the label, the label's placement, the accuracy and appropriateness of the content, the narrative style and flow, and ultimately the context within which the label will be used.

While its usefulness on its own is limited, a readability index can help identify potential problem areas. If, for example, the readability level comes out high, chances are good that a significant number of visitors will have difficulty reading the label, even among a college-educated audience, especially if it is read while a visitor is with friends or family, standing, or on the move. On the other hand, just inserting a bunch of one- and two-syllable words to reduce the index will not ensure the text is ultimately more readable. As Schultz (1998) explains, "A low readability index does not guarantee readable writing. We must still look at our writing to see how it flows. The fog index is a nice tool, but writing is still an art." Even Gunning (1968) himself cautions against overreliance on a readability formula: "The Fog Index is a tool, not a rule. It is a warning system, not a formula for writing" (xiii). And Serrell (1996a) makes a good point that readability indexes are unable to "detect writing with annoying perkiness, pompousness, sappiness, or a casual attitude toward accuracy" (200).

Strategy 6.2: Provide answers.

Many museum exhibits ask questions of visitors. After all, museum professionals have heard repeatedly that asking questions is a good way to engage visitors and get them thinking about the content. It's a commonly used technique, but what is its effect on visitors' confidence?

While many visitors enjoy the challenge of thinking about and figuring out the answers to questions, most quickly become frustrated when they can't tell if the answer they have come up with is correct. At one science museum exhibit, visitors were encouraged to put together an electrical circuit and then were presented with two different possible theories to explain the resulting phenomenon. They were asked, *Which theory best explains what's going on?* Many visitors put together a circuit, carefully read and thoroughly discussed the different theories, and eventually selected one that seemed the most plausible to them. At that point, however, there was no information to tell them whether they were correct, and they left the exhibit in frustration. Not telling visitors if they were correct undermined visitor confidence and ability to succeed. It can be argued in certain cases that there is no one right answer and that, for example, both theories are equally plausible. In that case, the exhibit must explain this to the visitors. Visitors want and need to know if they are right and when they are not (Gutwill 2006). If the museum is going to ask the question, it is obligated to provide the answer. Visitors to *The Color Connection* exhibit expressed their appreciation at having a question answered:

> You get that [answer] from that little thing right here [a label]. That's what I like about it. It's all explained. (Perry 1989, 191)

Undoubtedly some questions don't require answers. And providing answers to visitors does not always mean just telling them. Indeed, in the best situation visitors will closely examine an object or phenomenon, and the answer will become obvious (Serrell 1996a, 169). But this "obvious answer" phenomenon needs to be carefully tested with visitors to make sure it is in fact as obvious to visitors as museum professionals believe it is or should be. If visitors are either in doubt about the accuracy of their answer or think they are right but are in fact wrong, we have inhibited their ability to be successful. Following are three strategies for ensuring answers are provided to visitors.

Strategy 6.2a: Answer questions visitors ask.

Before visitors can attend to ideas museums are interested in communicating, their own questions must be answered. Taylor (1986) conducted an extensive study into visitors' questions and concluded that "the information presented in most labels represents answers to questions that visitors do not ask" (92). Even though "visitors' interests are predictable and fall into a few discrete categories . . . the kinds of questions that visitors seek answers to are not those which are addressed by the information in the majority of interpretive labels" (Taylor 1986, 94).

Taylor goes on to advocate for labels that are concrete and related to what visitors are looking at and have questions about. He explains that "visitors' questions about the exhibits . . . are based on those aspects of the exhibit that immediately catch their attention and the way in which the visitors relate what they see to their own knowledge and past experiences" (Taylor 1986, 94–95).

Until their own questions are answered, visitors won't be able to move on to more complex messages and ideas. Our job as designers and developers of visitor

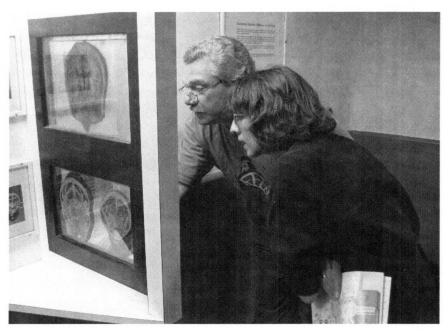

FIGURE 6.5.
At the Museum of Science and Industry, visitors wanted to know where the bodies
came from.

experiences is to craft a meaningful bridge between visitors' initial questions and
interests and the more complex educational goals of the exhibit. Answering visitors' questions is the first step in creating this bridge. Serrell (1996a) explains that
"knowing what your visitors know and what their top-of-mind questions are can
help plan the best order and emphasis of information" (109).

At the Museum of Science and Industry in Chicago, a stairwell showcased
thin slices of actual human bodies (figure 6.5). While the exhibit was a fascinating look inside the human body, visitors first of all wanted to know, "Where
did these come from?" The museum wisely answered this question clearly. An
accompanying label on the wall next to the exhibit explained, *These sections were
prepared in the 1940s from a man and a woman who died of natural causes. Their
bodies were frozen and cut into ½-inch sections with a power saw. The sections are
preserved in a solution of chloral hydrate, glycerin, potassium acetate, and water.*

Strategy 6.2b: Design labels that ensure at least one member
of the visitor group knows the answers to the questions.

An effective technique for providing visitors with answers to questions is to capitalize on a typical visitor engagement pattern whereby one visitor—often an adult but not always (Diamond 1980)—tends to take on the reader role at a particular exhibit while others in the group tend to engage physically with the exhibit.

At the original *Colored Shadows* exhibit, one of the first labels visitors encountered was on the side of the exhibit (see figures A.2 and A.3). In order to successfully answer the question posed—*What color do you think your shadow will be when you block one or more colored lights with your hand?*—visitors needed to (a) understand that colored lights were shining onto the tabletop, and (b) be able to locate those lights. In fact, as described previously, we found that most visitors did not notice the colored lights hanging over the exhibit at all. Without noticing the lights *and* correctly identifying which was blue, green, or red, it was virtually impossible to be successful at the exhibit. Furthermore, we found that when we tried to direct visitors' attention to the colored lights, because there were many other lights hanging in the gallery, visitors often made mistakes about which lights were for this exhibit in particular, often (incorrectly) thinking that the reason the table was white was because there were "white" lights across the room.

In *The Color Connection* exhibit, a simple computer module was developed to take over the function of the *Colored Shadows* label discussed (figures A.2 and A.3). Note that although the original label (figures A.2 and A.3) and the new computer module (figure A.18) both began with an initial question, the computer module ensured that at least one member of the visitor group (i.e., the person reading the monitor) had the answers to the question that was posed.

At the original label (figures A. 2 and A.3) visitors were confused by the question *What color do you think your shadow will be when you block one or more colored lights with your hand?* As mentioned, many visitors thought the colors were being projected from inside the table, were created in response to heat from their body, or were reflected off their clothes, so blocking them did not make sense. Being diligent visitors, they sometimes still came up with an answer to the question, but they had no way of telling whether they were on the right track and instead often concluded that they just weren't any good at science.

Replacing this original question with the question *Where do you think the colored shadows come from?* and then providing the answer at the bottom of the screen *Look up! There are 3 colored lights shining on the table* (figure A.18) enabled the visitor group to be successful in a way that was not happening before the revisions. It did not reduce the discussion or hypothesizing about where the colored shadows might be coming from. In fact, it empowered the group to have more meaningful conversations because at least one person was aware when the group was getting off track. Because the answer was clear and available, visitors were able to feel safe and smart.[6]

Strategy 6.3: Provide feedback.

One reason that providing answers is so important in educational settings such as museums is that answers provide important feedback to visitors to let them know when they are on the right track, thereby helping them to feel safe, smart, and capable of learning. Keller and Burkman (1993), in discussing classroom learning, stress that teachers should "help students build confidence by providing . . . feedback," and they go on to explain that "it is very demotivating to never know how well you are performing" (20). Csikszentmihalyi (1990) describes the importance of clear and immediate feedback in reaching and maintaining flow experiences, that is, those situations where one is so engrossed in and focused on an activity that all track of time is lost.

> Flow activities usually provide immediate and unambiguous feedback. One always knows whether one is doing well or not. . . . This constant accountability for one's actions is another reason one gets so completely immersed in a flow activity. (Csikszentmihalyi and Hermanson 1995, 36)

A wealth of researchers and theorists from the fields of learning and cognitive science, instructional design, and education echo the need for clear feedback in order for people to learn.

Providing answers to questions is not the only kind of feedback that is important. In order to be successful at an exhibit, visitors also need to know if they are using the exhibit in the intended manner—if they are noticing and paying attention to the intended things. Feedback in this case includes starting with where the visitors are and letting them know when they are on the right track. A label that directs attention, a keyboard that clicks when an item is selected, a photograph modeling how to use an exhibit—all of these interpretive strategies give visitors valuable feedback to let them know that they are using the exhibit in the intended manner.

Another kind of feedback essential to visitor success is This Exhibit Is Broken signs. All too often when visitors can't be successful at an exhibit—even when the exhibit is broken—they assume there is something wrong with themselves rather than with the exhibit.

The bottom line is that visitors will not feel safe and smart if they are wondering if they did something correctly, or if they got it right, or if they were using the exhibit in the intended way. This is not to say that there aren't many fine examples of open-ended exhibits and exhibitions that provide rich and meaningful visitor experiences. But the best of these are those that clearly communicate to visitors through their design that they are open-ended with multiple outcomes and no one right answer. They do this by providing useful feedback that lets visitors know clearly that this is how the exhibit is to be used and/or experienced.[7]

Strategy 6.4: Guide the visitor through a series of minisuccesses.

Another way of instilling a sense of competence and confidence in visitors is to carefully guide them through a series of small opportunities to succeed. Visitors feel smarter and more capable when the exhibit is carefully designed to allow them to (a) know immediately what they are supposed to do, (b) let them know that they can do it, (c) tell them what the exhibit is about, and (d) communicate that they will be able to get it. When visitors experience a quick minisuccess, they feel safe and smart and will be more likely to engage with the exhibit for a longer period. Learning guidance such as this was a popular technique that was effectively employed in the era of programmed text (Gagne and Briggs 1979, 161–70).[8]

Providing many opportunities for early minisuccesses is an important component of building feelings of confidence and competence. If visitors don't experience success, they will move to a different exhibit. In the final version of *The Color Connection* exhibit, minisuccesses were built into the revised computer program, which quickly guided visitors through a series of steps modeling how to engage with the colored lights (see figure A.18).

Strategy 6.5: Never dead-end the visitor.

Museum professionals spend a lot of time discussing ways to instill confidence and help visitors to feel safe, smart, and successful while within the museum itself, but less attention is paid to helping the visitor easily connect to additional resources to ensure their continued success once they leave the exhibition. As museums are institutions of lifelong learning, it is optimal that when visitors leave exhibits and galleries, they take with them a sense of connectedness to other resources within as well as outside the museum, whether these are other museum exhibits, classes, library books, or community programs.

An often overlooked consideration in the museum field is the exhibit's role not only in sparking an interest in something visitors didn't know about but also supporting visitors so that they can carry that interest and curiosity to the next level. Museums often assume that if visitors become interested in something in the museum, they will find ways to extend that experience. In fact, museums are but one small piece in the overall educational infrastructure that visitors avail themselves of (St. John and Perry 1993). As such, they have an opportunity to guide and support visitors on their learning journeys. Martin and Briggs (1986) discuss the importance of developing continuing motivation with learners:

> Continuing motivation refers to sustained effort, the tendency for an individual to work on a particular task or a similar task when . . . away from the instructional context. Continuing motivation implies that an individual voluntarily chooses to maintain or sustain activity toward a task over a period of time. (200)

When exhibits provide appropriate guidance and support and make it easy for them to avail themselves of additional opportunities, visitors are able to be successful and feel confident in their newly developed interest (Falk 1998). Following are six techniques for helping visitors succeed at developing their new interests.

Strategy 6.5a: Direct visitors to other exhibits
that deal with a similar or related topic.

A simple strategy that can be very effective in providing support for continued motivation as described above is simply pointing out other exhibit units related to a particular topic. At an exhibit exploring a particular artistic technique, visitors could be directed to see works in a different gallery by a different artist in order to see other examples of this same technique. In an exhibit about what makes a mammal a mammal, visitors could be directed to visit the wild animal hall to see additional examples of mammals. Sometimes it could be as simple as suggesting visitors turn around and look at another exhibit case that also deals with a related topic.

Another caution when using this technique is that one must be specific. It's not enough to suggest, "Want to know more? Explore other exhibits in this museum." Visitors are most successful when clear and specific directions are included with brief explanations of how these other opportunities relate to what they are learning. Ideally, these suggested links to other exhibits will anticipate what visitors have become interested in and lead them to places in the museum where this new interest is nurtured. Wolf (1986) goes a step further and suggests that such conceptual cross-linking is an essential instructional strategy that should always be included within galleries: "Conceptual labels must be cross-referenced with each other throughout the exhibit to help visitors comprehend conceptual relationships" (141).

Strategy 6.5b: Develop resource rooms to accompany exhibitions.

Another technique that museums have used to avoid dead-ending visitors includes the addition of resource rooms. While these are becoming quite rare in museums, they can provide a rich source of additional information for museum visitors. One study conducted at The Field Museum in Chicago generated strong evidence that visitors appreciated having a resource center available as part of the museum's larger exhibition on Native American peoples (Anderson and Roe 1993). Although the center was not used by very many visitors, the level of involvement among those who did use it was high, with 87 percent of respondents indicating they were "thinking, discovering, discussing, getting curious and looking up information" and only 13 percent indicating their primary use was to relax or take a break from the rest of their visit (Anderson and Roe 1993, 5–4).

Another study conducted at the National Zoo exploring visitor use of some of its discovery rooms (a close cousin to the resource center) also reported positive findings: "Visitors to discovery rooms seem to have more fun, do more, and learn more than visitors to traditional exhibits" (White 1990, 7). In conducting follow-up interviews with visitors to the zoo's discovery rooms, this study also found that almost all of the respondents "reported having done something—purchased a book, had a discussion with friends—as a result of the [discovery room] visit" (White 1990, 8). These are preliminary indicators that discovery and resource rooms may be useful techniques for extending the visitor experience.

Interestingly, in The Field Museum study mentioned, only a very few respondents said they came in looking for a particular bit of information or to find out something specific. This study concluded with the following:

> The visitor needs stimulation to form questions that can be answered in the Resource Center. Perhaps prompts located throughout the surrounding American Indian exhibit[ion] will lead visitors to the Resource Center with questions to be answered and can stimulate interest in fun activities. More visible signs at the entrance and within the Center may help visitors learn about available resources. Redesigning the room to alleviate the library look, and making the staff more accessible, may invite more participation from visitors. (Anderson and Roe 1993, 5-5)

Postings on a popular museum Listserv a few years ago also indicated that while there are not a lot of resource centers and discovery rooms in museums, the staff and visitors seem to appreciate them, especially being able to extend their gallery visits by touching real objects and further exploring areas of interest.

Instead of topic- or exhibition-specific resource rooms, some museums have set up lending libraries where visitors can check out books and other materials (P. Gupta, personal communication, September 7, 2005). Again, while apparently used by a relatively small percentage of the visiting public, they tend to be highly valued by those visitors who frequent them. Hopefully before resource/discovery rooms and lending libraries become even rarer commodities in museums, additional research will be conducted to see how they can more effectively extend visitors' exhibition experiences and nurture budding interests in new topics.

Strategy 6.5c: Develop relationships with local
public libraries and other community resources.

Another technique that can effectively extend a visitor's museum experience is to make visitors aware of, and encourage them to participate in or use, other community activities or resources. Some museums have gone as far as developing reciprocal relationships with local public libraries such that visitors can check out and return books from both organizations at both facilities. Among the people who use this type of service, it appears that the reciprocal relationship is valued.

There are many opportunities for museums and related community organizations to develop integrated networks of experiences with a single focus.

In the fall of 2005, an interesting model for this was developed by the city of Chicago. Over a two-month period, five cultural institutions participated in *Commit to Memory: A City-Wide Exploration of the Vietnam War*, culminating in the unveiling of the city's new Vietnam Veteran's Memorial. In the months leading up to the dedication, people were encouraged to "explore the complex history, memory and legacy of the Vietnam War through visual imagery, theatre, film and public discussion."[9]

While something of this scale obviously takes a large amount of resources and coordination, other smaller opportunities abound. A science museum exhibition about human anatomy could encourage visitors also to explore artists' depictions of the human body at the local art museum or to attend a lecture series at the natural history museum about recent human fossil finds. A zoo or natural history bird exhibition could include local bird-watching websites or Listserves.

Strategy 6.5d: Capitalize on computer and Internet resources.

Other techniques for not dead-ending the visitor capitalize on computer and Internet technologies. When museums include computers as part of an exhibition, visitors can view and find out information about the museum's collections or participate in a museum blog. Participating in social media opportunities can also help extend a museum visit or virtual visit in powerful ways.[10]

The bottom line is that when visitors leave an exhibit with a good idea of where they can easily get more information or see something else related to what they just saw, their experience is extended, they feel more confident, and they will be more likely to continue exploring.

Strategy 6.6: Be redundant. Present the same content in a variety of ways.

In a museum environment important messages must be repeated in different ways to ensure that the message is communicated to as large a number of persons as possible. . . . The skill in providing redundant information suggests that presentation formats and semantic constructions should vary so as to avoid boredom and at the same time be sufficiently similar to communicate critical aspects of the desired message. (Wolf 1986, 138)

When covering educational material in a textbook or other instructional material, it is often sufficient to present the information once and be done with it.

Research in informal learning environments, however, has shown that visitors are very selective about where they will focus their attention. One obvious reason the strategy of redundancy is so important in museums is that, if visitors are given only a single shot at some bit of information or exhibit message, chances are good they will miss it entirely. Each added opportunity provides an additional chance for visitors to encounter the message. Ash (2003, 12), in her discussion on the importance of dialogic inquiry within social groups, also stresses the importance of repeating key thematic content and principles across exhibits within an exhibition. This idea is further reinforced by research conducted by McManus (1987), who found that people who visit museums by themselves tend to read labels pretty extensively, but they tend not to engage with many interactive exhibits. These visitors in particular will likely miss out on key concepts if that information is included only as part of an interactive. McManus also points out that this penchant for reading and away from playing also tends to be typical among people who are visiting as part of a couple.

The likelihood of missing key concepts due to the configuration of one's social group is not the only reason to present the same content in a variety of ways. Some museum and education professionals frame this issue in terms of learning styles (Dierking 1991; Schaller et al. 2002; Serrell 1990, 1996a; McCarthy 1987). As Serrell (1996a) points out, however, "Learning styles, along with other educational models and theories, have some important, but limited, applications for the unconventional, informal, fast-paced nature of learning from museum exhibitions, which takes place in seconds, not semesters" (51). She goes on to recommend providing a variety of choices as a way of appealing to the widest range of learning styles among visitors. Wolf (1986) agrees: "Variety of formats used to present information increases the probability that a wider range of individuals will benefit from the stimulus" (138).

Layered on top of preferred learning style is visitors' learning modality, that is, whether they tend to be kinesthetic, auditory, or visual learners. Providing opportunities for visitors to engage with the same content in a variety of ways helps ensure that most visitors will be able to succeed. Additionally, by being redundant and presenting the same content in a variety of ways, museum professionals expose visitors to the same ideas repeatedly in slightly different forms and slightly different contexts, giving visitors plenty of opportunities to practice these ideas.

Redundancy of information is a powerful educational strategy that has a lot of support in the research literature (Feher and Rice 1985; Fleming and Levie 1978; Wolf 1986). It's important to remember that the redundancy strategy is not about having x for one type of learner and y for another; rather, when all learners encounter the same concept in different ways, their learning is enhanced. In other words, even if someone has a preference for, for example, auditory learning, that person will be a more successful learner when he or she also encounters a particular concept visually and kinesthetically.

> To foster the enhanced understanding that will yield more sophisticated explanations of an effect, it is desirable to expand the kinesthetic experience of the visitor. One way we can do this is by ensuring that the exhibit is usable in many different ways, that it has variable parameters that can be explored. . . . Another way of expanding the visitor's experience is to have available other exhibits that show interrelated effects. A set of exhibits showing different aspects of the same phenomenon forms a richer learning atmosphere, in terms of understanding, than a set of exhibits showing unrelated phenomena. . . . [Such a set of exhibits will foster] transfer of learning and concept formation. (Feher and Rice 1985, 45)

Interestingly, research from the field of instructional design indicates that learners "often learn best from the form of instruction they prefer the least" (Clark 1982, 92; Fleming and Levie 1993).

The takeaway lesson here is that it's important to employ many different types of learning opportunities that cover the same content so that visitors have multiple opportunities for success and can develop rich and meaningful understandings. *The Color Connection* exhibit provided one example of this. In at least four different parts of the exhibit, visitors could experience the idea that red, green, and blue lights combine to make white light: the opportunity to make hand shadows and block different colored lights; the What's Going On? computer module, which encouraged visitors to use the light switches to turn on and off different colored lights; the computer module that encouraged visitors look closely at a color TV display to see that it's comprised of only red, green, and blue lights; and the computer explanation comparing mixing colored lights with mixing colored paint.

Strategy 6.7: Eliminate unnecessary or extraneous information
that serves to confuse or intimidate visitors.

When visitors encounter text that they don't readily understand or that appears to be only minimally related to the main message, they become confused or frustrated. All too often, in our desire to make sure there is something for everyone, we as museum professionals include extraneous information "for those who might want it." Serrell (1996a, 75–82) discusses the danger of this approach at length and cautions us all that leaner text is more effective text.[11]

The *Colored Shadows* research clearly demonstrated this. As described in Appendix A, the original exhibit included a movable stanchion with a large Parent Information label which contained complex content about color, wavelengths, and subjective sensations (see figures A.6 and A.7). When concerns were raised that the information might be too complex for most visitors, the response was that it would be good information for those who wanted it. The data, however, clearly indicated otherwise. It was found that "many visitors read this label. Most of them were confused by it. Others used it to try to explain the concepts of the exhibit to other members of their visitor group. When they did this, the explanations were always at too high a level for the audience" (Perry 1989, 273–74).

This phenomenon is also demonstrated in instructional-design research. In discussing the optimal size, spacing, and pacing for instructional units, Fleming and Levie (1978) caution against trying to include too much extraneous information:

> The teacher/designer's tendency is typically toward trying to cover too much in a given time. For persons enthusiastic about their subject, there is always something very interesting or apparently essential which should be added to the unit. . . . There are apparently outside limits to human ability to process information. (123)

While these authors refer to research conducted in formal educational settings, their warnings are of even more importance in informal settings where distractions are high, motivations are intrinsic, and audiences are extremely diverse. When extra information is included, it often contributes to visitor conceptual overload and fatigue (Bitgood 2011, 252–269. In the worst cases, it erodes confidence and is ultimately counterproductive by serving to demotivate the very visitors museums are trying to attract.

Strategy 6.8: Anticipate visitors' physical needs and provide for them.

Maslow's hierarchy of needs explains that, at the most basic level, people cannot learn or ultimately feel satisfied and competent if their basic needs (for such things as food, water, shelter, rest, and restrooms) are not attended to. While most of us are familiar with Maslow's basic premise, I mention it here because it is such an important and fundamental concept, yet one that museums continue to neglect. Some might even say visitors' physical needs have a greater impact on visitor learning than the actual design of the exhibit itself. As Maslow (1943) himself said,

> [The] physiological needs are the most pre-potent of all needs. . . . If . . . the organism is then dominated by the physiological needs, all other needs may become simply non-existent or be pushed into the background. (373)

The bottom line is that if visitors don't feel comfortable, they won't engage in meaningful ways (Rand 2001). This strategy includes having adequate restroom facilities, plenty of benches and comfortable seating, a variety of eating options, tested and effective way-finding systems, and meeting (and exceeding) the requirements of the Americans with Disabilities Act for accessibility for all visitors.

PRINCIPLE 7: EXPEDIENCY
Visitors will feel more confident and competent when they experience success quickly.

The previous section focused on ways to help ensure that visitors experience success. It is just as important that they experience success quickly. In our zeal to develop rich and meaningful experiences for visitors, we often unintentionally make success theoretically achievable but highly unlikely because of the amount of effort and time required to experience that success. In formal educational arenas, educators have the luxury of taking the time to prepare learners up front, set the stage, and lay the foundation for what will follow. When we do this in museums, we run the very real risk of creating too large a space between what the visitor initially perceives and any sense of success or accomplishment. This expediency of success is an essential component of meaningful visitor experiences.

Rounds (2004) goes one step further and explains that expediency is essential so that visitors can quickly decide whether they will choose to engage with the exhibit. He talks about an exhibit's "scent" as being the initial information it communicates that enables visitors to make an accurate judgment about whether to engage or not based on the likelihood that they will find something to hold their interest. Rounds (2004) posits that, as important as it is to design exhibits that attract visitors and hold their attention, it is just as necessary—if not more so—to design exhibits that "facilitate accurate decisions by the visitor to reject engagement with specific exhibit elements" (411). When dealing with what he terms "curiosity-driven visitors" (i.e., the majority of visitors to the majority of museums), Rounds argues, museum professionals need to recognize that there are many things competing for their attention and that failure to attend to an exhibit, or even a decision to reject a particular exhibit, does not in and of itself connote a design failure.

One of the jobs of exhibit developers, however, is to help visitors become interested in things they didn't know they were interested in. It is perfectly natural and desirable for visitors to chose one well-designed exhibit in a museum over another, and their doing so does not mean that the museum has failed the visitor. The fact that some exhibits will be visited by lots of people and others will appeal to fewer visitors is also a natural state of affairs.

One way to encourage visitors to engage with an exhibit about a topic in which they may not have a preexisting interest is to ensure that they experience an immediate success. Following are a number of strategies for ensuring early and immediate visitor success.

Strategy 7.1: Ensure that the exhibit is immediately understandable.

It is not unusual for visitors to believe that, although they would likely succeed at an exhibit, they would need to invest more time and effort than they care to at that time. We've all heard visitors say things like, "I didn't spend much time at the exhibit," or "I didn't take the time to read all that." When visitors perceive that an exhibit will take too long or too much effort to engage with, the opportunity for them to experience confidence and success is reduced. Keller and Suzuki (1988) refer specifically to students using computer-based courseware, but their words ring even more true in the museum setting: "If they find that success comes at too high a cost, they will tend to move on to other activities" (416). Two techniques are suggested for helping ensure that exhibits are immediately understandable.

Strategy 7.1a: Develop labels that can be read at a glance.

McManus stresses that, contrary to many museum professionals' beliefs, visitors can and do read museum labels, and, in fact, "a visitor can read 20 words or more in five seconds while walking toward an exhibit" (1989, 186). She also found, however, that when groups of adults and children visited the museum together, the reading tended to be "brief, glance-at-text, in manner" (McManus 1987, 266). When exhibit labels are designed such that important content is quickly communicated in the first five seconds as a visitor is approaching, then at the moment of arriving at the exhibit, the visitor will already be well equipped to engage with the object and content in a meaningful way. Large letters that can be read from a distance and short, easy-to-read words that are straightforward and easy to understand go a long way toward instilling early confidence in visitors.

Reading at a glance is not limited to words on a label, however. Graphics, icons, charts, photographs—all of these can be read at a glance if they are (a) designed to communicate clearly and unambiguously, and (b) are large enough and noticeable enough to be understood from a distance. When using graphic images, it is even more important to test them with visitors as they can easily be misunderstood.[12]

Strategy 7.1b: First answer the questions, "What is it?"
and "What am I supposed to do?"

McManus (1990), in discussing the ways in which visitors to museums read (and don't read) interpretive labels, points out that visitors often use labels to engage in a conversation with the exhibit. She identifies "What's this?" and "What's going on?" as "the two most common questions" (McManus 1990, 5). At many museums, "What am I supposed to do?" is also top of mind for most visitors. Until these primary questions are answered, visitors can't engage in meaningful ways with the exhibit. When museum exhibits answer these questions quickly and up front, visitor confidence is increased, and meaning-making can proceed. McManus refers to this as museums keeping up their end of the conversation.

This is one reason identification labels at zoos are so important. A familiar sight is a group approaching an exhibit and a child running up to the enclosure, asking, "What is it? What is it?" An adult quickly scans the environment, looking for a sign or label that can be read at a glance to (a) answer the child's question, and (b) ensure that he or she doesn't look stupid in front of the child. Answering that first question immediately is a simple yet essential first step toward insuring feelings of confidence and competence.

With interactive exhibits, instead of asking, "What is it?" visitors tend to want to know what they are supposed to do. Confidence is increased when the visitor is able to quickly scan the exhibit and immediately understand how to use it (see also strategy 8.1b). This doesn't always have to be accomplished with text; in fact, in the most successful exhibits, the design itself will communicate instantly and seamlessly what the visitor is supposed to do (Norman 1988).

Strategy 7.2: Have no obstacles between the visitor and the content.

Time is an important commodity in museums. In fact, a number of years ago, Falk (1981) proposed that visitors to museums use time as currency. In other words, visitors spend time in a museum as shoppers spend money in a shopping mall. Visitors have a finite amount of time; hence, they dole it out carefully, spending it where they perceive a big payoff and choosing not to spend it in places that will cost too much (Bitgood 2011).

Because their time is a precious commodity, museum visitors need to get to what's important quickly. In other leisure and educational settings, such as at the movies, at a baseball game, or in a classroom, time is not perceived on the same scale as it is in a museum. At a movie, patrons are willing to sit through tens of minutes of promotion, titles, credits, and other introductory material. Similarly, at a baseball game everyone stands to sing the national anthem before the game begins, and in a classroom concepts are introduced over days and weeks. These strategies are extremely useful for setting the stage, for getting people in the right frame of mind, or even for laying a solid conceptual foundation or framework for what will be coming next. In museums, however, introductory material gets in the way and sets up unnecessary barriers between the visitor and the content, barriers that too often discourage the visitor from engaging. Hein refers to this as an "activation energy barrier" (G. Hein, personal communication, December 8, 2006).

Strategy 7.2a: Eliminate title screens on computer interactives
and other technology presentations.

As I was working with the *Colored Shadows* exhibit, I spent many hours designing and testing various versions of title screens, some with minimal text, some with blinking lights, some with scrolling questions designed to stimulate cognitive curiosity, all with simple and easy-to-read vocabulary. I also experimented with having a brief (eleven-screen) What's Happening? introductory sequence that visitors would go through before being taken to a screen with five menu choices. The sequence was designed to give visitors a good foundation for learning the rest of the content in the exhibit. Nothing I did, however, got visitors to stay longer than a few seconds.

After repeated tests, revisions, retests, and observations of visitors approaching, staying for a few seconds, and then moving away, I tried the interactive with no title or introductory screen and no introductory information. It was surprising how quickly and enthusiastically visitors now engaged with the interactive. Eventually, the title screen was eliminated entirely and replaced with a simple display with six menu options (see figure A.16):

- What's happening?
- Where does this happen in my home?
- What can I do with my preschooler at this exhibit?
- What are the primary colors?
- Why are there colored shadows?
- Where can I get more information?

I'm reminded of the father and daughter group discussed in chapter 1. If the dad had had to read a title screen or negotiate a series of menus, he probably wouldn't have bothered.

The data indicated that including a title screen or a prescribed introductory unit set up an unnecessary obstacle to visitors using the computer interactive.[13] "The title screen/introductory unit were both impediments to the visitor being able to . . . get involved in the exhibit" (Perry 1989, 282). I'm not saying that there isn't a place for title screens, instructions, or introductory units in some museum computer interactives or video presentations. All too often, however, such devices serve as obstacles rather than gateways.

Strategy 7.2b: Eat dessert first.

When The Field Museum in Chicago acquired the famous Tyrannosaurus rex skeleton now known as Sue, the institution wisely mounted her in the main entry hall, where all could see her and become more curious about and interested in all the evolutionary changes that led up to such a magnificent creature.

Some exhibitions, on the other hand, are set up in such a way as to require visitors to negotiate a wealth of information and less interesting artifacts and objects in order to "get to the good stuff." But visitors come to museums to see cool stuff. When the cool stuff is presented first, it serves as a jumping off point to get visitors excited about many of the less inherently interesting (at least to some visitors) objects and concepts.

Strategy 7.2c: Use advance organizers carefully and cautiously.

A number of years ago, David Ausubel proposed a three-step process for facilitating meaningful learning. In the first step, Ausubel suggested presenting learners with what he termed an "advance organizer"—an overarching conceptual framework based on ideas already familiar to the learner—upon which students could scaffold subsequent content and meaningful learning. The second step of Ausubel's (1968) instructional model was the presentation of the content itself, followed by a third step relating the content back to the original advance organizer.

Many museum professionals have enthusiastically embraced the notion of advance organizers (see, for example, Korn 1987; Griggs 1986; Screven 1986). Over the years, an advance organizer—at least in the museum field—has come to mean any kind of content overview presented at the beginning of an exhibition. While such advance organizers can serve the useful function of giving visitors a sneak preview of what they are about to see, two cautionary points need to be made.

First, an advance organizer isn't just an overview or introduction to what the visitor will experience in the exhibition. In fact, Ausubel (1978) has argued extensively about the difference between an advance organizer and an "overview . . . a summary presentation of the principal ideas in a passage . . . [which] achieves its effect largely by the simple omission of specific detail" (252). An advance organizer, according to Ausubel, is a deliberate strategy to connect what visitors already know with what they will see and experience in the exhibit.[14]

> In designing the advance organizer, recall of previous knowledge relevant to the new knowledge is important. It should provide a bridge that links the known to the unknown, by including an abstract outline of the new information and a restatement of old knowledge. Theoretically, this will encourage transfer and application of old knowledge, to make the new knowledge more meaningful to the learner. (Postrech 1998)

One example of such an advance organizer was at the entrance to *Underground Adventure*, a large exhibition about the importance of soil, at The Field

Museum in Chicago. As visitors walked down a relatively long hallway to enter the exhibition, they passed four glass cases containing jeans, medicine, soda cans, and cereal boxes with a few noticeable labels pointing out that none of this stuff would be possible without soil. Using objects that are familiar and readily recognizable to visitors, the exhibition made a nice connection between what visitors already knew and were familiar with and the main educational messages visitors would be experiencing in the rest of the exhibition.

The second caveat relates directly to the principle of expediency and ensuring that there are no obstacles between the visitor and the content. When an advance organizer becomes an obstacle, it can violate the expediency principle and erode visitors' confidence by making it appear that there will be too much to "learn." Advance organizers that are heavily text laden, written in language that is unfamiliar, or positioned in such a way (e.g., at the entrance to an exhibition) that visitors think they need to read the whole thing before they get to the good stuff (i.e., the compelling objects, artifacts, and phenomena they came to see) can end up being counterproductive by placing an obstacle between the visitor and the cool and interesting stuff of the museum. Rather than facilitating meaning making, they actually make it more difficult for visitors who are trying to be "good" but are really preoccupied with getting into the exhibition. The result is an erosion of feelings of confidence and competence.

> The rationale for using organizers is based primarily on: (a) the importance of having relevant or otherwise appropriate established ideas already available in cognitive structure to make logically meaningful new ideas potentially meaningful and to give them stable anchorage; (b) the advantages of using the more general and inclusive ideas of a discipline as the anchoring ideas or subsumers (namely the aptness and specificity of their relevance, their greater inherent stability, their greater explanatory power, and their integrative capacity); and (c) the fact that they themselves attempt both to identify already existing relevant content in cognitive structure (and to be explicitly related to it) and to indicate explicitly both the relevance of the latter content and their own relevance for the new learning material. In short, *the principal function of the organizer is to bridge the gap between what the learner already knows and what he needs to know before he can successfully learn the task at hand.* (Ausubel 1968, 148; italics in original)

> If I had to reduce all of educational psychology to just one principle, I would say this: The most important single factor influencing learning is what the learner already knows. Ascertain this and teach him accordingly. (Ausubel 1968, vi)

Screven (1986) calls for the use of conceptual preorganizers, which are related to advance organizers. Following up on Screven's recommendation, Morrissey (1991) conducted an interesting experiment to see if by engaging with a video preorganizer, visitors would end up spending less time in the exhibition, thereby reducing their learning. She found, however, that the opposite was true: subsequent time spent in the exhibit was significantly greater among those visitors who chose to use the organizer, debunking the theory that the time spent with the preorganizer would compete for time spent in the exhibition. Morrissey (1991) concludes by stating, "These results do not suggest that interactive video *should* be used in a museum environment, but rather that it *can* be used effectively as a pre-organizer for an exhibit without competing with the exhibit for visitors' attention" (117; italics in original).

In conclusion, museum professionals are encouraged to be thoughtful about the use of advance organizers and preorganizers in museum exhibitions; to use them selectively and only when appropriate; and if a decision is made to include them, to make sure they (a) don't violate the principle of expediency by creating barriers—or perceived barriers—between the visitor and the content; (b) don't rely too heavily on text but instead also use visual elements such as objects, graphics, floor plans, and the like; and (c) carefully bridge the gap between what visitors know and what they will be learning.

NOTES

1. When Paul Martin was an exhibit developer for the Minnesota History Center's *Minnesota from A to Z* exhibition, he insisted that the team's mantra be about making sure visitors felt "safe and smart." The result was a popular exhibition that connected with visitors on many levels. The exhibition closed on July 4, 2004.

2. It would be interesting to see what percentage of museum visitors leave an exhibit either having been unsuccessful or feeling that they have been unsuccessful.

3. There are many other useful techniques out there, and I encourage readers to seek out Beverly Serrell's (1996a) excellent book on exhibit labels for a much more comprehensive treatment of this issue. Additional resources are the easy-to-use, research-based *Guidelines for Document Designers* (Felker et al. 1981) and the fall 1989 special issue of *Visitor Behavior* (Vol. 4, no. 3).

4. This latter example demonstrates the care one must take when replacing longer words with shorter words. In this case, the word "potent" is actually more difficult than its longer counterpart "powerful."

5. When using the readily available Flesch-Kincaid Index included as part of the Microsoft Word software, keep in mind that the Kincaid formula was developed for navy training manuals, and the Flesch formula was developed primarily for assessing school textbooks. Like the Fry and FORCAST measures, these are more applicable to technical and instructional reading, as described above, and

hence will actually underestimate the reading level of museum interpretive text, thereby overestimating its overall readability. See www.readability.info/info.shtml for additional information.

6. While the usefulness of this interpretive technique has been clearly demonstrated with this type of interactive science exhibit, it is not limited to such a venue. It can be used just as effectively in, for example, art museums, history museums, dioramas, and other object-based exhibits.

7. As examples, see some of the *Going APE!* exhibits at the Exploratorium in San Francisco (Humphrey and Gutwill 2005) and the Science Museum of Minnesota's *Experiment Benches* (Perry 1994b).

8. I am in no way advocating for the intensely structured and highly organized format of programmed instruction for museum settings. The strategy of ensuring minisuccesses, however, is a useful technique that, when used appropriately, has an important place in museums for helping visitors feel safe, smart, and successful.

9. The five institutions were Gene Siskel Film Center (a film), Museum of Contemporary Photography (exhibitions), Pritzker Military Library (public discussion), Steppenwolf Theatre Company (a play), and the National Vietnam Veterans Art Museum (exhibitions).

10. See, for example, some of the many ways that the North Carolina Museum of Life and Science is incorporating a Web presence and social-networking opportunities into its visitor experiences, such as with the *Animal Keepers' Blog* and *Flickr Plant Project* (www.ncmls.org). Other examples include the Science Museum of Minnesota's *Science Buzz* (www.sciencebuzz.org), which includes kiosks integrated into many of its exhibits; the Minneapolis Institute of Art and Walker Art Center's collaborative *Arts Connected* project, which puts information about their entire collections online (www.artsconnected.org); and the Indianapolis Museum of Art's *Art Babble* project (www.artbabble.org).

11. See pages 75–82 of Serrell's book *Exhibit Labels* for a thoughtful and insightful discussion on the dangers of including extra information for those who might want it and designing different experiences for very specific audiences.

12. Felker et al. (1981, 89–105), in *Guidelines for Document Designers*, do an excellent job of presenting a brief overview of some of the research on the use of charts, tables, graphs, and other images as part of instructional messages. Included are clear and concrete recommendations.

13. Even though the computer program was designed to provide a deeper level of content, it was also based on the principles of success and expediency; in other words, it too was designed so that visitors could quickly read and understand it. It required more investment of energy than read-at-a-glance information that visitors could glean as they approached the exhibit. Providing opportunities for early and immediate successes, then carefully bridging visitors into deeper levels of engagement, however, is an effective instructional strategy that is particularly powerful for museums.

14. This relates directly to strategy 5.2 discussed earlier under the interest principle in chapter 5.

Challenge

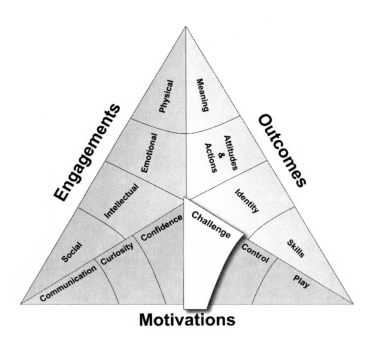

The previous chapter made the point that visitors will be motivated to learn and will have meaningful and enjoyable experiences when they feel safe and smart. Furthermore, it was posited that confidence and a feeling of personal competence are essential motivating constructs for visitors to have satisfying educational experiences in museums.

In this chapter, I argue that, while feeling confident in one's ability to succeed is essential, it's also important that confidence be carefully balanced with a certain element of uncertainty and challenge. "If success or failure is guaranteed, then there is little incentive to engage in the activity" (Perry 1989, 66). Hein (1998) describes this as "intellectual challenge":

> People need to connect to what is familiar, but learning, by definition, goes beyond the known; it leads to new "agreeable places." . . . [This] is the lure of a challenge. The trick, of course, is to find just the right degree of intellectual challenge to leave the learner slightly uncomfortable but sufficiently oriented and able to recognize the challenge that she will accept it. This central dilemma of all learning . . . needs to be emphasized in every exhibition. (176)

Hein (1998) suggests that in designing exhibits, museum professionals should ask themselves, "Will this challenge our visitors but provide them with enough familiar context so they can rise to the challenge?" (176)[1]

This chapter discusses two principles that contribute to visitors feeling challenged: the importance of both setting appropriate expectations and designing for an appropriate level of uncertainty.

PRINCIPLE 8: EXPECTATIONS
Visitors will feel appropriately challenged when they know what is expected of them.

We are all familiar with the old adage about how we can't know when we've arrived if we don't know where we are going. Visitors to museums likewise want to know where they are going, or, more specifically, what it is they are supposed to be doing, learning, or paying attention to. When they can't figure this out, they often become frustrated or, worse, intimidated, which leads to feelings of dissatisfaction, ultimately ending in aborted visits. During the research on the *Colored Shadows* exhibit, it was not unusual for visitors to express a lack of understanding regarding what the exhibit was about:

> What was the purpose [of the exhibit]?

> It was neat . . . but I don't know what it was supposed to do.

> I guess [I would not give it a very high rating] because I wasn't too sure what the point of it was.

> I don't know what it is doing, to tell you the truth. (Perry 1989, 185)

Without clear expectations for the exhibit, visitors were not able to be appropriately challenged. As stated previously, when visitors approach a new exhibit, they often ask themselves two questions: What is it? and What am I supposed to do?[2] Once visitors know what to expect (i.e., what the exhibit is about and what they should do), they are able to engage with it in meaningful ways. When expectations aren't clearly communicated, frustration sets in, and visitors leave to have an enjoyable experience elsewhere. One of the easiest ways to set up appropriate expectations is to have a clearly stated goal.

Strategy 8.1: Include a clearly stated goal.

Csikszentmihalyi (1990) talks of the importance of clear and meaningful goal setting for achieving a state of what he refers to as "flow." While not all museum experiences are, or should be, flow experiences, the clear communication of goals is essential to visitor learning and enjoyment, a premise well supported in the research literature (Keller and Burkman 1993, 16–18). Following are three techniques for clearly communicating the goals of an exhibit or exhibition to visitors.

Strategy 8.1a: Ensure that the title of the
exhibit is descriptive and goal oriented.

In discussing the role of titles, it's important to differentiate between titles of exhibitions and titles of exhibits. When dealing with the former, the main purpose of the title is to quickly communicate the overall content area: "The best titles [for exhibitions] will arouse interest and curiosity and give enough information to enable visitors to decide whether they are interested enough in the subject matter to enter" (Serrell 1996a, 22). Exhibit titles, on the other hand, can serve a more specific purpose; they are an opportunity to communicate not only what the exhibit is about but also what visitors are expected to do. *Lens Play* at the Exploratorium, for example, quickly lets visitors know that this exhibit is about lenses and optics and that they are supposed to play with the lenses.

In exhibit titles, onomatopoeia, alliteration, double entendre, and puns are all common and yield results generally considered positive. Such titles, however, while clever, can sometimes mislead visitors. In the best cases, a title will first clearly communicate the goal of the exhibit and only secondarily be clever. Titles deserve our careful attention as they are often the first thing to cue visitors as to what the exhibit is about and what is expected of them. In too many instances, titles are missed opportunities to communicate with visitors quickly and succinctly. In other situations, titles actually mislead and confuse.

One example of this was the title of the original *Colored Shadows* exhibit. While the phrase "colored shadows" accurately described what visitors were seeing at the exhibit and in fact served to communicate to visitors that the exhibit was about something cool, exciting, and novel, it also served to focus visitors on something that the exhibit was not about. The exhibit wasn't really about colored shadows at all; it was about mixing colored lights. The title *Colored Shadows* served more as an identification label than a title. The result was that visitors expected the exhibit to be about shadows, and they expected to learn something about shadows. In this situation, the title was counterproductive to achieving the goals of the exhibit.

Shadows are a complex and difficult phenomenon for most museum visitors, at least partly because they are about the absence of something. Considering this together with the fact that much of the visiting public has a naïve understanding of shadows,[3] it's not surprising that so many respondents expressed a limited understanding of what the exhibit was about.

It turns out that the purpose of the *Colored Shadows* exhibit was to help visitors understand that white light is made up of red, green, and blue light, and when you mix colored lights, you get different colors. Calling the exhibit *Colored Shadows*, not surprisingly, focused visitor attention on shadows. When the exhibit then attempted to communicate, for example, that red plus blue plus green equals white, visitors became confused, as evidenced by the quotes at the beginning of this section. That's not to say the exhibit shouldn't have made any mention of shadows. Obviously, visitors are going to notice and make shadows and have lots of fun doing so. But the title *Colored Shadows* led visitors to expect that the exhibit would be about shadows when in fact the shadows were just a neat side benefit of messing around with the lights. When the title was changed to *The Color Connection: Mixing Colored Lights* (see figure A.10), there was less confusion (Perry 1989, 203). Granted, this title isn't as catchy as *Colored Shadows*, but it's not bad, and it served to clearly communicate the goal of the exhibit and reduce visitor confusion.

Strategy 8.1b: Tell visitors directly what they are expected to do and/or learn.

At many exhibits, it is unclear what the visitor is expected to do. And when visitors are confused about what they are supposed to do or learn, they find it difficult to feel appropriately challenged. In these cases, a clearly worded statement can help (figure 7.1).

FIGURE 7.1.
This label clearly tells visitors what is expected of them.

In other situations, such as at many interactive exhibits with buttons, if it's already clear what a visitor is expected to do, text instructions just get in the way. Testing exhibit labels for their ability to clearly and quickly communicate what visitors can expect to do and learn is an important aspect of exhibit design.

In addition, at the entrance to an exhibition, it can sometimes be helpful to include some brief information about what visitors can expect to learn: "In this exhibition you'll find out about Monet's everyday life as reflected in his paintings" or "In this exhibit you will learn how bats are not as scary as you may think."

Strategy 8.1c: Use carefully designed, implicit (nonverbal) goals whenever possible.

The best type of goal is one that clearly communicates but doesn't use words. Norman (1988) talks about the *affordances* of objects and explains that the best-designed objects naturally communicate what is expected. He gives the example of doors that are designed with flat plates if they are to be pushed open and handles if they are to be pulled. He argues that flat plates are affordances, telling folks that they should push rather than pull. Likewise, flat horizontal surfaces are for sitting or putting things on.

> Affordances provide strong clues to the operations of things. Plates are for pushing. Knobs are for turning. Slots are for inserting things into. Balls are for throwing or bouncing. When affordances are taken advantage of, the user knows what to do just by looking: no picture, label, or instruction is required. Complex things may require explanation, but simple things should not. (Norman 1988, 9)

While Norman is talking particularly about the operation of things, this same principle of affordances also works in the design of museum exhibits.

In *The Color Connection*, one successful label was the reading rail with pictures of hand shadows (see figure A.15). As visitors approached the exhibit, they immediately knew what they were supposed to do and began making hand shadows.

Labels with clear affordances are more of an issue in museums that have hands-on and interactive exhibits than in, for example, many collections-based museums, which tend to have a more limited range of desired physical engagements. In many museums, it's instantly clear that the visitor is expected to look at an object, artifact, or work of art. But in museums that offer a variety of ways of interacting with an exhibit, visitors can have satisfying experiences only when they know clearly what is expected of them.

Strategy 8.2: Direct visitors' attention to the
important parts of the exhibit, object, or artifact.

Museums are environments composed of a variety of stimuli all clamoring for visitors' attention. Many times visitors don't know what to pay attention to. Directing visitors' attention to the important parts of an exhibit is an important instructional strategy for setting up appropriate visitor expectations. As described previously, directing attention is best achieved subtly through exhibit design, artifact position, and/or the use of color, sound, and lighting.

In other situations the attention-focusing strategy is more obvious—such as the use of an arrow or spotlight—but still doesn't involve the use of words. In still other situations, the use of a verbal cue is necessary (see figure A.13). And sometimes the best attention-directing devices take the form of a question (Serrell 1996a, 172). When directing attention, it's important to not talk down to visitors. In other words, avoid the temptation to tell them to look at something that they are already looking at.

A number of years ago, Borun and Adams (1992) conducted a series of interesting explorations into the design of exhibit labels that would help visitors overcome their naïve understandings about the relationship between the physical force of gravity and the phenomena of the earth spinning. After many failed attempts, they found that when they deliberately rethought the purpose of the exhibit label, they were finally able to reduce visitor misconceptions. They eventually designed an exhibit label that "created a loop, sending the visitor back to the device to test the information, then back to the label to interpret the experience," thereby creating a dynamic relationship between the visitor, the label, and the object or phenomenon (Borun and Adams 1992, 118). One reason that the label in figure A.13 was effective was that it directed visitors' attention in such a way as to create exactly this type of dynamic relationship. This kind of dialogue between visitor, label, and object, helps clarify for visitors what to expect from the exhibit.

PRINCIPLE 9: UNCERTAINTY
Visitors will feel appropriately challenged when they perceive that success is not automatic.

Despite their needing to know what to expect, in order for visitors to feel challenged, they must not feel that the exhibit is too easy or that they already understand everything about the topic. In other words, success must not be automatic;

it must require a certain investment of energy. This is not an easy goal to accomplish as visitors must also perceive that success is (a) achievable, and (b) worth the effort (see chapter 6 on confidence). In other words, for example, if visitors feel that they could succeed if they spent more time, but they are unwilling to spend that time, the challenge bar has been set too high.

> It was pretty neat. I'm sure if you spent a little bit more time at it [you could] learn more.

> It's interesting. I mean if people really want to delve into it they can and they'll probably learn a lot more about the spectrum and the colors. But I'm not that in-depth into it. (Perry 1989, 189)

Both of these quotes indicate that while these particular visitors understood that success was not automatic, and they would likely succeed if they engaged further, neither wanted to invest the amount of time necessary to succeed. In a more desirable scenario, the exhibit would be designed in such a way that visitors would perceive that success was not automatic, but that it was worth whatever was required to succeed. There are two ways to achieve this: (a) increase the payoff, or (b) reduce the amount of perceived effort, for example, by making the task smaller.

Csikszentmihalyi (1990) talks about "the golden ratio between challenges and skills" and emphasizes that "enjoyment appears at the boundary between boredom and anxiety, when the challenges are just balanced with the person's capacity to act" (52). It's important to note that this point, this boundary, is different in different environments. In a formal learning situation, such as a continuing education class, the optimal point between comfort and challenge for any particular learner may be in a very different place than when that exact same person is in a museum environment rife with competing sensory stimuli, physical needs, and interesting companions.

Two strategies have proven effective for stimulating appropriate levels of challenge in museum visitors: (a) the use of questions, and (b) the selective disclosure of information.

Strategy 9.1: Ask questions.

Research from the field of instructional design comes out overwhelmingly in favor of using questions to stimulate learner interest and engagement and increase learning (Fleming and Levie 1978, 135–37; Fleming and Levie 1993, 216–17, 261–62). There have been many studies investigating the differential effectiveness and usefulness of various types of questions and their placement— that is, as preinstructional text, postinstructional text, or embedded within instructional text. In museum environments, questions are likewise revered as important techniques for attracting and engaging visitors (Serrell 1996a), and a few excellent studies have supported their effectiveness. For example, Hirschi and Screven (1988) found that visitors spent significantly more time reading labels that had questions as titles, and Litwak (1996) demonstrated that visitors learn more when exhibit titles are presented in the form of a question as opposed to a statement. Gutwill (2006) found that, as compared to labels that asked a question only and labels that made a suggestion only, visitors preferred labels that posed a question followed immediately by a suggestion for how to go about answering it (e.g., "Can you . . . " followed by "Try . . . "). He concluded that visitors appreciated the balance between the uncertainty posed by the question and the comfort of the subsequent guidance.

> While posing questions in labels may lead to visitor discomfort, it appears that adding a suggestion for how to answer the question may alleviate that discomfort. The hybrid format with Question and Suggestions seemed most agreeable to visitors, providing them with guidance while also encouraging thinking. (Gutwill 2006, 8)

As Serrell (1996a, 105–10, 169–70) points out, however, there are good questions and bad questions. I refer the reader to her excellent discussion on the appropriate use of questions in labels for both static as well as interactive exhibits.

It's also important to note that different types of questions are more or less effective in different contexts. For example, "Can you get the largest ring to stumble around?" (Gutwill 2006, 5) is very different from "What does heat look like?" (Serrell 1996a, 170), which is very different from "What do the burr and wool have in common with the pieces of Velcro?" (Serrell 1996a, 170). Gutwill and Allen (2010) demonstrated the effectiveness of using "juicy questions" to stimulate deeper intellectual engagements and scientific inquiry. Questions can contribute to a sense of uncertainty and challenge, as well as to other motivations such as intellectual curiosity. More important than the type of question, however, is its authenticity.[4]

It is clear that when thoughtfully designed and appropriately used, questions can be an extremely effective tactic for creating a sense of uncertainty and enhancing learning in museum environments.[5]

Strategy 9.2: Have hidden information (that is revealed
only after further investment of energy).

Another strategy that is particularly effective at stimulating appropriate feelings of uncertainty and challenge is the use of hidden information. Following are three suggested techniques for working with hidden information.

Strategy 9.2a: Use flip labels.

A commonly used technique in museums is flip labels or other progressive-disclosure techniques (see strategy 4.2b). Serrell (1996a, 107–10) describes a variety of interesting and effective ways of using flip labels to use hidden information that is revealed only after visitors do something, even if that is simply to lift the label. When using flip labels, it's important to keep in mind the level of "payoff" for visitors once they have invested the energy. What's behind the flip label or the next screen of the computer interactive has to be worth it.

Strategy 9.2b: Take advantage of the limited size of computer screens.

Computer interactives can also be an effective way to have hidden information. Because visitors understand that each screen is limited in its capacity to carry information, we can use this to our advantage by requiring frequent, easily achievable input by the user. One example of this was at *The Color Connection* exhibit.

At the original *Colored Shadows* exhibit, one of the computer modules, What To Do And Notice, consisted of a single computer screen (see figure A.8, screen 3). This single screen had a very high concept density. (See Strategy 6.1d for a discussion of concept density.) At the revised *The Color Connection* exhibit, this single-screen module was replaced with a ten-screen module called What's Happening? with each screen requiring some investment of energy by the visitor— that is, pressing a "next screen" button (see figure A.18). Because information was hidden, a sense of uncertainty was created and visitors felt appropriately challenged without feeling overwhelmed.[6]

Strategy 9.2c: Use "less noticeable" text.

Information can also be hidden in plain sight. One of the reasons the computer labels in figures A.17 and A.18 worked so well for visitors was that the information below the square was "hidden." Actually, it wasn't really hidden; it was just less noticeable due to the smaller font size and muted color, which created the illusion that it was not quite as easily accessible as the other text on the screen. This strategy also contributed to the perception of uncertainty.

NOTES

1. Hein (1998) goes on to advocate for testing any design proposed with the end users to ensure that the appropriate balance between comfort and challenge is achieved: "The answer to this question resides not in some theoretical principle, but in empirical results from trying out various exhibition components with visitors" (176).

2. See a discussion of this as part of strategy 7.1b, under the confidence principle of expediency in chapter 6.

3. Some common misconceptions about shadows include the following: a shadow is something that exists on its own; light pushes the shadow away from the object to a wall, the ground, or other surface where the shadow lies; shadows are "dark reflections" of objects (Hapkiewicz 1992, 1999). See also http://homepage.mac.com/vtalsma/syllabi/2943/handouts/misconcept.html#light.

4. See Serrell's (1996a, chs. 10 and 15) excellent discussions on the authenticity of questions.

5. See also strategy 6.2 (chapter 6) about the importance of providing visitors with answers. This supports Gutwill's (2006) research on the use of question and suggestion labels rather than question labels alone.

6. Notice that this type of interactive label sets up the sort of dynamic relationship between the visitor, label, and object (in this case, the colored lights) that Borun and Adams (1992) advocate for, as discussed in strategy 8.2.

8

Control

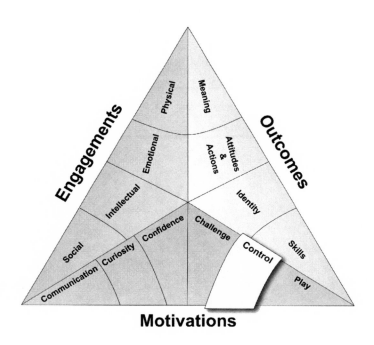

Much has been written about the role control plays in learning, life, and the design of educational experiences (for example, Csikszentmihalyi 1990; Deci 1980; Keller and Burkman 1993; Martin and Briggs 1986; Reigeluth 1983), and much of what has been written describes how particular learners' perception of control relates directly to their expectations of success. It is not surprising, then, that control is an important component of any model for the design of intrinsically motivating informal learning experiences.

Because museums are free-choice environments, it is imperative that visitors feel in charge of their experiences. Control over when they come, the things they do, the order they do them in, and when they leave is an essential component of all successful visitor experiences. This chapter discusses two constructs that contribute to control: choice and power.

PRINCIPLE 10: CHOICE
Visitors will feel in control when they are given appropriate choices.

The most obvious choice that visitors have is selecting which exhibits and exhibitions to engage with, in what order, and for how long. It is not uncommon, however, for visitors—especially novice visitors—to become easily weighed down by the sheer number of choices they must make, sometimes as soon as they enter a museum or exhibition gallery. While providing choices is important, most visitors need additional information to ensure they don't become overwhelmed and to maximize the likelihood of their making choices that ultimately lead to satisfying experiences.

Strategy 10.1: Make sure visitors have the
right information to make wise choices.

The right information can include computer menu items that give a brief but accurate description of what each item is about (see figure A.16), labels that can be "read" at a glance (see figure A.15), exhibit titles that describe what the exhibit is about (figure A.10), and brief statements about how long a video program is. Such information provides visitors with what they need to know in order to make wise decisions.

On a larger scale, orientation spaces can give visitors information that will help them make choices by laying out what kind of information will be covered and perhaps including a floor plan. While helpful, sometimes orientation spaces can create a barrier, thereby violating the confidence principle embodied in strategy 7.2. When orientation spaces are optional rather than required, and when they clearly communicate what the benefit of using them will be, they can help provide visitors with the information they need to make wise choices.

Museum websites can also provide visitors with important decision-making information. Some websites even include information not only about why you might want to visit but also about why you might not—for example, "This is a particularly large exhibition without easy access to bathrooms. You might want to do this exhibition early in your trip when everyone is fresh." Or "This exhibition is filled with lots of really cool objects, but there are few hands-on activities. Visitors who like to touch things may want to also visit exhibition x, which has more interactive exhibits."

Another successful and yet simple strategy employed in many exhibits is to display the length of a video presentation so that visitors can decide if they want to invest that amount of time.

Strategy 10.2: Ensure that the exhibit includes a choice of activities.

When exhibits include a variety of activities, visitors perceive that they have a choice. For example, when visitors engaged with the computer at *The Color Connection*, the first thing they saw was a menu of six activities or topics they could select. Visitors appreciated being able to choose among these options.

Strategy 10.3: Provide a variety of different types of activities.

By making exhibits that contain a variety of approaches to learning and giving people with different learning styles access to the same information, visitors can make clear decisions about where to spend their attention and time. (Serrell 1990, 30)

In addition to having a choice among the different options listed on the computer menu, visitors to *The Color Connection* could also choose from among a variety of types of activities. The exhibit unit had four sides with three different labels. Each label encouraged an entirely different way of engaging with the exhibit, but the content of each overlapped with and complemented the others. Visitors could use the computer, make hand shadows, try to make different colored shadows, or play with the switches to turn the lights on and off. All of these activities contributed to visitors developing a greater understanding of and appreciation for mixing colored lights.

The *Nature Walk* dioramas at The Field Museum in Chicago provide another good example of including multiple types of activities that visitors can choose from. In contrast to more traditional dioramas where the primary way of engaging is by looking and perhaps reading a label, in this presentation, randomly located dioramas along a simulated nature walk encourage you to look at the specimens, find different objects hidden in the cases, listen to bird calls, read the labels, and flip up sections of logs to discover critters hiding inside.

Strategy 10.4: Become very familiar with the magic number 7 +/− 2.

> The so-called 'magic number' of 7 +/− 2 has been found across a wide variety of stimuli and across modalities: vision, audition. It appears to be a reliable measure of human capacity (Miller, 1968). (Fleming and Levie 1978, 54)

While it is desirable to provide visitors with choices, it is also easy to overwhelm them with too many. As risky as it is to provide insufficient choices, it is equally ineffective to provide too many choices .

> There is a potential danger in believing that additional choices will always enhance motivation. Instead, we believe, there is probably some optimal, intermediate number of choices that will be maximally motivating. Faced with more choices than we can reasonably discriminate among (perhaps 5–7 alternatives [cf. Miller 1956]), for instance, we are likely to devalue the importance of choice, and to experience frustration instead of satisfaction. (Malone and Lepper 1987, 239)

Miller (1956) discusses the "magical number seven, plus or minus two" as being the upper limit of humans' capacity for memory and perceptual tasks. It stands to reason that five to seven items, i.e., the lower end of the range, would be an appropriate number of menu (and other) choices confronting visitors. Research has indicated that while this number is remarkably stable across situations, it is also significantly affected by the size of the "unit" and the individual's familiarity with the item (Fleming and Levie 1978, 55). In other words, choosing between ten or twenty large exhibition galleries in a totally unfamiliar museum that covers unfamiliar content could easily be overwhelming for visitors. In these situations, narrowing the choices down for visitors can be particularly helpful, such as has been done at the Detroit Institute of Arts with a series of brochures, each focusing on specific visitor interests.

Malone and Lepper (1987) go on to write specifically about the challenges of freer-form learning environments:

> These considerations should also help us to understand both the potential benefits, and the possible dangers, of more open-ended, exploratory learning environments

(e.g., Brown 1983; Lepper 1985). On the one hand, the availability of choices at each level of analysis, at every step in the process of selecting and completing a project, can be highly intrinsically motivating (Lepper and Greene 1978). On the other, a total lack of structure may leave many learners overwhelmed and unable to make effective choices. (239)

PRINCIPLE 11: POWER

Visitors will feel in control when they are able to expend relatively minor amounts of energy and produce significant results.

While the importance of providing choices and multiple ways for visitors to engage with an exhibit or exhibition has been discussed frequently in the professional museum literature, the issue of feeling powerful has received significantly less attention. Being in charge of an experience consists of more than just the ability to make good choices; it also entails the ability to be powerful.

The most obvious example of this can be observed by watching youngsters in museums running from exhibit to exhibit, pushing buttons, waiting for something to happen, and then rushing on to the next unit. Young visitors in particular don't have many opportunities to feel powerful, but museums with buttons provide a smorgasbord of opportunities to make big things happen. In fact, it can be argued that the popularity of hands-on interactive exhibits is due at least in part to the ability to do something rather simple, requiring minimal effort, and to produce a rather powerful effect.

Two design strategies to help visitors feel powerful are outlined below.

Strategy 11.1: Allow the visitor to manipulate the object or artifact.

While most objects in a museum setting can't be touched, many can still be manipulated. In some cases this might entail pushing a button to rotate an object so you can see the other side of it. Or it could entail turning on a light to illuminate a part of an object you wouldn't otherwise notice. The Brooklyn Children's Museum had a stuffed bird in a glass case and asked the provocative question, "Is it dead or alive? Is it real or fake?" For children just learning the differences between alive and dead and fake and real, the ability to push a button and rotate the bird to show the back of it cut open to reveal the stuffing was a powerful experience that enabled them to learn in a meaningful way.

Feeling powerful can also be achieved by handling a reproduction, turning it over, and comparing what's in your hands with what's on display. Even something as simple as feeling a facsimile of the velvet on a deer's antlers can impart a sense of power.

Strategy 11.2: Allow visitors to interact with the exhibit at their own pace.

This strategy may seem obvious in a museum setting where visitors typically have little choice but to interact with the exhibit at their own pace. In numerous places, however, it's easy to violate this principle. A few examples come to mind—for instance, many audio tours and video presentations and even some exhibitions with a strict, linear path along which visitors often feel compelled to move with "the group" so as not to create bottlenecks or be perceived as exhibit hogs. This is not to say that linear, sequential treatments are an anathema in museums but rather that they need to be carefully managed to enable visitors to progress at their own pace.

The Colored Connection exhibit provided one example of an effective self-paced, linear interpretive treatment. The label directing visitors to look up (see figure A.13) laid out a linear instructional sequence that allowed visitors to engage at their own pace. There was nothing there to rush them along. Many of the exhibits at the Exploratorium in San Francisco use this strategy by setting up the interpretation so that visitors can progress at their own pace. And at the Detroit Institute of Arts, many exhibits include flip books to provide this type of opportunity. Other examples often seen in museum settings are the computer programs that present a small amount of information and then an opportunity to progress to the next screen when the visitor is ready. (This overlaps with strategy 9.2b.)

Museums are now including audio guides that allow you to stop the guide when you want; even better, they are replacing predetermined, step-by-step sequences through a gallery with the ability to go to any object in any order, press a button to hear about that object, and then move on.

Designing exhibits so that visitors experience feelings of control presents its own unique challenges. At the original *Colored Shadows* exhibit, visitors experienced some control over how they used the exhibit, but we noted that they were not able to turn the lights on and off. Because the exhibit was about mixing colored lights, we hypothesized that enabling them to turn the lights on and off would make it easier for them to be powerful, to experiment and take charge of their learning. A wooden box was built with large red, green, and blue buttons on top. Visitors could press, for example, the red button and turn on or off the red light. This box turned out to be a popular feature of the exhibit because (a) visitors had a choice about which lights were on or off at any particular time, and (b) they could produce powerful effects, that is, colored lights.

We were surprised, however, to observe visitors repeatedly pounding somewhat mindlessly on the buttons, creating rapid-fire light shows, but not engaging in any intellectually meaningfully way. One young visitor in particular was very enthusiastic: this teenage boy leaned on the tabletop and settled in with the box, pounding on the buttons for a full fifteen minutes, creating a brilliant light show. Although he was enjoying himself, his enjoyment had nothing to do with the educational goals of the unit.

We were interested in analyzing this interaction. After all, as long as he was having fun, so what if he wasn't learning anything? It could even be argued that because he was having such a great time, he might decide to study light waves later on in life. On closer observation and analysis, however, we realized that by designing the exhibit to allow—and even subtly encourage—visitors to engage in this type of experience, we were drawing their attention away from the fun they could experience by mixing colored lights. This pounding on the buttons also prevented other visitors from using the exhibit, except as passive observers. Furthermore, other visitors were beginning to think that the exhibit was primarily about making flashy light shows.

We experimented by replacing the large buttons with wall light switches (see figure A.12), making it slightly more difficult to turn on and off the lights, yet still enabling experimentation and the power to control them. Subsequent observation and interviews with visitors indicated that this strategy effectively gave visitors the opportunity to be powerful—without being too powerful or disruptive of other visitors' experiences—and had the added benefit of relating the exhibit to something visitors were familiar with (see strategy 5.2, p. 109). In other words, this relatively minor change resulted in a substantial improvement in visitor engagement with mixing colored lights, while not significantly reducing visitor enjoyment.

Play

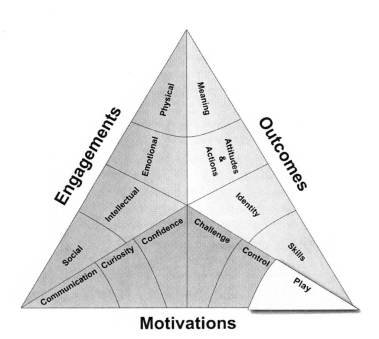

We often envision play as the fun, lighthearted recreation of children: dress-up and make-believe, parks and playgrounds, games and sports. While frequently engaged in for its pure, intrinsic joy, this type of play can also be thought of as a requisite, preformal learning stage, that is, as a phase or process that is part of learning other important skills (Sykes 1992, 1993; Göncü and Gaskins 2007; Singer, Golinkoff, and Hirsch-Pasek 2006). It's the play that puppies engage in as they tumble with their littermates; it's playing with dolls as part of learning how to be a parent; it's playing softball to learn about cooperation and how to be part of a team. As Richman and Lansdown (1988) explain, "Play is not merely a way of passing time . . . but an integral part of development, and an important precursor of more formal learning" (218).

A concrete example of play as a precursor to more formal learning was the playful childhood experience described in a research study about museum professionals' memorable museum learning experiences:

> I grew up in the Bay Area in California and remember really clearly playing with a particular exhibit at the Lawrence Hall of Science that had ramps on hinges so that they would alternatively be bridges or valleys, and bridges and valleys, and bridges and valleys. And this machine would go up and down. And you could control the rate at which the bridges would turn into valleys, and there would be balls rolling around. And the point that I thought was always . . . to get the right rate, so it just got faster and faster and faster and faster and faster. But I just loved letting the ball run around and trying to see what I could do with it. And I liked watching it and listening to it.
>
> And I put it out of my mind for about twenty years, until I was in a physics class and found out what a cyclotron was. And all of a sudden I realized that I had a model, a real visceral physical model, of what a cyclotron did, and what each of these electromagnets did to the part—to the charged particles floating around. . . . Each of these little valleys was like the magnet accelerating it down hill all the time, and it gave me a way to understand a cyclotron. And I don't think any other way could have. And it struck me as being important that this had stayed in my memory for more than twenty years. (Perry 2002, 23)

Without the opportunity to play with the ramps on hinges, learning about a cyclotron later in life would likely have been a very different experience for this respondent.

There is a large body of research on play, but while play is easy to recognize, it can be notoriously difficult to define. Hirsh-Pasek and Golinkoff (2008, p. 2) present a list of eight features that tend to characterize play:

> Play (a) is pleasurable and enjoyable, (b) has no extrinsic goals, (c) is spontaneous, (d) involves active engagement, (e) is generally engrossing, (f) often has a private reality, (g) is nonliteral, and (h) can contain a certain element of make believe. (2)[1]

Except in the context of exhibits at many children's museums, play is often missing from discussions about the development of museum experiences; yet, it remains an essential component of intrinsically motivating visitor experiences. When play is discussed in the context of exhibit development, it is often limited to experiences for children or ones that are a little goofy. While these types of experiences can be important to include, the premise of this chapter is that—at least in the context of designing intrinsically motivating visitor experiences— play does not have to be limited to children or to goofiness. Rather, play in this context can—and should—be thought of quite broadly to include any of a variety of types of experiences, for adults and children and everyone in between, that include a sense of playfulness, even if it's only in one's mind .

> Play is usually associated with children, but despite all of the differences between adults and children, play is a suitable and respectable way to describe intense and meaningful adult learning (Kerr and Apter 1991). (Rieber 2001, 2)

Rieber (2001) goes on to advocate for the use of the phrase "serious play" to distinguish it from the trivial way many of us use the word play:

> I like the oxymoronic sound to this phrase—it sounds contradictory. Play sounds fun and even frivolous, but never serious. But I use the term serious play . . . [because] it also conveys a certain amount of respect for play in learning for both children and adults. . . . A simple way of understanding serious play in education is with the advice of "experience first, explain later." (4)

I take the stand that in museum settings, those visitors who have the most satisfying and enjoyable experiences are those who feel the most playful—playful with actions yes, but also playful with ideas, playful with thoughts, playful all over. It can even be argued (and I do!) that when doing the most serious work as scientists, art historians, or researchers, many professionals are actually engaged in play. For example, when the Spirit rover landed on Mars in 2004, some of the first words uttered by Charles Elachi, director of NASA's Jet Propulsion Laboratory, were, "Mars is our sandbox, and we are ready to play and learn" (*Chicago Tribune*, January 16, 2004, 10). Unfortunately, all too often play is pitted against learning as if they were opposite ends of a continuum. In fact, in the best cases, they are intimately intertwined, essential characteristics of rich and meaningful, intrinsically motivating experiences.

When we as museum professionals take our educational missions and ourselves too seriously, we run the risk of brushing aside the joys and importance of play as an educational and instructional strategy—as something that we can design for. This is not to say that play for play's sake is what museums are or should be about. Museums have educational missions; certain ideas and content are core to what they do and vital to the experiences they offer their publics. In the best situations, play experiences in museums are inseparable from the educational messages (Everett and Piscitelli 2006). In reality, however, when play is incorporated, if at all, it is often done as an afterthought to an educational message. At the opposite end of the spectrum, some experiences are designed to be almost exclusively about play with little or no attention to content.

As mentioned previously, at the *Colored Shadows* exhibit we found that visitors enjoyed the original exhibit immensely. It was one of the most popular exhibits in the gallery, and—as described in chapter 5 on curiosity—visitors found the bright colors compelling and attractive. They enjoyed waving their hands in the lights and were surprised and delighted when they made colored shadows. There was no question that this was a playful experience. But early interviews with visitors revealed that most didn't see the exhibit as a place where they could learn about mixing colored lights; rather, they saw it primarily as an opportunity to play in the lights and make colored shadows. One of the overarching research questions for that study, therefore, was whether the exhibit could be redesigned in such as way as to (a) maintain its popularity and the playfulness that visitors enjoyed, while (b) simultaneously increasing learning about mixing colored lights. In other words, while playing in the lights was important, it would be even better if that activity concomitantly contributed to visitors learning about how colored lights mix to make other colors. This is the proverbial challenge facing museum exhibit developers: how to design for playfulness in such a way as to facilitate intended learning rather than as separate from it.

Play, for all its association with lightheartedness, free-spiritedness, and the simple pleasures of life, is a surprisingly complex and serious business. One has only to search the educational research literature to realize that there are almost as many definitions of play as there are people interested in learning more about it. The wealth of descriptions of and attempts to study this elusive construct is impressive. I do not intend this book as any kind of comprehensive or definitive treatment of play in particular; rather, it is about the design of rich and satisfying visitor experiences, play being only one of their many different facets. This discussion focuses very specifically on two aspects of play that emerged from the *Colored Shadows* research and evolved from Malone and Lepper's (1987, 248–49) original set of heuristics: fantasy and sensory experiences. I include this chapter on play to encourage all of us to think seriously, thoughtfully, and creatively about how to incorporate playful imagination and sensory enjoyment in ways that are fully integrated with educational messages.

PRINCIPLE 12: IMAGINATION
Visitors will feel playful when they use their imaginations.

Many researchers agree that using one's imagination is an important aspect of being playful (Diamond, n.d.; Göncü and Gaskins 2007; Singer, Golinkoff, and Hirsch-Pasek 2006). In this case, I define "using one's imagination" broadly to include situations that "[evoke] mental images of physical or social situations not actually present" (Malone and Lepper 1987, 240). This can include creative thought and intellectual exploration.

> Strategy 12.1: Ensure that the exhibit includes activities
> that encourage visitors to use their imaginations.

Children's museums in particular tend to be rich environments to stimulate fantasy and imaginative play. One young mother described a program that was perfectly suited to her and her preschool-age son:

I was new to the community and I was searching out opportunities for my son. He was three and a half at the time. . . . Upon arriving at the Children's Museum [I] encountered a very wonderful gentleman, who was there with his child in tow, who was the story teller for the day. . . . We all gathered around and after just a few brief introductions this man began leading a story about . . . [an] imaginary fishing trip. And we gathered all our gear together and we talked about the fishing rods and where the bait comes from and what other equipment we were going to need. And we talked about where we would go to fish. And then . . . we arrived at the fishing spot and . . . went through the process of, bait[ing] our hooks, casting out our line, reeling in our fish. . . . This man then congratulated us all on having caught our fish, and opened up an ice chest where he had brought fish to the museum that morning. And these were fish fully intact with their heads and their tails and the scales, and everything was there, and all of us gathered around as he proceeded to clean them and to bone them and to filet them, and to show the children all the various parts of the fish that we had just caught in our imaginations. And then he also hooked up a little frying pan and put in the cooking oil and filleted these fish, and cut them into small pieces and breaded them, and proceeded to fry these little chunks of fish which we then, a few minutes later, had the opportunity to all sample. And when I left that day, I mean it was—it was an incredible experience; having this moment of sharing, and then having it culminate in this moment that engaged so many other senses. (Spock 2000, 28–30)

While fantasy and imagination are relatively easy to incorporate into children's museums' programs such as the fish story above, including meaningful fantasy into museum exhibits can be more of a challenge. At the original *Colored Shadows* exhibit, fantasy was not an integral part of the original design. The labels explained interactive ways to understand the content, but there was no explicit attempt to get visitors to use their imaginations. It was interesting, however, that when most visitors arrived at the exhibit, one of the first things they did was start creating hand shadows—typically a duck or wolf head. Almost as quickly, these duck and wolf heads would start attacking one another in mock battle. Unfortunately, this particular type of play proved disruptive and, ultimately, counterproductive to learning. In other words, most visitors tended to (a) make hand shadows they already knew how to make (thereby reducing any meaningful challenge), and (b) focus exclusively on "the battle," thereby paying little attention to the colored lights, the focus of the exhibit. Here was a clear case of visitors using their imaginations and engaging in fantasy play, but in a less-than-optimal manner, or as Lepper and Malone (1987, 279) would say, in a way that competes with rather than reinforces the educational goals.

Our first attempt to improve the imaginative play at the exhibit was a failure. We designed prototype cardboard cutout figures—for example, a sun and a pony—with stick handles and the following accompanying text: "Can you make a yellow sun travel across a blue sky? Can you make a red pony gallop across a green field?" The intention was for visitors to take the cardboard sun and hold it just right so as to block out the blue light and cast a yellow (red plus green) shadow of a sun on a blue (actually cyan, blue plus green) background. The intended "fantasy" was to imagine the cyan background as the sky. The red pony fantasy involved a similarly convoluted idea. It's a good thing these were developed as prototypes because we quickly found out that most visitors totally ignored our "challenge" and chose instead to use the paddles to play chase-my-younger-siblings-and-hit-them-as-they-run-around-the-table.

Our next attempt was more successful. Because making hand shadows was such a natural activity for most visitors, we decided to stick with it but to gently guide visitors away from the fighting-duck-and-wolf scenarios. We figured that visitors made the duck and wolf figures not because that's what they wanted to make but because they didn't know what else to do. We designed an interpretive panel with pictures of less common hand shadows of varying degrees of difficulty.

We were delighted when we found visitors of all ages engaged in various forms of sophisticated fantasy play, such as making shadow mouths talk, making birds fly, and even creating miniplays. While this example of incorporating imaginative play into an exhibit was not directly related to the educational goals of the exhibit (i.e., to learn about mixing colored lights) it did enable visitors to engage in imaginative play that focused their attention on the colors and the shadows.

Evoking fantasy and imagination is not solely the realm of science or children's museums. Art and history museums also have unlimited opportunities to engage visitors' imaginations. Based on Malone and Lepper's (1987) definition of fantasy as "mental images of things not present to the senses or within the actual experience of the person involved" (240), many experienced visitors to art and history museums probably engage in fantasy to a great extent naturally. Asking them to imagine what it would feel like to be in a painting or to be a historical figure is a simple and yet effective strategy for helping visitors feel playful. For someone already well versed in the content, play might involve interesting ideas or juxtapositions.

Dioramas are another effective technique for engaging visitors' imaginations and stimulating playfulness. Visitors to the dioramas at the Chicago Academy of Sciences described the experience perfectly:

> It was like I was in the big fat middle of it! . . . It seems like I'm walking 100 yards into the diorama.

> [The diorama] puts you in the middle of a place where you could not otherwise be. . . . This is what it would feel like . . . a sense of immediacy of a place where you're not likely to go. (Perry, Garibay, and Edington 1995, 7)

Strategy 12.2: Incorporate endogenous (as opposed to exogenous) fantasy whenever possible.

Malone and Lepper (1987) talk about the difference between endogenous and exogenous fantasy in educational computer games. They describe endogenous fantasy as including those imaginative scenarios that are intrinsic to the educational content—for example, the *Downhill Race* exhibit at the Exploratorium where you race two wheels down a slope to learn that the distribution of weight within a wheel makes it roll faster or slower. In this case, the exhibit uses a race fantasy to add a layer of playfulness to the educational experience, and the race itself is a natural and integral (i.e., endogenous) part of the learning experience. Another example of an endogenous fantasy is a museum exhibit that engages visitors in a mocked-up crime scenario to teach them about forensic science.

Exogenous fantasy, on the other hand, entails an imaginative overlay that has little to do with the educational goal. An example of an exogenous fantasy might be a game to help people learn about the different painting styles of various artists. Each time you correctly identify the painting style, you get to add a color to your pallet until all the colors are filled in. In this case, the color pallet is an imaginative record-keeping device, but it has little to do with identifying painting styles. Any number of other fantasies could be used just as easily: a worksheet with check boxes, colored chips deposited into a "bank," and so on. In other words, the fantasy is extrinsic to the learning itself.

While any kind of fantasy can enhance the playfulness of a museum experience, Malone and Lepper (1987) assert that "in general, endogenous fantasies are both more interesting and more educational than exogenous fantasy" (240).

It should be noted that while endogenous fantasy can be the more powerful learning strategy, the making of hand shadows in the above example definitely falls into the exogenous fantasy camp. In other words, making a particular figure—for example, a bird, funny face, or rabbit—is not directly related to the science of mixing colored lights. This is a clear example of how exogenous fantasy can still be an effective strategy. Did visitors learn about, for example, mixing red and green to make yellow by making the hand shadows? Probably not. But a strong argument can be made for providing this type of imaginative and playful experience, whereby visitors are challenged and can be successful while also becoming familiar with light. In many ways, playful experiences like this can still serve as a precursor to more formal learning later on, as mentioned at the beginning of this chapter.

PRINCIPLE 13: SENSORY EXPLORATION
Visitors will feel playful when they use multiple senses to explore the exhibit.

Strategy 13.1: Include playful ways visitors of all
ages can use their senses to explore the exhibit.

Sensory experiences are a powerful component of many memorable learning moments, and different types of exhibits include experiences that engage different senses. The power of sensory experiences was demonstrated in a front-end evaluation for the *Underground Adventure* exhibition at The Field Museum in Chicago. When asked what dirt made them think of, visitors' shared the following:

> You can smell the dirt when it rains. Like the first spring rain . . . you can smell the earth. . . . It's really nice.

> I have to be barefoot all the time. . . . I'm the first person in the spring to get my shoes off.

> You know, if you go down to the first part of the water at the beach [it feels the way] mud feels. I like that. . . . It feels nice and cool.

> [Playing in the mud] feels good. It feels squishy . . . kind of like Play-Doh. . . . You can make something out of it. . . . Sometimes I make mud pies.

> In Georgia you've got . . . soil that you can eat. It's sort of . . . clumpy, light red dirt. . . . You just eat it by itself. . . . My mom ate it. She grew up in the South. . . . It's sweet.

> I like squishing mud between my toes.

> I have days where I'm walking in the city. . . . I'd do anything to walk in that sand and feel the [warm sand] between my toes and lie in it. [It's] warm and soothing.

> I just took a class . . . [where] they actually made you taste the different soil types. And you can tell the difference. . . . I use that as a metaphor now. . . . I say that if you want to tell the real story of the earth, that you need to taste the soil. (Perry and Garibay 1996, 33)

What if the museum had decided to include samples of dirt that visitors could taste? Or buckets of mud for visitors to dip their hands into? Obviously not all museums are equipped to deal with the mess accompanying such visitor experiences, but we should not be too hasty in discarding opportunities for engaging the senses in creative ways.

In the previous section, a visitor shared a story about a museum program that used an imaginary fishing trip to engage many different senses: sight, sound, and especially smell and taste. While we can probably think of more museum program experiences that engage many senses, with some creativity exhibits can too. At The Field Museum, the developers of the *Nature Walk* exhibition wanted to retain the existing natural history dioramas, but they also wanted to encourage visitors to be more playful by having them explore the exhibits with as many senses as possible (Serrell and Becker 1990, 1991). They positioned the dioramas so visitors could walk around them on all sides, thereby improving their visual experience. They included search-and-find activities that encouraged visitors to look more intently at the details of the carefully crafted scenes, and they included buttons for visitors to press to hear the sounds of different animals they were looking for. Developers also added floor-level reproductions of bumpy logs visitors could touch and open to reveal hidden critters.

An exhibition about an abstract concept like photosynthesis presents its own set of challenges. During the development of its *Sugar from the Sun* exhibition, the Garfield Park Conservatory in Chicago employed many creative ways to incorporate smell, sound, touch, and even imagined taste into an aesthetically appealing visual display of plants. In one prototype interpretive label, visitors were encouraged to "blow on a plant" and think about how they were "feeding" it. In another area, even though having visitors taste real food was too difficult to incorporate, the exhibition included familiar edible plants such as bananas, pineapples, and cacao to create a virtual-taste experience.

It's important to keep in mind that sensory experiences incorporated into an exhibition need to be authentic so as not to violate feelings of trust. This is particularly an issue in immersive environments in which it's not clear to visitors when something is real or recreated. The summative evaluation of *Sugar from the Sun* explored this issue with respondents. Data indicated that they enjoyed the sights (real fruit in the trees), sounds (birds, frogs, and insects), and other sensory opportunities, as long as they were authentic. In other words, artificial elements were accepted as part of the *Sugar from the Sun* experience as long as (a) visitors didn't feel tricked into thinking the artificial elements were real, and (b) they did not intrude too much on the soothing, naturalistic feelings induced by the immersive environment (Gyllenhaal 2008, 32).

Authenticity may be part of the reason the exogenous fantasy of making hand shadows described above worked well, whereas using cardboard cutout figures didn't. Using one's hands to make shadows is an authentic experience whereas using paddles is less so.

Incorporating sensory experiences not only adds to enjoyment but can also improve visitor understandings. When the Boston Museum of Science revised its diorama exhibits to include more sensory experiences, one study reported, "The time visitors spend in the gallery has increased, the manner in which they interact with the exhibits has become more active, and they learn more from their visit to the exhibit" (Davidson, Heald, and Hein 1991). As an additional benefit of retrofitting the diorama cases, many more people with disabilities (a large and important segment of all museum audiences) were able to have meaningful experiences.

Other examples of effectively incorporating sensory experiences for visitors are the many opportunities at the Detroit Institute of Arts. In its expansive, institution-wide redesign and renovation efforts, the museum was committed to engaging visitors in meaningful and creative ways. Its galleries are full of opportunities for auditory, immersive, tactile, and visual experiences (Penney 2009; Hennes 2009). For example, in its *Fashionable Living* exhibition, a virtual eighteenth-century banquet is laid out on a large dining room table. Visitors sit down to an exquisitely prepared meal, complete with all the sounds of clinking glasses, muted dinner table conversation, and settings being arranged. It is a powerful experience.

It should be pointed out that while there is a tendency to dismiss many sensory experiences as primarily for kids, they are just as important for adults. An excellent example of this comes from the *Sounds from the Vault* exhibition at The Field Museum in Chicago. The museum wanted to display the fragile musical instruments in its collections, but the exhibit developers didn't want to design a passive experience in which visitors might—at best—get to hear recordings of the instruments. Instead, they designed electronic interactive devices so that visitors were actually able to "play" the instruments. Instruments encased in large Plexiglas boxes had plenty of interfaces where visitors could mimic the actual motions required to play the instrument, whereupon they would hear prerecorded sounds made by that very same instrument.

Sensory exploration can provide powerful and memorable visitor experiences, and we have only begun to tap this area.

NEXT STEPS

The What Makes Learning Fun? framework was developed as a way to structure and guide our thinking about successful visitor experiences. By providing research, principles, and strategies, it helps us, as museum professionals, expand our thinking about, and practice of, creating visitor-centered exhibits that facilitate active visitor participation in the interpretive process. Thoughtful consideration and integration of these tools into the design process will maximize the likelihood that a museum's educational mission is not at odds with the social agenda museum visitors bring with them, or vice versa. In other words, museum visitors will have fun learning. Thus, we all become interpretive activists.

The strategies and techniques described in this book are not static; like our profession, they are dynamic and evolving as we learn from each other and from our visitors. This is just the beginning of the conversation about interpretive activism. Design discussions will advance the conversation and contribute to the evolution of these ideas, as well as the development of more concrete examples and techniques. For additional photographs, examples, and ongoing discussions and updates, please visit www.selindaresearch.com/wmlf. I look forward to seeing you there.

NOTE

1. This list of eight features can also be found in Hirsh-Pasek, Golinkoff, Berk, and Singer (2009).

Descriptions of the *Colored Shadows* and *The Color Connection* Exhibits

THE *COLORED SHADOWS* EXHIBIT

The focus of the original research that provided the foundation for the What Makes Learning Fun? (WMLF) framework was the *Colored Shadows* exhibit, a version of the familiar and popular exhibit that came from the Exploratorium Cookbook and that is found in many science museums around the world (Bruman, 1975). At the Children's Museum of Indianapolis, the exhibit consisted of a large white table—actually a cube—with three floodlights (one red, one green, and one blue) suspended from the ceiling. Because the colored lights combined to wash the tabletop in white light, the exhibit looked, to visitors who approached, like a simple white table or cube (figure A.1). When visitors waved their hands over the top of the table however, their hand shadows would be brilliantly colored.[1] The popular exhibit surprised and delighted many visitors.

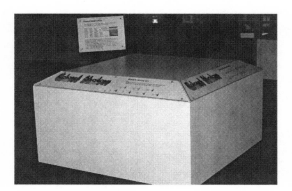

FIGURE A.1

The *Colored Shadows* exhibit looked like a plain white cube with interpretive text on the sides. Off to the side of the cube was a movable stanchion that contained a *Parent Information* sign. (The computer that was usually alongside the table was out for repair the day this photograph was taken.)

Goals and Objectives

Four goals were articulated for the *Colored Shadows* exhibit.

The goals of this exhibit are:

1) for the museum visitor to go away questioning his or her basic assumptions about the characteristics of light.
2) to stimulate adult/child interaction about scientific phenomenon.
3) to encourage the museum visitors to engage in playful exploration of some of the physical characteristics of light.
4) for the museum visitor to learn something about light (Perry, 1989, 252).

In addition, the exhibit had many educational objectives. These were divided into those for the adult visitor (e.g., the adult visitor will "state that red plus green light makes yellow," "attempt to describe to the child(ren) how colored lights combine to form different colored lights," and "engage in playful exploration with the child(ren) with the colored lights") and those for the child visitor (e.g., the child visitor will "perceive that colored lights combine to form different colors," and "enjoy manipulating and playing with colored lights and shadows of colored lights") (Perry, 1989, 252–53).

The Labels

Interpretative text was included on the four angled "reading rails," one on each side of the table. The four panels all included the title of the exhibit (*Colored Shadows*) in brightly colored letters. Two of the panels contained interpretive text with the heading: What is Going On (figures A.2 and A.3), and the other two were labeled What To Do And Notice (figures A.4 and A.5). In addition to the reading rails, off to the side of the exhibit was a movable stanchion with a sign reading Parent Information (figures A.6 and A.7).

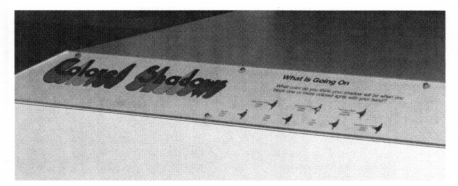

FIGURE A.2
Two of the reading rails contained the label *What Is Going On.*

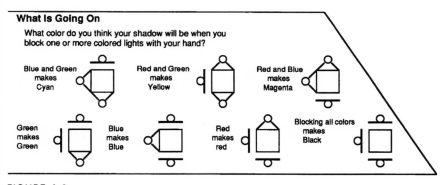

FIGURE A.3
The text on the *What is Going On* label.

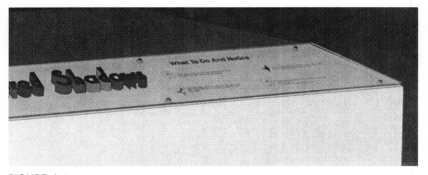

FIGURE A.4
Two of the reading rails (on opposite sides of the table) contained the label *What To Do And Notice*.

What To Do And Notice

1. Place your hand over the white table top and notice the different colors made by your shadow.

2. The three lights above the table are red, green and blue. Notice that all three together make the table look white.

3. If your hand blocks out all three colors, then no light hits the table and your shadow is black.

4. What colored shadows can you make by blocking different lights? You should see eight different colors.

FIGURE A.5
The text on the *What To Do And Notice* label.

FIGURE A.6
The *Parent Information* label included detailed information about light waves.

Parent Information

The chart shows what color the shadow is when your hand blocks out one or more of the lights.

White – Red = Blue + Green (Cyan)
White – Blue = Red + Green (Yellow)
White – Green = Red + Blue (Magenta)
White – Red – Blue = Green
White – Red – Green = Blue
White – Blue – Green = Red
White – Red – Green – Blue = Black

Colors are subjective sensations that can be produced by light of a certain wavelength and by combinations of different wavelengths. The sensation of yellow can be produced by either light of a wavelength we call yellow or by a combination of more than one, such as red and green. The color we call white is a balance of all the wavelengths we can see.

FIGURE A.7
The text on the *Parent Information* label.

The Computer Program

Most of the time, a computer was attached to one side of the exhibit to provide additional interpretive information to visitors. The computer program comprised twenty-six screens, including a title screen, a menu screen, and five short units (figure A.8) (Perry, 1989, 236–48).

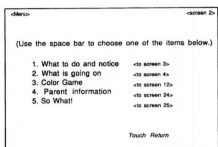

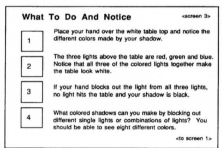

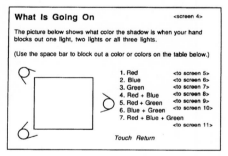

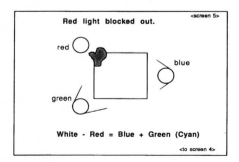

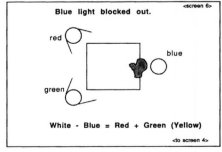

FIGURE A.8.
Selected screen designs for the *Colored Shadows* computer program: (a) title screen (1 screen); (b) menu screen (1 screen); (c) first module, *What To Do And Notice* (1 screen); and (d) second module, *What Is Going On* (8 screens).

FIGURE A.8.
(*continued*)

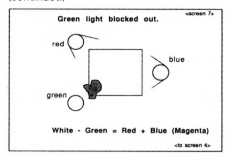

Green light blocked out.

<screen 7>

red

blue

green

White - Green = Red + Blue (Magenta)

<to screen 4>

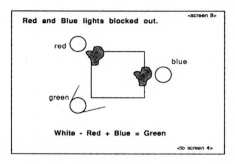

Red and Blue lights blocked out.

<screen 8>

red

blue

green

White - Red + Blue = Green

<to screen 4>

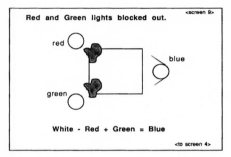

Red and Green lights blocked out.

<screen 9>

red

blue

green

White - Red + Green = Blue

<to screen 4>

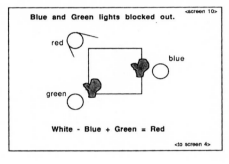

Blue and Green lights blocked out.

<screen 10>

red

blue

green

White - Blue + Green = Red

<to screen 4>

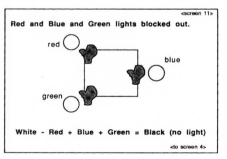

<screen 11>

Red and Blue and Green lights blocked out.

red

blue

green

White - Red + Blue + Green = Black (no light)

THE COLOR CONNECTION EXHIBIT

A primary focus of the research was the evolution of the *Colored Shadows* exhibit over time into a new exhibit called *The Color Connection*. At first glance, *The Color Connection* looked similar to *Colored Shadows*: the same white table was used, there were interpretive reading rails on all four sides, and the same Apple computer was along one side of the table (figure A.9). The goals and objectives remained the same, and the exhibit was in the same location in the physical sciences gallery of the Children's Museum.

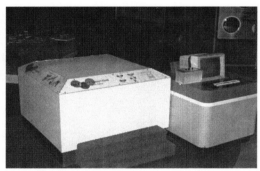

FIGURE A.9
The Color Connection exhibit looked similar to the *Colored Shadows* exhibit and even used the same table and computer. The changes were in the interpretive components that incorporated the principles and strategies of the WMLF framework.

The major difference between the two exhibits was that the revised exhibit, *The Color Connection*, deliberately and systematically incorporated the motivation principles and strategies from the WMLF framework. The process used is described in detail in Appendix B. Following is a brief overview of some of the major revisions made to the *Colored Shadows* exhibit as it evolved into *The Color Connection* exhibit.[2]

The Title

During the research study, interviews and observations revealed that because the title of the exhibit was *Colored Shadows*, many visitors thought the exhibit was primarily about shadows, rather than the mixing of colored lights. The title of the exhibit was changed from *Colored Shadows* to *The Color Connection* to more clearly communicate the goal of the exhibit (strategy 8.1a) and to help focus attention on the process of mixing colored lights rather than on creating colored shadows (figure A.10).

FIGURE A.10
Changing the title of the exhibit helped visitors understand that the exhibit was about mixing colored lights.

The Lights

In the original *Colored Shadows* exhibit, the lights shining on the tabletop were floodlights that most visitors were not aware of. They just saw a white tabletop. During our conversations with visitors, we found that most visitors had trouble connecting the colored shadows on the tabletop with the lights hanging overhead. Without this conceptual connection, it was difficult for many visitors even to begin thinking about mixing colored lights. To them, the exhibit was more about the surprise of having colored shadows.

One of the first changes made was to replace the floodlights with spotlights that projected colored and overlapping circles of light (figure A.11). This was done to clarify that the light on the table was coming from the lights overhead and to stimulate sensory curiosity (strategy 3.1). It also served to provide feedback to the visitor (strategy 6.3) by making it clear when someone's hand was blocking a particular color of light.

FIGURE A.11
Replacing the flood lights with spot lights reinforced the idea that
the colors on the table were coming from the lights overhead.

One limitation of the original (*Colored Shadows*) exhibit was that visitors were not able to control the lights. Because we wanted to facilitate playfulness (principles 12 and 13) and also give the visitors control (principles 10 and 11), we added switches (figure A.12). In the revised *The Color Connection* exhibit, visitors were able to turn the lights on and off.

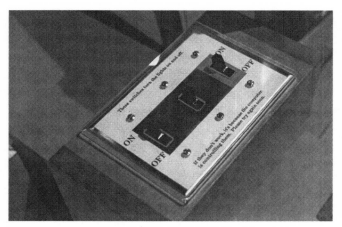

FIGURE A.12
Adding color-coded switches facilitated playfulness and control.

The Labels

Major revisions were also made to the interpretive labels. Each label from the original *Colored Shadows* exhibit was carefully analyzed to identify ways in which the label incorporated or violated the WMLF principles. Many of the original labels were found to violate the success and expediency principles in particular, often leaving visitors feeling frustrated and intimidated. We decided to not include the Parent Information sign in *The Color Connection* exhibit, as it proved to inhibit motivation for many visitors. The remaining interpretive labels were revised to systematically incorporate WMLF strategies. The two interpretive labels for the original *Colored Shadows* exhibit were ultimately replaced with three labels for *The Color Connection* exhibit (figures A.13 to A.15). The Did you know? label (figure A.14) was repeated on two sides.

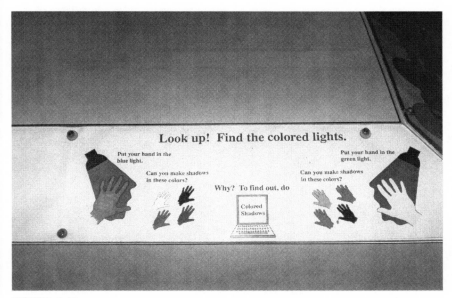

FIGURE A.13
The revised exhibit interpretation deliberately incorporated strategies from the WMLF framework.

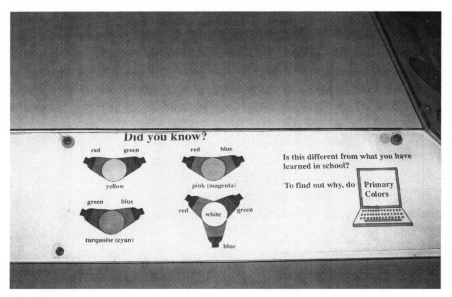

FIGURE A.14
This revised label was on two of the four reading rails.

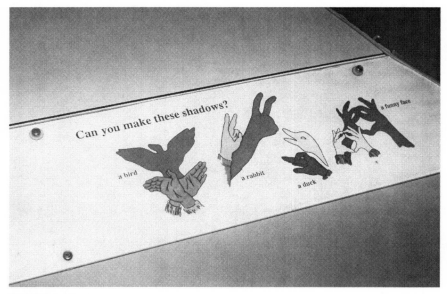

FIGURE A.15
This revised label incorporated Play and Challenge principles.

The Computer Program

In talking with visitors to the original *Colored Shadows* exhibit, we discovered that—like the labels—the computer program often violated WMLF principles and resulted in less-than-optimal visitor experiences. The final, revised computer program included six menu offerings, each unit designed to incorporate specific principles and strategies (figure A.16).[3]

- What's happening? (10 screens)
- Where does this happen in my home? (8 screens)
- What can I do with my preschooler at this exhibit? (12 screens)
- What are the primary colors? (23 screens)
- Why are there colored shadows? (16 screens)
- Where can I get more information? (7 screens)

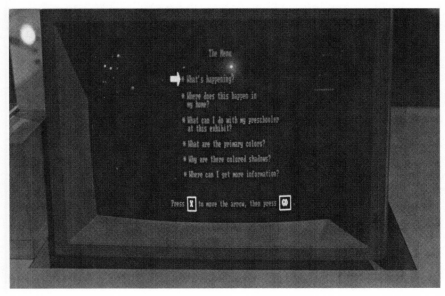

FIGURE A.16
The menu for *The Color Connection* computer program had six module offerings. This was the initial screen that visitors saw.

An important goal of the re-design of the computer program was to facilitate social interaction and group meaning-making. Many WMLF strategies were incorporated including chunking the information, modeling effective teaching/ learning strategies, using questions, and making sure at least one of the members of the social group knew the answers to the questions. The screens were designed so the read-at-a-glance information was in bold, easy-to-see text, and the answers and feedback were more subtle (figure A.17). Each module was repeatedly tested with visitors and revised until it was effective at facilitating social group interactions and jump-starting meaningful exploration.

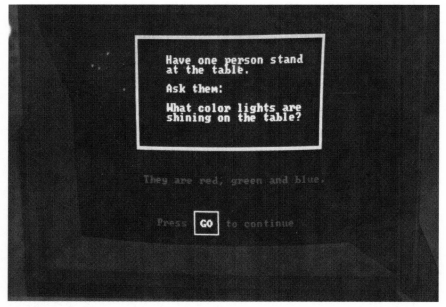

FIGURE A.17
The first screen from the *Why are there colored shadows?* module.

Most visitors who used the computer program started with the What's happening? module. The entire set of screen designs for this module is included as figure A.18.

Ask your child:

Where do you

think the

colored shadows

come from?

Look up! There are 3 colored lights shining
on the table.

Press GO to continue

Put your hand in the white light.

How many shadows

are there?

Why?

There are 3 shadows of your hand because
there are 3 lights shining on the table.

Press GO to continue

Look at the

white circle of light

on the table.

Press GO to continue

Where is the

white light on the table

coming from?

The only lights shining on the table are red, green and
blue. When red, green and blue lights mix, they make
white light.

Press GO to continue

Now what color is

the light on the table?

How many shadows do you have?

What color is it?

Only the red light is on, and the shadow is black. When you
have one color and you block it out, you see no light, or black.

Press GO to continue

And now the table

is

green!

What color is your shadow?

The green light is the only light that's on. Again your
shadow is black.

Press GO to continue

FIGURE A.18

Screen designs from the *What's happening?* computer module.

Let's turn on both

the red and green

lights together.

The table is yellow!

The table is yellow, but there is no yelow light.
Red and green mix to make yellow.

Press GO to continue

How many shadows do
you have now?

Why?

What color are the
shadows?

You have two shadows because there are two
lights. The shadows are red and green.

Press GO to continue

The table is white
again.

Where is the white
light coming from?

There is no white light shining on the table. When red,
blue and green lights mix, they make white light.

Press GO to continue

Now it's your turn!

Use the switches next to
the computer.

See what colors you can make!

Press GO to return to the menu.

FIGURE A.18
Continued.

The second computer module, Where does this happen in my home? (figure A.19), was a more didactic treatment but still incorporated many of the WMLF strategies including chunking information, asking questions, providing answers, connecting to something familiar, presenting information that contradicts what they know, and not dead ending the visitor. This module was also tested repeatedly with visitors until it was effective at stimulating curiosity. The complete set of screen designs for Where does this happen in my home? is included as figure A.19.[4]

You can see that red, green
and blue lights mix together
to make white light.

Where do you think this happens
in your home?

Press GO to continue

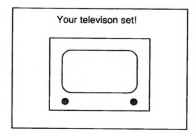

Your televison set!

Press GO to continue

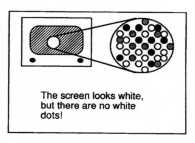

The screen looks white,
but there are no white
dots!

Press GO to continue

What would happen if

there were no blue dots,

only red and green?

Press GO to continue

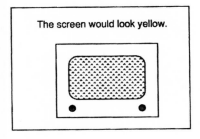

The screen would look yellow.

Press GO to continue

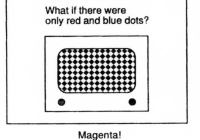

What if there were
only red and blue dots?

Magenta!

Press GO to continue

FIGURE A.19
Screen designs from the *Where does this happen in my home?* computer module.

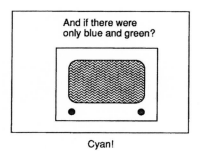

And if there were
only blue and green?

Cyan!

Press GO to continue

When you go home today,

look at your TV screen

with a magnifying glass.

The red, green
and blue dots will be very clear.

Press GO to return to The Menu.

FIGURE A.19
Continued.

NOTES

1. When red, green, and blue lights mix, they make white light. When someone's hand blocks out one of the colors of light, the remaining two colors combine to make another color, resulting in hand shadows of many different colors.

2. For a more complete description of the changes made to the original exhibit, see Perry (1989, 254–84).

3. See Perry (1989, 304–25) for the entire set of screen designs that made up this revised computer program. They can also be found at www.selindaresearch.com/wmlf

4. Note that now that television pictures have improved in quality, this no longer works.

Overview of Original Research

BACKGROUND OF THE STUDY

This book came about as a result of an extensive research study conducted to better understand museum visitors' experiences and how to design for them in order to maximize the potential for learning and enjoyment. It is based on the assumption that the most meaningful learning that takes place in informal settings is that which advances visitors' understandings while also being enjoyable, intrinsically motivating, and meaningful; furthermore, these two goals (learning and enjoyment) are assumed, by definition, to be intimately intertwined and inseparable in informal educational venues. The research study was based on the hypothesis that if we could unpack and understand what makes learning fun and apply those principles and strategies to the design of informal learning experiences, the educational potential of museums and other informal educational environments would improve. The following is a brief summary of the research. For a complete description including citations, see Perry (1989).

THEORETICAL FOUNDATION

The study began in the mid-1980s with a review of existing research that identified the following four basic premises upon which the study was based.

1. *Visitors learn in museums by engaging with an artifact or phenomenon.* Although often a physical interaction or manipulation, this engagement can also be intellectual, aesthetic, or emotional. There is much in the research literature to support the value of hands-on and minds-on interaction.
2. *Visitors learn in museums through social interactions.* This premise states that when people visit museums as part of small social groups, their learning takes place primarily through social interactions with each other. Museum

professionals often design exhibits with the assumption that visitors learn in museums primarily by reading labels. Research studies indicate, however, that within social groups, one person typically reads the labels quickly and then initiates a discussion with their visiting companions, blending what they already know with the new information gleaned from the labels. The quality and richness of the learning that takes place and the meanings that are made are a direct result of the quality of the conversations.

3. *A primary difference between schools and museums as educational institutions is motivation.* Generally speaking, people go to school because they have to, and their participation is based on a system of external rewards and punishments. People who go to museums, on the other hand, tend to go because they want to go, and their learning experiences are guided, to a large extent, by intrinsic motivation. In other words, they are free to attend to whatever they want, terminate their interaction at any point, and engage with exhibits in whatever order and with whatever intensity they choose. Relying primarily on models from formal education and instruction limits our effectiveness at designing meaningful informal learning experiences.

4. *The design of exhibits has traditionally focused on learning and aesthetics and paid relatively less attention to issues related to intrinsic motivation.* The premise of the research behind this book was that until we incorporate motivational theory into exhibit designs, exhibits' potential as educational opportunities will not be fully realized.

DESIGN AND FINDINGS

Based on these four premises, a research study was designed to create and validate a development model grounded in theories of intrinsic motivation that, when used to revise a popular museum exhibit, would increase the learning that took place while simultaneously maintaining the popularity of the exhibit. The study sought to improve learning by increasing the amount and quality of both physical interactions with the exhibit and social interactions among visitors.

The phases of the research included (a) developing a theoretical model to describe the essential components of what makes learning fun, (b) revising a popular exhibit to incorporate as many of the components of the model as possible, and (c) verifying the efficacy of the model by comparing visitors' experiences at the revised exhibit with those at the original configuration.

The work began with an existing, empirically validated model for the design of intrinsically motivating educational computer games (Malone 1980, 1981;

Malone and Lepper 1987; Lepper and Malone 1987). This model included seven major categories: challenge, curiosity, control, fantasy, cooperation, competition, and recognition. Based on a number of predetermined criteria, the popular *Colored Shadows* exhibit located in the physical sciences gallery of the Children's Museum of Indianapolis was selected as the focus of this research. The research design consisted of two distinct phases, a developmental research phase to refine the model and adapt it to a museum setting, followed by a quasi-experimental, interrupted time-series study to test and verify the efficacy of the model.

Developmental Phase of the Study

Over a period of four months, a formal formative evaluation/prototyping process was used to develop and revise the theoretical model and to develop an exhibit that incorporated its principles and strategies. Visitors were observed and interviewed, and revisions were repeatedly made until it was determined that the effectiveness of both the model and exhibit had been maximized.

After the prototyping was completed, a final (revised) version of the model was developed that included six motivations identified as important for the design of intrinsically motivating educational museum exhibits: communication, curiosity, confidence, challenge, control, and play. In addition, a final (revised) exhibit (now called *The Color Connection*) was produced. This exhibit included new lights and light switches, new interpretive labels, and a new, six-module computer program. The original furniture and computer hardware were retained, so at first glance the revised exhibit looked almost identical to the original.

Verification Phase of the Study

A quasi-experimental, interrupted time-series design was used to test the effectiveness of the model by comparing visitors' experiences at the original exhibit (*Colored Shadows*) with their experiences at the revised exhibit (*The Color Connection*). During this verification phase, eight trained data collectors observed visitors over a span of 12.5 hours spread out over four weekends—a total of 100 people-hours of observation. Data collectors recorded 611 visitor groups at the exhibit—380 groups at the original (*Colored Shadows*) version and 231 at the revised (*The Color Connection*) version. Of these groups, 99 were interviewed, and 466 were observed. Of the groups that were observed, time at exhibit was measured, as were the quantity and quality of social interactions, interactions with the exhibit itself, and learning behaviors. In addition, a knowledge hierarchy was used to assess exit knowledge about the primary exhibit concepts of the 99 groups that were interviewed. Their levels of enjoyment were also determined.

Many interesting results emerged from the verification phase of the study. The following are a few highlights (see Perry [1989] for a comprehensive description of the findings).

At the revised exhibit (*The Color Connection*), the average visit length increased from thirty-five to seventy-five seconds. The longest visit of any respondent increased from three to nine minutes. The proportion of visitors who left the exhibit with at least the basic understanding that red, green, and blue lights combine to form white light increased from 52 to 75 percent, while the proportion of visitors who left the exhibit with a fairly sophisticated understanding of the basic principles increased from 26 to 47 percent. In addition, the number of visitors who left the exhibit with no knowledge and/or interest in the scientific concepts (Level 0 on the knowledge hierarchy) decreased from 15 to 2 percent. The data also indicated that both the quantity and quality of visitor interactions with the exhibit increased. These interactions included putting hands in the lights in a purposeful manner, playing in the lights, making hand shadows, blocking out the lights with hands, looking from the table to the lights overhead, turning the lights on and off purposefully, reading the labels silently, and using the computer program.

There was also an increase in the quality and quantity of social interactions, including explaining and teaching behavior, developmentally appropriate social interactions, asking and answering questions, directing someone else's behavior, directing someone else's attention, verbal exchanges, and reading and interpreting labels. Finally, the overall enjoyment of the exhibit did not appear to decrease.

CONCLUSIONS

This study demonstrated that when a popular museum exhibit was designed to deliberately incorporate the six intrinsic motivations of communication, curiosity, confidence, challenge, control, and play, time at the exhibit increased, as did the quality and quantity of learning behaviors, including social and physical engagements, as well as knowledge, without an accompanying decrease in enjoyment, indicating an overall improved visitor experience, where learning was maximized and enjoyment remained high. While this study was conducted in a single museum with a single stand-alone exhibit, many additional opportunities since the original research was conducted have provided for further testing and refinement of the model.

The What Makes
Learning Fun? Framework

COMMUNICATION

Visitors to museums want to make sense of objects, phenomena, and experiences.

Principle 1—Collaboration

Meaningful communication is enhanced when visitors collaborate on a group task or meaning-making venture.

Strategy 1.1:   Design spaces that encourage members of visiting social groups to stay together and in close proximity.
Strategy 1.2:   Ensure there is something for everyone.
Strategy 1.3:   Pose a problem that encourages input from a number of visitors working together.

Principle 2—Guidance

Visitors will experience more meaningful communication when they engage in active teaching/learning processes, guidance and direction.

Strategy 2.1:   Guide the visitor group through a successful teaching/learning process.
Strategy 2.2:   Model appropriate teaching/learning strategies.
Strategy 2.3:   Use visitor-spoken language.

CURIOSITY
Visitors to museums want to be surprised and intrigued.

Principle 3—Perceptual Curiosity
Visitors will be attracted to an exhibit when their perceptual curiosity is aroused.

Strategy 3.1:   Stimulate perceptual curiosity by using audio, visual, and other sensory effects.
Strategy 3.2:   Use a variety of these effects, but use them wisely.

Principle 4—Intellectual Curiosity
Visitors will become interested in and engage with an exhibit when their intellectual curiosity is piqued.

Strategy 4.1:   Present information that contradicts what visitors already know.
Strategy 4.2:   Present incomplete information.
    4.2a: Leave some things unsaid.
    4.2b: Use progressive disclosure.
    4.2c: Use questions to stimulate intellectual curiosity, but use them carefully.

Principle 5—Interest
Visitors will be attracted to and engage with an exhibit that deals with a topic that is already of interest to them.

Strategy 5.1:   Cover topics that are already of interest and relevant to visitors.
Strategy 5.2:   Relate new information to past knowledge and things that are already familiar to the visitor.
    5.2a: Use metaphors and analogies, but choose them carefully and use them wisely.
    5.2b: Display the artifact or object in context.
Strategy 5.3:   Balance the familiar with the novel.
Strategy 5.4:   Ensure the exhibit is personally meaningful and relevant to visitors.
Strategy 5.5:   Ensure the exhibit includes things of interest to everyone.

CONFIDENCE

Visitors to museums want to feel safe and smart.

Principle 6—Success

Visitors will feel confident and competent when they experience success.

Strategy 6.1:	Use clear, straightforward, and easy-to-read text.
6.1a:	Use simple and non-exclusionary vocabulary.
6.1b:	Use white space to chunk information.
6.1c:	Use short sentences.
6.1d:	Minimize concept density.
6.1e:	Define unfamiliar terms and include pronunciation guides.
6.1f:	Use readability indexes, but recognize their limitations.
Strategy 6.2:	Provide answers.
6.2a:	Answer questions visitors ask.
6.2b:	Design labels that ensure at least one member of the visitor group knows the answers to the questions.
Strategy 6.3:	Provide feedback.
Strategy 6.4:	Guide the visitor through a series of minisuccesses.
Strategy 6.5:	Never dead-end the visitor.
6.5a:	Direct visitors to other exhibits that deal with a similar or related topic.
6.5b:	Develop resource rooms to accompany exhibitions.
6.5c:	Develop relationships with local public libraries and other community resources.
6.6d:	Capitalize on computer and Internet resources.
Strategy 6.6:	Be redundant. Present the same content in a variety of ways.
Strategy 6.7:	Eliminate unnecessary or extaneous information that serves to confuse or intimidate visitors.
Strategy 6.8:	Anticipate visitors' physical needs and provide for them.

Principle 7—Expediency

Visitors will feel confident and competent when they experience success quickly.

Strategy 7.1:   Ensure that the exhibit is immediately understandable.
    7.1a: Develop labels that can be read at a glance.
    7.1b: First answer the questions: "What is it?" and "What am I supposed to do?"
Strategy 7.2:   Have no obstacles between the visitor and the content.
    7.2a: Eliminate title screens on computer interactives and other technology presentations.
    7.2b: Eat dessert first.
    7.2c: Use advance organizers carefully and cautiously.

CHALLENGE

Visitors to museums want to be challenged.

Principle 8—Expectations

Visitors will feel appropriately challenged when they know what is expected of them.

Strategy 8.1:   Include a clearly stated goal.
    8.1a: Ensure that the title of the exhibit is descriptive and goal-oriented.
    8.1b: Tell visitors directly what they are expected to do and/or learn.
    8.1c: Use carefully designed implicit (nonverbal) goals whenever possible.
Strategy 8.2:   Direct visitors' attention to the important parts of the exhibit, object, or artifact.

Principle 9—Uncertainty

Visitors will feel appropriately challenged when they perceive that success is not automatic.

Strategy 9.1:   Ask questions.
Strategy 9.2:   Have hidden information (that is revealed only after further investment of energy).
    9.2a: Use flip labels
    9.2b: Take advantage of the limited size of computer screens.
    9.2c: Use "less noticeable" text.

CONTROL
Visitors to museums want to feel in charge of their experiences.

Principle 10—Choice
Visitors will feel in control when they are given appropriate choices.

Strategy 10.1:   Make sure visitors have the right information to make wise choices.
Strategy 10.2:   Ensure that the exhibit includes a choice of activities.
Strategy 10.3:   Provide a variety of different types of activities.
Strategy 10.4:   Become very familiar with the magic number 7 +/– 2.

Principle 11—Power
Visitors will feel in control when they are able to expend relatively minor amounts of energy and produce significant effects.

Strategy 11.1:   Allow the visitor to manipulate the object or artifact.
Strategy 11.2:   Allow visitors to interact with the exhibit at their own pace.

PLAY
Visitors to museums want to be playful.

Principle 12—Imagination
Visitors will feel playful when they use their imaginations.

Strategy 12.1:   Ensure that the exhibit includes activities that encourage visitors to use their imaginations.
Strategy 12.2:   Incorporate endogenous (as opposed to exogenous) fantasy whenever possible.

Principle 13—Sensory Exploration
Visitors will feel playful when they use multiple senses to explore the exhibit.

Strategy 13.1:   Include playful ways visitors of all ages can use their senses to explore the exhibit.

Sample Knowledge Hierarchies

Here are a few sample knowledge hierarchies from actual studies. Additional examples of knowledge hierarchies can be found in Perry (1993d).[1]

This hierarchy describes visitor learning at a *Whispering Dishes* exhibit at an unnamed science center.

0   No awareness or interest in how the sound was being projected across the room
1   An explanation, but incorrect (misconception)
2   An explanation of what you had to do, but not how it operated
3   An understanding that sound or sound waves traveled across the room
4   An understanding that sound waves were reflected from the dish across the room
5   An understanding that sound waves were reflected across, focused and heard by the partner's ear at the focal point (McClafferty 1995).

The following hierarchy presents visitors' awareness of and understandings about the behind-the-scenes research that was portrayed in a temporary exhibition on spiders at The Field Museum in Chicago.

0   These visitors didn't know much about spiders, and they didn't care to learn more. (They were often being dragged through the exhibition by other members of their group.)
1   These visitors didn't know much about spiders, but they were interested in learning more.
2   These visitors knew some things about spiders, but they had incomplete understandings, or some of what they knew was incorrect.

3   These visitors knew quite a bit about spiders—they had a pretty good idea about how spiders live their lives, and how spiders fit into the worlds of nature and humans. But they hadn't recognized the collections and research themes of the Curator's Office.

4   These visitors knew about spiders in general, and they also knew how the spiders that were on display in this exhibition had been captured. However, their knowledge didn't go much beyond the techniques used to capture spiders in the field.

5   These visitors knew that the scientists who caught spiders brought them back to labs where they separated them, preserved them, and categorized them. However, they didn't know much about the later stages of research, and they don't know that the labs are at The Field Museum.

6   These visitors knew that the spider labs were at The Field Museum, and that the scientists who caught and categorized spiders worked there, behind the scenes. They also realized that the museum stored at least some of the spiders for use in later exhibits and for educational programs, but they did not understand that these collections mostly were used for research.

7   These visitors knew that the scientists who caught and stored spiders used them mainly for research. They also knew that the museum's behind-the-scene's collections were very large and used mainly for scientific research. (Gyllenhaal 1998a, 21–22)

This hierarchy describes visitors' understandings of the diversity and interconnectedness of life in the soil as portrayed in the *Underground Adventure* exhibition at The Field Museum.

0   This level indicated no knowledge about or interest in dirt and soil. "I don't know much about soil, and truthfully, I don't care much."

1   This level represented limited knowledge but an interest in finding out more. "I don't know much about soil, but now I'm curious."

2   Visitors indicated a preliminary understanding of soil and dirt, but their understanding tended to be superficial and incomplete. "Lots of stuff lives underground, but I don't know much about it."

3   Visitors indicated a basic understanding that all things underground are interrelated and interconnected. "All that stuff that lives underground is interrelated in some way."

4   This level included a realization and appreciation of the fact that human beings are part of the equation, and that what goes on underground is not just something that humans observe as outsiders. "I am part of that interrelationship."

5   These visitors indicated a more sophisticated understanding of the interrelationship between soil, humans, and the health of the planet, including a deep appreciation for soil and a desire to do something proactive. "I appreciate how important all of these interrelationships are to the health of the planet." (Schaefer, Perry, and Gyllenhaal 2002, 33–36)

The following hierarchy is included because it's an interesting example of a different use of the technique. Rather than describing visitor understandings, this hierarchy demonstrates the range of ways on-the-floor interpretive staff engaged with the public as part of the *Traveling Experiment Gallery* at the Denver Museum of Nature and Science.

0   "I don't want to interact with visitors right now." Probably everyone feels like Level 0 from time to time—hopefully, these people either get to go on break or go home!

1   "I'll just answer visitors' questions, giving facts and explanations." This seems to be the "traditional" kind of docent interaction at many museums.

2   "I'll ask the visitors questions, but I'll just request factual knowledge." We saw a few volunteers functioning at this level.

3   "I'll ask questions that help visitors make good observations of the phenomena that I show them." This may be the most appropriate level to work at with younger children.

4   "I'll ask questions that guide visitors towards a pre-determined explanation (whatever answer seems to be appropriate for their age and background)." Level 4 seemed to be achieved by some well-trained and well-motivated volunteers.

5   "I'll try to help visitors ask better questions so that they can develop their own explanations, even if they disagree with what I consider to be 'correct.' (I'm just the 'coach,' and I have to be accepting of a range of outcomes, as long as the visitors develop them themselves.)"

6   "I'll help visitors ask questions that take them beyond just developing an explanation—I'll also help them to re-examine and challenge their explanations, and to test them using experiments." (Gyllenhaal 1998b, 42)

NOTE

1. This article is also available from the Visitor Studies Association online archive (www. visitorstudiesarchives.org).

Acknowledgments

This undertaking would not have been possible without the contributions and support of many individuals and organizations. I am profoundly grateful to you all. At the risk of omitting some, I'd like to thank in particular, the following:

Kris Morrissey was an unfailing advocate, muse, contributor, and personal champion, and provided immeasurable support and guidance. Beverly Serrell contributed valuable ideas and set a high standard to reach for. Additional support, photographs, examples, ideas, encouragement, and feedback came from Gene Dillenburg, Daryl Fischer, Preeti Gupta, Josh Gutwill, Judy Koke, Francie Muraski-Stotz, Brooke Portmann, Lisa Roberts, Diana Ryan, Matt Sikora, Lois Silverman, Mike Spock, and Marcella Wells. Rebecca Reynolds gently pushed, and pushed some more. Ryan Crow produced the WMLF graphic. Cecilia Garibay, Eric Gyllenhaal, Lorrie Beaumont, Carey Tisdal, Jane Schaefer, and all the Selinda research associates over the years gave support, encouragement, ideas, and dedication.

Reviewers of various drafts included Josh Gutwill, Eric Gyllenhaal, Kris Morrissey, and Marcella Wells. Gail Merrit helped smooth the rough edges, in this manuscript and in so much more.

Thomas Malone and Mark Lepper provided the essential initial organizing framework. The original study would not have been possible without the generous support of the Children's Museum of Indianapolis, including John VanAusdal, Ann Ray, and Nikki Anderson, as well as many colleagues at Indiana University.

In addition to those mentioned, I am deeply indebted to all the rest of my family, friends, and colleagues whom I have neglected to mention by name, but who were consistently with me throughout this project.

Finally, I'd like to thank my parents Karyl S. Perry and Herbert B. Perry for instilling the curiosity, passion, and love of learning necessary to undertake this journey, the Milbury family for teaching me so much along the way, and most importantly, Greg Maravolo for being such a significant part of it.

References

Abbey, D. S. (1968). Kids, kulture, and curiosity. *Museum News* (46): 30–33.

Abu-Shumays, M., and Leinhardt, G. (2002). Two docents in three museums: Central and peripheral participation. Pp. 401–23 in G. Leinhardt, K. Crowley, and K. Knutson (Eds.), *Learning conversations in museums.* Mahwah, NJ: Lawrence Erlbaum Associates.

Anderson, P., and Roe, B. C. (1993). *MIES: The Museum Impact and Evaluation Study: Roles of affect in the museum visit and ways of assessing them.* Vol. 3: *Individual site research reports.* Chicago: Museum of Science and Industry.

Ansbacher, T. (1998). John Dewey's *Experience and Education*: Lessons for museums. *Curator, 41*(1): 36–49.

Ansbacher, T. (1999). Experience, inquiry, and making meaning. *Exhibitionist, 18*(2): 22–28.

Ansbacher, T. (2002a). Misunderstandings of meaning making. *Exhibitionist, 21*(1): 53–55.

Ansbacher, T. (2002b). What are we learning? Outcomes of the museum experience. *Informal Learning Review, 53* (March–April): 1, 4–7.

Ansbacher, T. (2005). Rethinking our goals: Putting process first. *Informal Learning Review, 74* (September–October): 13–18.

Ansbacher, T., Hein, G., McLean, K., Rounds, J., and Spock, M. (2000). Meaning making: The conversation continues. *Exhibitionist, 19*(2): 38–47.

Argyle, M., and Kendon, A. (1967). The experimental analysis of social performance. In L. Berkowitz (ed.), *Journal of Advances in Social Psychology, 3*: 55–98.

Ash, D. (2002). Negotiations of thematic conversations about biology. Pp. 357–400 in G. Leinhardt, K. Crowley and K. Knutson (Eds.), *Learning conversations in museums.* Mahwah, NJ: Lawrence Erlbaum Associates.

Ash, D. (2003). Dialogic inquiry and biological themes and principles: Implications for exhibit design. *Journal of Museum Education, 28*(2): 8–13.

Ausubel, D. P. (1968). *Educational psychology: A cognitive view.* New York: Holt, Rinehart & Winston.

Ausubel, D. P. (1978). In defense of advance organizers: A reply to the critics. *Review of Educational Research, 48*(2): 251–57.

Bandura, A. (1977). *Social learning theory.* Englewood Cliffs, NJ: Prentice Hall.

Beck, L., and Cable, T. (2002). *Interpretation for the 21st century: Fifteen guiding principles for interpreting nature and culture* (2nd ed.). Champaign, IL: Sagamore.

Berlyne, D. E. (1960). *Conflict, arousal, and curiosity.* New York: McGraw Hill.

Bitgood, S. (2000). The role of attention in designing effective interpretive labels. *Journal of Interpretation Research, 5*(2): 31–45.

Bitgood, S. (2009a). When is "museum fatigue" not fatigue? *Curator, 52*(2): 193–202.

Bitgood, S. (2009b). Museum fatigue: A critical review. *Visitor Studies, 12*(2): 1–19.

Bitgood, S. (2009c). "Museum fatigue": A new look at an old problem. *Informal Learning Review,* (97): 18–22.

Bitgood, S. (2011). *Social design in museums: The psychology of visitor studies; Collected essays Volume One.* Edinburgh, UK: MuseumsEtc, Ltd.

Borun, M., and Adams, K. A. (1992). From hands on to minds on: Labeling interactive exhibits. *Visitor studies: Theory, research and practice.* Vol. 4: *Collected papers from the 1991 Visitor Studies Conference.* Jacksonville, AL: Visitor Studies Association, 115–20.

Borun, M., Chambers, M., and Cleghorn, A. (1995). Family learning in four science museums: Preliminary results. *Current Trends in Audience Research, 9:* 116–24.

Borun, M., Chambers, M., and Cleghorn, A. (1996). Families are learning in science museums. *Curator, 39*(2): 123–38.

Borun, M., Chambers, M. B., Dritsas, J., and Johnson, J. I. (1997). Enhancing family learning through exhibits. *Curator, 40*(4): 279–95.

Borun, M., and Dritsas, J. (1997). Developing family-friendly exhibits. *Curator, 40*(3): 178–96.

Borun, M., Dritsas, J., Johnson, J. I., Peter, N. E., Wagner, K. F., Fadigan, K., et al. (1998). *Family learning in museums: The PISEC perspective.* Philadelphia: Philadelphia/Camden Informal Science Education Collaborative (PISEC), Franklin Institute.

Borun, M., Massey, C., and Lutter, T. (1993). Naive knowledge and the design of science museum exhibits. *Curator, 36*(3): 201–19.

Brown, A. L., and Campione, J. C. (1994). Guided discovery in a community of learners. Pp. 229–70 in K. McGilly (Ed.), *Classroom lessons: Integrating cognitive theory and classroom practice.* Cambridge, MA: MIT Press.

Brown, J. S. (1983). Learning-by-doing revisited for electronic learning environments. In M. A. White (Ed.), *The future of electronic learning.* Hillsdale, NJ: Lawrence Erlbaum Associates.

Bruman, R., (1975). *Exploratorium cookbook: A construction manual for Exploratorium exhibits.* Vol. 1. San Francisco: Exploratorium.

Bruner, J. S. (1966). The will to learn. Pp. 113–28 in *Toward a theory of instruction.* Cambridge, MA: Belknap Press.

Callison, D. J. (1983). *A simulation of random access video technology: Reaction to premastered multimedia interactive programmed instruction in a children's museum free inquiry learning environment.* Unpublished doctoral dissertation, Indiana University, Bloomington.

Carlson, S. P. (1993). *Cognitive model for learning in educationally oriented recreation facilities.* Unpublished doctoral dissertation, Michigan State University, East Lansing.

Chance, P. (1979). *Learning and behavior.* Belmont, CA: Wadsworth.

Clark, R. E. (1982). Antagonism between achievement and enjoyment in ATI studies. *Educational Psychologist, 17*(2): 92–101.

Collins, A. M., and Loftus, E. F. (1975). A spreading-activation theory of semantic processing. *Psychological Review, 82:* 407–28.

Crowley, K. (2000). *Building islands of expertise in everyday family activity: Musings on family learning in and out of museums* (Technical Report No. MLC-05). Pittsburgh, PA: Museum Learning Collaborative.

Crowley, K., and Callanan, M. (1998). Describing and supporting collaborative scientific thinking in parent-child interactions. *Journal of Museum Education, 23*(1): 12–17.

Csikszentmihalyi, M. (1988). Human behavior and the science center. Pp. 80–87 in P. G. Heltne and L. A. Marquardt (Eds.), *Science learning in the informal setting.* Chicago: Chicago Academy of Sciences.

Csikszentmihalyi, M. (1990). *Flow: The psychology of optimal experience.* New York: Harper & Row.

Csikszentmihalyi, M., and Hermanson, K. (1995). Intrinsic motivation in museums: What makes visitors want to learn? *Museum News, 74*(3): 34–37, 59–60, 62.

Davidson, B., Heald, C. L., and Hein, G. L. (1991). Increased exhibit accessibility through multisensory interaction. *Curator, 34*(4): 273–90.

Deci, E. L. (1980). *The psychology of self-determination.* Lexington, MA: D. C. Heath & Company.

Designing exhibits that motivate. Pp. 25–29 in M. Borun, S. Grinell, P. McNamara, and B. Serrell (Eds.), *What research says about learning in science museums.* Washington, DC: Association of Science-Technology Centers.

Diamond, J. (n.d.) Playing and learning. Association of Science-Technology Centers . Retrieved April 10, 2011 (www.astc.org/resource/education/learning_diamond.htm).

Diamond, J. (1980). The ethology of teaching: A perspective from the observations of families in science centers. *Dissertation Abstracts International* (UMI No. 8113012).

Diamond, J. (1986). The behavior of family groups in science museums. *Curator, 29*(2): 139–54.

Diamond, J. (1999). *Practical evaluation guide: Tools for museums and other informal educational settings.* Walnut Creek, CA: AltaMira Press.

Dierking, L. (1991). Leaning theory and learning styles: An overview. *Journal of Museum Education, 16*(1): 4–6.

Dierking, L. D., Jones, M. C., Wadman, M., Falk, J. H., Storksdieck, M., and Ellenbogen, K. (2002). Broadening our notions of the impact of free-choice learning experiences. *Informal Learning Review, 55*: 1, 4–7.

Dierking, L. D., and Pollock, W. (1998). *Questioning assumptions: An introduction to front-end studies in museums.* Washington, DC: Association of Science and Technology Centers.

Doering, Z. D., and Pekarik, A. J. (2000). Questioning the entrance narrative. Pp. 261–67 in J. S. Hirsch and L. H. Silverman (Eds.), *Transforming practice.* Washington, DC: Museum Education Roundtable.

Dotzour, A., Houston, C., Manubay, G., Schulz, K., and Smith, J. C. (2002). *Crossing the bog of habits: An evaluation of an exhibit's effectiveness in promoting environmentally responsible behaviors.* Unpublished master's thesis, University of Michigan, Ann Arbor.

Dunbar, I., and Blanchette, I. (2001). The in vivo/in vitro approach to cognition: The case of analogy. *Trends in Cognitive Sciences, 5*(8): 334–39.

Durbin, G. (Ed.). (1996). *Developing museum exhibitions for lifelong learning.* London: Stationery Office.

Everett, M., and Piscitelli, B. (2006). Hands-on trolleys: Facilitating learning through play. *Visitor Studies Today, 9*(1): 10–16.

Falk, J. H. (1981). The use of time as a measure of visitor behavior and exhibit effectiveness. *Museum Education Roundtable: Roundtable Reports, 7*(4): 10–13.

Falk, J. H. (1998). A framework for diversifying museum audiences. *Museum News, 77*(5): 36–39, 61.

Falk, J. H. (2009). *Identity and the museum visitor experience.* Walnut Creek, CA: Left Coast Press.

Falk, J. H., and Dierking, L. D. (1992). *The museum experience.* Washington, DC: Whalesback Books.

Falk, J. H., and Dierking, L. D. (2000). *Learning from museums: Visitor experiences and the making of meaning.* Walnut Creek, CA: AltaMira Press.

Falk, J. H., and Dierking, L. D. (2002). *Lessons without limit: How free-choice learning is transforming education.* Walnut Creek, CA: AltaMira Press.

Feher, E., and Diamond, J. (1990). Science centers as research laboratories. Pp. 26–28 in B. Serrell (Ed.), *What research says about learning in science museums.* Washington, DC: Association of Science-Technology Centers.

Feher, E., and Rice, K. (1985). Development of scientific concepts through the use of interactive exhibits in a museum. *Curator, 28*(1): 35–46.

Felker, D. B., Pickering, F., Charrow, V. R., Holland, V. M., and Redish, J. C. (1981). *Guidelines for document designers.* Washington, DC: American Institutes for Research.

Fenichel, M., and Schweingruber, H. A. (2010). *Surrounded by science: Learning science in informal environments.* Board on Science Education, Center for Education, Division of Behavioral and Social Sciences and Education. Washington, DC: National Academies Press.

Fienberg, J., and Leinhardt, G. (2002). Looking through the glass: Reflections of identity in conversations at a history museum. Pp. 167–211 in G. Leinhardt, K. Crowley and K. Knutson (Eds.), *Learning conversations in museums.* Mahwah, NJ: Lawrence Erlbaum Associates.

Finamore, E. B., and Perry, D. L. (1995). *Prototyping final report: Prejudice and discrimination/name calling event* (unpublished manuscript). Chicago: Chicago Children's Museum.

Fiske, J. (1987). *Television culture.* London: Methuen.

Fleming, M., and Levie, H. W. (1978). *Instructional message design: Principles from the behavioral sciences.* Englewood Cliffs, NJ: Educational Technology Publications.

Fleming, M., and Levie, H. W. (1993). *Instructional message design: Principles from the behavioral and cognitive sciences.* 2nd ed. Englewood Cliffs, NJ: Educational Technology Publications.

Friedman, A. (Ed.). (2008). Framework for evaluating impacts of informal science education projects. Center for Advancement of Informal Science Education, March 12. Retrieved September 16, 2011 (http://insci.org/resources/Eval_Framework.pdf).

Gagné, R. M. (1965). *The conditions of learning.* New York: Holt, Rinehart and Winston, Inc.

Gagne, R. M., and Briggs, L. J. (1979). *Principles of instructional design.* 2nd ed. New York: Holt, Rinehart & Winston.

Garibay, C., and Perry, D. L. (1998). *Living together at The Field Museum: Summative evaluation* (unpublished manuscript). Chicago: The Field Museum.

Göncü, A., and Gaskins, S. (Eds.). (2007). *Play and development: Evolutionary, sociocultural, and functional perspectives.* Mahwah, NJ: Lawrence Erlbaum Associates.

Gottfried, J. L. (1979). *A naturalistic study of children's behavior in a free-choice learning environment.* Unpublished doctoral dissertation, University of California, Berkeley.

Gould, S. J. (1995). *Dinosaur in a haystack: Reflections in natural history.* New York: Three Rivers Press.

Greene, D., and Lepper, M. R. (1974). Intrinsic motivation: How to turn play into work. *Psychology Today, 8*(5): 49–54.

Griggs, S. A. (1986). Orienting visitors within a thematic display. *International Journal of Museum Management and Curatorship, 2*: 119–34.

Gunning, R. (1968). *The technique of clear writing.* New York: McGraw-Hill.

Gutwill, J. (2006). Labels for open-ended exhibits: Using questions and suggestions to motivate physical activity. *Visitor Studies Today, 9*(1): 1, 4–9.

Gutwill, J. P., and Allen, S. (2010). Facilitating family group inquiry at science museum exhibits. *Science Education, 94*(4): 710–42.

Gyllenhaal, E. D. (1998a). Communicating behind-the-scenes research to museum visitors: Evaluations of temporary exhibits at The Field Museum. Pp. 15–24 in *Current Trends in Audience Research and Evaluation.* Vol. 11. Los Angeles: American Association of Museums/Committee on Audience Research and Evaluation. Also available at www.selindaresearch.com/Gyllenhaal 1998BehindTheScenes.pdf.

Gyllenhaal, E. D. (1998b). *Traveling Experiment Gallery: Final evaluation report* (unpublished manuscript). St. Paul: Science Museum of Minnesota . Also available at www.selindaresearch .com/Traveling%20ExperimentGallerySummative.pdf.

Gyllenhaal, E. D. (2001). *CARING Study at the Brookfield Zoo: A preliminary report* (unpublished manuscript). Chicago: Brookfield Zoo.

Gyllenhaal, E. D. (2002a). Aaron's treasures: How to nurture your child's urge to collect (without letting it drive you nuts). *Chicago Parent* (July). Available at Salt the Sandbox. Retrieved September 16, 2011 (http://saltthesandbox.org/ChicagoParentArticle1.htm).

Gyllenhaal, E. D. (2002b). Islands of expertise: Why do children become such specialists? *Chicago Parent* (September). Available at Salt the Sandbox. Retrieved April 29, 2006 (http://saltthe sandbox.org/ChicagoParentArticle2.htm).

Gyllenhaal, E. D. (2006). Memories of math: Visitors' experiences in an exhibition about calculus. *Curator, 49*(3): 345–64.

Gyllenhaal, E. D. (2008). *Remedial/summative evaluation of the Sugar from the Sun exhibition.* Chicago: Garfield Park Conservatory Alliance. Also available from www.informalscience.org/ evaluation/show/171.

Gyllenhaal, E. D., and Perry, D. L. (2005). *Old Faithful Visitor Education Center formative evaluation: Summary of prototype testing at Old Faithful Geyser* (unpublished manuscript). Mammoth, WY: Yellowstone National Park. Also available from http://selindaresearch.com/OldFaithfulVisitor EducationCenterPrototypeTestingReport.pdf.

Haden, C., Ornstein, P. A., Eckerman, C. O., and Didow, S. M. (2001). Mother-child conversational interactions as events unfold: Linkages to subsequent remembering. *Child Development, 72*(4): 1016–31.

Halpern, R. (2004). *Confronting the big lie: The need to reframe expectations of afterschool programs.* New York: Partnership for After School Education.

Hapkiewicz, A. (1992). Finding a list of science misconceptions. *MSTA Newsletter, 38* (winter): 11–14.

Hapkiewicz, A. (1999). Naïve ideas in earth science. *MSTA Journal, 44*(2) (fall): 26–30.

Hein, G. E. (1998). *Learning in the museum.* New York: Routledge.

Hein, G. E., and Alexander, M. (1998). *Museums: Places of learning*. Washington, DC: American Association of Museums.

Hennes, M. L. (2009). The renovated DIA: A docent's perspective. *Curator, 52*(1): 77–80.

Hensel, K. A. (1987). Families in a museum: Interactions and conversations at displays. *Dissertation Abstracts International, 49*(09A): 2612 (UMI No. 8824441).

Hensel, K. A. (1991). Learning through a lens. *Journal of Museum Education, 16*(1): 13–14.

Hilke, D. D. (1988). Strategies for family learning in museums. *Visitor studies: Theory, research and practice*. Vol. 1: *Proceedings of the first annual Visitor Studies Conference*. Jacksonville, AL: Visitor Studies Association, 120–34.

Hipschman, R. (1980). *Exploratorium cookbook II: A construction manual for Exploratorium exhibits*. Vol. 2. San Francisco: Exploratorium.

Hipschman, R. (1987). *Exploratorium cookbook III: A construction manual for Exploratorium exhibits*. Vol. 3. San Francisco: Exploratorium.

Hirschi, K. D., and Screven, C. G. (1988). Effects of questions on visitor reading behavior. *ILVS Review: A Journal of Visitor Behavior, 1*(1): 50–61.

Hirsh-Pasek K, and Golinkoff, R. M. (2008). Why play=learning. In R. E. Tremblay, R. G. Barr, R. De V. Peters, and M. Boivin, eds. Encyclopedia on Early Childhood Development [online]. Montreal, Quebec: Centre of Excellence for Early Childhood Development, 1–7. Available at www.child-encyclopedia.com/documents/Hirsh-Pasek-GolinkoffANGxp.pdf. Accessed November 5, 2011.

Hirsh-Pasek, K., Golinkoff, R. M., Berk, L. E., and Singer, D. (2009). *A mandate for playful learning in preschool; Presenting the evidence*. New York: Oxford University Press.

Hood, M. G. (1983). Staying away: Why people choose not to visit museums. *Museum News, 61*(4): 50–57.

Hood, M. G. (1989). Leisure criteria of family participation and nonparticipation in museums. *Marriage & Family Review, 13*(3–4): 151–70.

Housen, A. (1992). Validating a measure of aesthetic development for museums and schools. *ILVS Review: A Journal of Visitor Behavior, 2*(2): 213–38.

Humphrey, T., and Gutwill, J. P. (2005). *Fostering active prolonged engagement: The art of creating APE exhibits*. San Francisco, CA: Exploratorium.

Irvine, K. N., Saunders, C. D., and Foster, J. S. (2000). Using evaluation to guide the development of behavior change programs. *Visitor studies: Theory, research and practice: Selected papers from the 1995 Visitor Studies Conference, 8*(2): 47–55.

Iyengar, S. S., and Lepper, M. R. (1999). Rethinking the value of choice: A cultural perspective on intrinsic motivation. *Journal of Personality and Social Psychology, 76*(3): 349–66.

Jones, W. (1987). Characteristics of a good exhibit. *Visitor Behavior, 2*(2): 4.

Kaplan, S., Bardwell, L. V., and Slakter, D. B. (1993). The restorative experience as a museum benefit. *Journal of Museum Education, 18*(3): 15–17.

Keller, J. M. (1983). Motivational design of instruction. Pp. 383–434 in C. M. Reigeluth (Ed.), *Instructional-design theories and models: An overview of their current status*. Hillsdale, NJ: Lawrence Erlbaum Associates.

Keller, J. M. (1987a). Strategies for simulating the motivation to learn. *Performance & Instruction, 26*(8): 1–7.

Keller, J. M. (1987b). The systematic process of motivational design. *Performance and Instruction, 26*(9–10), 1–8.

Keller, J. M., and Burkman, E. (1993). Motivation principles. Pp. 3–53 in M. Fleming and W. H. Levie (Eds.), *Instructional Message Design: Principles from the behavioral and cognitive sciences.* 2nd ed. Englewood Cliffs, NJ: Educational Technology Publications.

Keller, J. M., and Suzuki, K. (1988). Use of the ARCS motivation model in courseware design. Pp. 401–35 in D. H. Jonassen (Ed.), *Instructional designs for microcomputer courseware.* Hilsdale, NJ: Lawrence Erlbaum Associates.

Kendon, A. (1977). *Studies in the behavior of social interaction.* Bloomington: Indiana University Press.

Kerr, J. H., and Apter, M. J. (Eds.). (1991). *Adult play: A reversal theory approach.* Rockland, MA: Swets and Zeitlinger.

Koran, J. J., and Koran, M. L. (1983). The roles of attention and curiosity in museum learning. *Journal of Museum Education, 8*(2): 14–17, 24.

Koran, J. J., Koran, M. L., Foster, J. S., and Dierking, L. D. (1988). Using modeling to direct attention. *Curator, 31*(1): 36–42.

Koran, J. J., Morrison, L., Lehman, J. R., Koran, M. L., and Gandara, L. (1984). Attention and curiosity in museums. *Journal of Research in Science Teaching, 21*(4): 357–63.

Korn, R. (1987). Motivating visitors with interactive labels. *Journal of Museum Education: Roundtable Reports, 12*(1): 15–16.

Korn, R. (1998). Making sure the time is right for front-end evaluation. *Visitor Studies Today!, 1*(1): 12–13.

Laetsch, W. M., Diamond, J., Gottfried, J. L., and Rosenfeld, S. (1980). Children and family groups in science centers. *Science and Children* (March):14–17.

Leinhardt, G., and Crowley, K. (1998). *Museum learning as conversational elaboration: A proposal to capture, code, and analyze talk in museums.* Pittsburgh, PA: Learning Research and Development Center, University of Pittsburgh.

Leinhardt, G., Crowley, K., and Knutson, K. (Eds.). (2002). *Learning conversations in museums.* Mahwah, NJ: Lawrence Erlbaum Associates.

Leinhardt, G., and Gregg, M. (2002). Burning buses, burning crosses: Student teachers see civil rights. Pp. 139–66 in G. Leinhardt, K. Crowley, and K. Knutson (Eds.), *Learning conversations in museums.* Mahwah, NJ: Lawrence Erlbaum Associates.

Leinhardt, G., and Knutson, K. (2004). *Listening in on museum conversations.* Walnut Creek, CA: AltaMira Press.

Leinhardt, G., Knutson, K., and Crowley, K. (2003). Museum Learning Collaborative redux. *Journal of Museum Education, 28*(1): 23–31.

Lepper, M. R. (1985). Microcomputers in education: Motivational and social issues. *American Psychologist, 40,* 1–18.

Lepper, M. R., and Greene, D. (1978). Overjustification and beyond: Toward a means-end analysis of intrinsic and extrinsic motivation. In M. R. Lepper and D. Greene (Eds.), *The hidden costs of reward.* Hillsdale, NJ: Lawrence Erlbaum Associates.

Lepper, M. R., and Malone, T. W. (1987). Intrinsic motivation and instructional effectiveness in computer-based education. Pp. 255–86 in R. E. Snow and M. J. Farr (Eds.), *Aptitude, learning, and instruction.* Vol. 3: *Conative and affective process analyses.* Hillsdale, NJ: Lawrence Erlbaum Associates.

Litwak, J. M. (1993). Enhancing museum learning by facilitating the visitor social agenda. *Visitor studies: Theory, research and practice.* Vol. 5: *Collected papers from the 1992 Visitor Studies Conference.* Jacksonville, AL: Visitor Studies Association, 111–15.

Litwak, J. M. (1996). Visitors learn more from labels that ask questions. *Current Trends in Audience Research and Evaluation, 10*: 40–50.

Malone, T. W. (1980). *What makes things fun to learn? A study of intrinsically motivating computer games.* Palo Alto, CA: Xerox Research Center.

Malone, T. W. (1981). Toward a theory of intrinsically motivating instruction. *Cognitive Science, 4*: 333–69.

Malone, T. W., and Lepper, M. R. (1987). Making learning fun: A taxonomy of intrinsic motivations for learning. Pp. 223–53 in R. E. Snow and M. J. Farr (Eds.), *Aptitude, learning, and instruction.* Vol. 3: *Conative and affective process analyses.* Hillsdale, NJ: Lawrence Erlbaum Associates.

Manning, R. E. (1999). *Studies in outdoor recreation: Search and research for satisfaction.* Corvallis: Oregon State University Press.

Manubay, G., Dotzour, A., Schulz, K., Smith, J. C., Houston, C., De Young, R., et al. (2002). *Do exhibits promote environmentally responsible behavior? An evaluation of the Bog of Habits.* (unpublished manuscript). Brookfield, IL: Brookfield Zoo.

Marsh, C. (n.d.). Visitors as learners: The role of emotions. Association of Science-Technology Centers. Retrieved November 18, 2009 (www.astc.org/resource/education/learning_marsh.htm).

Martin, B. L., and Briggs, L. J. (1986). *The affective and cognitive domains: Integration for instruction and research.* New Jersey: Educational Technology Publications, Inc.

Maslow, A. H. (1943). A theory of human motivation. *Psychological Review, 50*(4): 370–96.

McCarthy, B. (1987). *The 4MAT system: Teaching to learning styles with right/left mode techniques.* Rev. ed. Barrington, IL: EXCEL Inc.

McClafferty, T. P. (1995). *Did you hear the message? Visitors' use and understanding of a sound exhibit at interactive science centers.* Paper presented at the National Association for Research in Science Teaching Conference, San Francisco, California, April.

McLean, K. (1993). *Planning for people in museum exhibitions.* Washington, DC: Association of Science-Technology Centers.

McManus, P. M. (1987). It's the company you keep . . . : The social determination of learning-related behaviour in a science museum. *International Journal of Museum Management and Curatorship, 6*: 263–70.

McManus, P. M. (1988). Good companions: More on the social determination of learning-related behaviour in a science museum. *International Journal of Museum Management and Curatorship, 7*: 37–44.

McManus, P. M. (1989). Oh, yes, they do: How museum visitors read labels and interact with exhibit texts. *Curator, 32*(3): 174–89.

McManus, P. M. (1990). Watch your language! People do read labels. Pp. 4–6 in B. Serrell (Ed.), *What research says about learning in science museums.* Washington, DC: Association of Science-Technology Centers.

McManus, P. M. (1994). Families in museums. Pp. 81–97 in R. Miles and L. Zavala (Eds.), *Towards the museum of the future: New European perspectives.* London: Routledge.

Melton, A. W. (1996). *Problems of installation in museums of art.* Washington, DC: American Association of Museums.

Miles, R. S. (1987). Museums and the communication of science. In D. Evered and M. O'Connor (Eds.), *Communicating science to the public* (114–122). New York: John Wiley & Sons.

Miller, G. A. (1956). The magical number seven, plus or minus two: Some limits on our capacity for processing information. *Psychological Review, 63*: 81–97.

Miller, G. A. (1968). The magical number seven, plus or minus two: Some limits on our capacity for processing information. In R. N. Haber (Ed.), *Contemporary theory and research in visual perception.* New York: Holt, Rinehart, and Winston, Inc.

Morrissey, K. (1991). Visitor behavior and interactive video. *Curator, 34*(2): 109–18.

Myers, O. E., Jr, Saunders, C. D., and Birjulin, A. A. (2004). Emotional dimensions of watching zoo animals: An experience sampling study building on insights from psychology. *Curator, 47*(3): 299–321.

National Research Council. (2009). *Learning science in informal environments: People, places, and pursuits.* Committee on Learning Science in Informal Environments. Philip Bell, Bruce Lewenstein, Andrew W. Shouse, and Michael A. Feder, Editors. Board on Science Education, Center for Education, Division of Behavioral and Social Sciences and Education. Washington, DC: National Academies Press.

Nedzel, L. N. (1952). *The motivation and education of the general public through museum experiences.* Unpublished doctoral dissertation, University of Chicago.

Norman, D. A. (1988). *The design of everyday things.* New York: Doubleday.

Paris, S. G. (Ed.). (2002). *Perspectives on object-centered learning in museums.* Mahwah, NJ: Lawrence Erlbaum Associates.

Paris, S. G., and Mercer, M. J. (2002). Finding self in objects: Identity exploration in museums. Pp. 401–23 in G. Leinhardt, K. Crowley, and K. Knutson (Eds.), *Learning conversations in museums.* Mahwah, NJ: Lawrence Erlbaum Associates.

Penney, D. W. (2009). Reinventing the Detroit Institute of Arts: The reinstallation project 2002–2007. *Curator, 52*(1): 35–44.

Perry, D. L. (1989). The creation and verification of a development model for the design of a museum exhibit. *Dissertation Abstracts International, 50*(12A), 3926 (UMI No. 9012186).

Perry, D. L. (1992). Designing exhibits that motivate. *ASTC Newsletter, 20*(2): 9–10, 12.

Perry, D. L. (1993a). Beyond cognition and affect: The anatomy of a museum visit. *Visitor studies: Theory, research and practice.* Vol. 6: *Collected papers from the 1993 Visitor Studies Conference.* Jacksonville, AL: Visitor Studies Association, 43–47.

Perry, D. L. (1993b). Designing exhibits that motivate. In M. Borun, S. Grinell, P. McNamara, and B. Serrell (Eds.), *What research says about learning in science museums* (25–29). Washington, DC: Association of Science Technology Centers.

Perry, D. L. (1993c). *Evaluation of the Museum of Science and Industry's AIDS exhibit: Phase two report* (unpublished manuscript). Chicago: Museum of Science and Industry.

Perry, D. L. (1993d). Measuring learning with the knowledge hierarchy. *Visitor studies: Theory, research and practice.* Vol. 6: *Collected papers from the 1993 Visitor Studies Conference.* Jacksonville, AL: Visitor Studies Association, 73–77.

Perry, D. L. (1994a). The anatomy of a museum visit: What visitors really want. Pp. 67–73 in *The Sourcebook: 1994 Annual Meeting.* Washington, DC: American Association of Museums.

Perry, D. L. (1994b). *Experiment Benches: Summative evaluation report* (unpublished manuscript). St. Paul: Science Museum of Minnesota.

Perry, D. L. (2002). Profound learning: Stories from museums. *Educational Technology, 42*(2): 21–25.

Perry, D. L., and Edington, G. (1995). *Zap it! Research/evaluation study* (unpublished manuscript). Chicago: Chicago Academy of Sciences.

Perry, D. L., and Garibay, C. (1996). *Life underground at The Field Museum: Front-end evaluation* (unpublished manuscript). Chicago: The Field Museum.

Perry, D. L., Garibay, C., and Edington, G. (1995). *"It was like I was in the big fat middle of it!": The diorama experience* (unpublished manuscript). Chicago: Chicago Academy of Sciences.

Perry, D. L., Garibay, C., and Gyllenhaal, E. D. (1998). Front end evaluation for *Life Underground*, a Field Museum exhibition about life in the soil. *Current Trends in Audience Research and Evaluation, 11*: 59–67.

Perry, D. L., and Morrissey, K. (1999). *Designing for conversation.* Workshop presented at the Chicago Children's Museum as part of the Visitor Studies Association Annual Conference, July.

Perry, D. L., and Morrissey, K. (2005). *Designing for conversation.* Workshop presented to the Garfield Park Conservatory, Chicago, Illinois, May.

Perry, D. L., and Niehus, K. (1996). *Hunters of the Sky: Summative evaluation report.* (unpublished manuscript). St. Paul: Science Museum of Minnesota.

Postrech, R. (1998). Advance organizers. Montclair State University, April 30. Retrieved November 11, 2009 (http://chss2.montclair.edu/sotillos/_meth/00000012.htm).

Rand, J. (1990). *Fish stories that hook readers: Interpretive graphics at the Monterey Bay Aquarium* (Technical Report No. 90-30). Jacksonville, AL: Center for Social Design.

Rand, J. (2001). The 227-mile museum, or a visitors' bill of rights. *Curator, 44*(1): 7–14.

Reigeluth, C. M. (Ed.). (1983). *Instructional-design theories and models: An overview of their current status.* Hillsdale, NJ: Lawrence Erlbaum Associates.

Richman, N., and Lansdown, R. (1988). *Problems of preschool children.* New York: John Wiley & Sons.

Rieber, L. P. (2001). *Designing learning environments that excite serious play.* Paper presented at the annual meeting of the Australasian Society for Computers in Learning in Tertiary Education, Melbourne, Australia. Available at http://it.coe.uga.edu/%7Elrieber/publications.html.

Roberts, L. C. (1991). The elusive qualities of "affect." *ILVS Review, 2*(1): 133–36.

Roberts, L. C. (1997). *From knowledge to narrative: Educators and the changing museum.* Washington, DC: Smithsonian Institution Press.

Romiszowski, A. J. (1981). *Designing instructional systems: Decision making in course planning and curriculum design.* New York: Nichols Publishing Company.

Rosenthal, E., and Blankman-Hetrick, J. (2002). Conversations across time: Family learning in a living history museum. Pp. 305–29 in G. Leinhardt, K. Crowley, and K. Knutson (Eds.), *Learning conversations in museums.* Mahwah, NJ: Lawrence Erlbaum Associates.

Rounds, J. (2000). Why are some science museum exhibits more interesting than others? *Curator 43*(3): 188–198.

Rounds, J. (2004). Strategies for the curiosity-driven museum visitor. *Curator, 47*(4): 389–412.

Rounds, J. (2006). Doing identity work in museums. *Curator, 49*(2): 133–50.

Rowe, S. (2003). Visitors and voices: A dialogic approach to learning in science museums. *Journal of Museum Education, 28*(2): 3–7.

Salmi, H. S. (1993). *Science centre education: Motivation and learning in informal education.* Ann Arbor, MI: UMI Dissertation Services (UMI No. 9417665).

Saunders, C., Birjulin, A. A., and Myers, O. E. (1998). Developing caring attitudes at a new "children's zoo": Guiding principles and front-end studies. *Current Trends in Audience Research and Evaluation, 11:* 89.

Schaefer, J., Perry, D. L., and Gyllenhaal, E. D. (2002). *Underground Adventure: Final summative/ remedial evaluation* (unpublished manuscript). Chicago: The Field Museum. Available at www .selindaresearch.com/UndergroundAdventureSummative.pdf.

Schaller, D. T., Allison-Bunnell, S., Borun, M., and Chambers, M. B. (2002). How do you like to learn? Comparing user preferences and visit length of educational Web sites. *Visitors Studies Today!, 5*(2): 1, 5–10.

Schauble, L., Gleason, M., Lehrer, R., Bartlett, K., Petrosino, A., Allen, A., et al. (2002). Supporting science learning in museums. Pp. 425–52 in G. Leinhardt, K. Crowley, and K. Knutson (Eds.), *Learning conversations in museums.* Mahwah, NJ: Lawrence Erlbaum Associates.

Schultz, C. (1998). Vicissitudes in appraising reading difficulty. International Personnel Assessment Council, April. Retrieved April 10, 2011 (www.ipmaac.org/acn/apr98/reading.html).

Screven, C. G. (1974). *The measurement and facilitation of learning in the museum environment: An experimental analysis.* Washington, DC: Smithsonian Institution Press.

Screven, C. G. (1986). Exhibitions and information centers: Some principles and approaches. *Curator, 29*(2): 109–37.

Screven, C. G. (1992). Motivating visitors to read labels. *ILVS Review: A Journal of Visitor Behavior, 2*(2): 183–212.

Screven, C. G. (1993). *Behavior research and environmental graphic design.* Chicago: Society for Environmental Graphic Design.

Screven, C. G. (1999). *Visitor studies bibliography and abstracts.* 4th ed. Chicago: Screven & Associates.

Serrell, B. (1990). Learning styles and museum visitors. Pp. 29–31 in B. Serrell (Ed.), *What research says about learning in science museums.* Vol. 1. Washington, DC: Association of Science-Technology Centers.

Serrell, B. (1996a). *Exhibit labels: An interpretive approach.* Walnut Creek, CA: AltaMira Press.

Serrell, B. (1996b). Behind it all: A big idea. Pp. 1–8 in *Exhibit labels: An interpretive approach.* Walnut Creek, CA: AltaMira Press.

Serrell, B. (2006a). *Judging exhibitions; A framework for assessing excellence.* Walnut Creek, CA: Left Coast Press.

Serrell, B. (2006b, Spring). Comparing the "Excellent Judges Framework" to other methods of reviewing exhibitions. *Exhibitionist, 25*(1): 56–60.

Serrell, B. (1998). *Paying attention: Visitors and museum exhibitions.* Washington, DC: American Association of Museums, Technical Information Service.

Serrell, B., and Becker, B. A. (1991). Stuffed birds on sticks: Plans to re-do the animal halls at Field Museum. *Visitor studies: Theory, research and practice.* Vol. 3: *Proceedings of the 1990 Visitor Studies Conference.* Jacksonville, AL: Visitor Studies Association, 263–69.

Serrell, B., and Becker, B. A. (1990). *Stuffed birds on sticks: Evaluation of the animal halls as a planning tool for renovations* (unpublished manuscript). Chicago: The Field Museum.

Serrell, B., Ratcliffe, S., and Prager, M. (2001). Summary of the summative evaluations of The Changing Face of Women's Health. *Current Trends in Audience Research and Evaluation, 14:* 1–12.

Sheppard, B., Weil, S., and Rudd, P. (2000). *Perspectives on outcome based evaluation for libraries and museums.* Washington: DC: Institute of Museum and Library Services.

Shettel, H. (1973). Exhibits: Art form or educational medium? *Museum News, 52*(1): 32–41.

Shettel, H., Butcher, M., Cotton, T. S., Northrup, J., and Slough, D. S. (1968). *Strategies for determining exhibit effectiveness.* Report No. AIR E95-4/48-FR. Washington, DC: American Institutes for Research.

Sikora, M., Fischer, D., Serrell, B., Perry, D., and Morris, K. (2009). New roles for evaluation at the Detroit Institute of Arts. *Curator, 52*(1): 45–65.

Silverman, L. H. (1990). *Of us and other "things": The content and functions of talk by adult visitor pairs in an art and a history museum.* Unpublished dissertation, University of Pennsylvania, Philadelphia.

Silverman, L. H. (1995). Visitor meaning-making in museums for a new age. *Curator, 38*(3): 161–70.

Silverman, L. H. (2000). Making meaning together: Lessons from the field of American History. Pp. 230–39 in J. S. Hirsch and L. H. Silverman (Eds.), *Transforming practice.* Washington DC: Museum Education Roundtable.

Silverman, L. H. (2010). *The social work of museums.* New York: Routledge.

Simon, N. (2010). The participatory museum. Santa Cruz, CA: Museum 2.0.

Singer, D., Golinkoff, R. M., and Hirsch-Pasek, K. (Eds.). (2006). *Play = learning: How play motivates and enhances children's cognitive and social-emotional growth.* New York: Oxford University Press.

Spock, M. (Ed.) (2000). *Philadelphia Stories* [Video with study guide]. Washington, DC: American Association of Museums.

Spock, M., Perry, D. L., Leichter, H. J., Gyllenhaal, E. D., and Forland, E. (1997). Philadelphia stories: Listening to how museum professionals describe pivotal learning experiences in museums. Unpublished raw data.

Spock, M., Perry, D. L., and Lewis, S. (1997). *Philadelphia stories; Listening to how museum professionals describe pivotal learning experiences in museums.* Unpublished manuscript, Chapin Hall Center for Children at the University of Chicago, Illinois.

St. John, M., and Perry, D. L. (1993). Rethink role, science museums urged. *ASTC Newsletter, 21*(5): 1, 6–7.

Sykes, M. (1992). "Where learning is child's play": Exhibit evaluation in a children's museum. *Current Trends in Audience Research, 6:* 36–40.

Sykes, M. (1993). Evaluating exhibits for children: What is a meaningful play experience? Pp. 227–33 in D. Thompson, A. Benefield, S. Bitgood, H. Shettel, and R. Williams (Eds.), *Visitor studies: Theory, research and practice.* Vol. 5: *Collected papers from the 1992 Visitor Studies Conference.* Jacksonville, AL: Visitor Studies Association.

Taylor, S. M. (1986). Understanding processes of informal education: A naturalistic study of visitors to a public aquarium. *Dissertation Abstracts International, 48*(05): 1165 (UMI No. 8718179).

Tinsley, H. E. A., and Manfredo, M. J. (1991). The paragraphs about leisure and recreation experience preference scales: Results from two inventories designed to assess the breadth of the perceived psychological benefits of leisure. In B. L. Driver, P. J. Brown, and G. L. Peterson (Eds.), *Benefits of leisure.* State College, PA: Venture Publishing, Inc.

Tisdal, C. E. (2004). *Phase 2 summative evaluation of Active Prolonged Engagement at the Exploratorium* (unpublished manuscript). San Francisco: Exploratorium.

Tisdal, C. E., and Perry, D. L. (2004). *Going APE! at the Exploratorium: Interim summative evaluation report* (unpublished manuscript). San Francisco: Exploratorium.

Vygotsky, L. S. (1978). *Mind in society: The development of higher psychological processes.* Cambridge, MA: Harvard University Press.

Vygotsky, L. S. (1986). *Thought and language.* Cambridge, MA: MIT Press.

Wansley, T. S. (1995). Responsive constructivist evaluation of a self-guided activity trail at Cochran Mill Nature Center. *Dissertation Abstracts International, 56*(10A), 3901 (UMI No. 9602819).

Weaver, S. (2007). *Creating great visitor experiences: A guide for museums, parks, zoos, gardens, and libraries.* Walnut Creek, CA: Left Coast Press.

Weil, S. E. (2000). Transformed from a cemetery of bric-a-brac. Pp. 4–15 in B. Sheppard (Ed.), *Perspectives on outcome based evaluation for libraries and museums.* Washington, DC: Institute of Museum and Library Services.

Wells, M., and Butler, B. (2002). A visitor-centered evaluation hierarchy. *Visitor Studies Today!, 5*(1): 5–11.

Wells, M., and Butler, B. (2004). A visitor-centered evaluation hierarchy: Helpful hints for understanding the effects of botanical garden programs. *Public Garden, 19*(2): 11–13.

Wells, M., and Loomis, R. J. (1998). A taxonomy of museum program opportunities—adapting a model from natural resource management. *Curator, 41*(4): 254–64.

White, J. (1990). What have we discovered about discovery rooms? Pp. 7–9 in B. Serrell (Ed.), *What research says about learning in science museums.* Washington, DC: Association of Science-Technology Centers.

Wolf, R. L. (1986). The missing link: The role of orientation in enriching the museum experience. *Journal of Museum Education, 11*(1): 134–42.

Wood, D., Bruner, J. S., and Ross, G. (1976). The role of tutoring in problem solving. *Journal of Child Psychology and Psychiatry 17*(2): 89–100.

Index

About the Author

Deborah L. Perry is the director of Selinda Research Associates in Chicago and has conducted research and evaluation in informal learning settings for more than twenty-five years. With a background in instructional systems technology and a passion for what makes learning fun, she has served as a consultant, workshop leader, conference presenter, researcher, evaluator, and instructional designer. Before founding Selinda Research Associates, she was an elementary school media specialist.

CPSIA information can be obtained at www.ICGtesting.com
Printed in the USA
BVOW030043260412

288703BV00002B/1/P